Overleaf: Spareribs can go to the dressiest patio happening. Try our Southern Spareribs Specialty menu at your next poolside party. Menu and recipes start on page 85.

Outdoor Cookbook

Entertaining · Menus · Equipment

By the Editors of Southern Living

Book Division of The Progressive Farmer Company, P. O. Box 2463, Birmingham, Ala. 35202.

Southern Living Books

Vice President and Director	Leslie B. Adams, Jr.
Editorial Director	John Logue
Marketing Director	David M. North
Book Editor	Betty Ann Jones

Outdoor Cookbook

Foods Editor	Lena Sturges
Assistant Foods Editor	Jean Wickstrom
Entertainment Editor	Mary Whitfield
Building and Landscape Editor	Philip Morris
Editorial Assistants	Karen Phillips
	Susanna Van Hoose
Technical Consultants	Elkin Minter, Anne Sweaney, Home Economics Department, University of Alabama
Photography	Taylor Lewis and John Watson
Design and Illustrations	Philip T. Sankey

Library of Congress Catalog Card Number:
73-80503

Manufactured in the United States of America

First Printing 1973

Contents

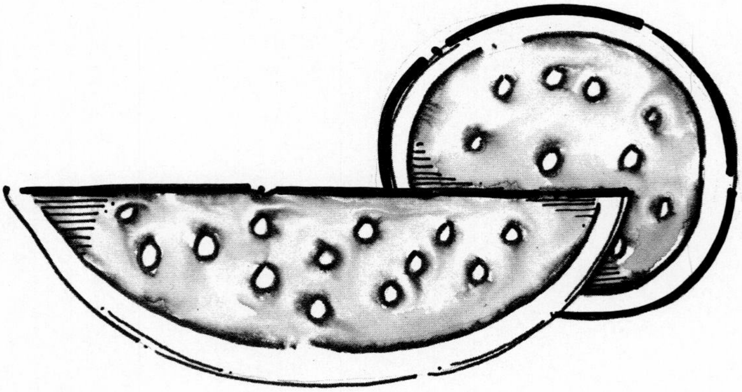

Introduction

Except for rain, nothing can dampen spirits at an outdoor cookout. For most in this country, the pleasure of cooking outdoors is limited to a few short months when the weather is agreeably warm.

Here in the South, we blend hospitality with Southern temperatures and have the perfect recipe for successful outdoor entertaining all year long. In fact, we prepared many recipes in this book *outdoors in February* while in other areas, people were warming their hands and food over hot ranges.

In the good old days most outdoor meals consisted of weiners and marshmallows — appetizing but humdrum after a while. Now, with gas and electric grills, charcoal smokers, and hibachis you can cook Glazed Pork Loin, Shrimp en Brochette, and Lobster Luau with side dishes like Celery Amandine and Orange Lotus Blossom . . . And smoke needn't get in your eyes.

A few basic rules outlined in this book will make things easier still when you eat outside. Remember that no matter how good your equipment is, it must be handled properly. Check the tips on the selection and care of your grill and pay special attention to the suggestions for getting the whole meal together. After you have read the book, it's time to try out the delicious recipes for yourself. The backdrop of nature will save you the trouble of decorating. You can enjoy the sights and sounds of the out-of-doors, while savoring the smell and taste of good food. With all of nature providing you with a casual, relaxed atmosphere and a great appetite, no wonder you'll overeat.

Outdoor Menus

There's a lot of outdoors and a lot of eating in the South. Combine the two, and you've learned one of the South's secrets for home entertaining. It's a year-round pleasure and there's a never-ending search for new ideas and new combinations of foods and surroundings.

Combinations for a barbecue meal are purely a matter of preference, and there are as many possibilities as there are recipes. Preferences may vary within a neighborhood, or even within a family. Some prefer to cook the meat outdoors, prepare the vegetables and salad indoors, and assemble it all outside for the "come and get it" signal. Others prefer to cook every single item outdoors, and it is possible to cook meat, vegetables, and bread on the grill, quite successfully.

We see no reason why you should use these menus as suggested if there happens to be a particular food your family doesn't like. We've selected foods that "go together," but there's no bound rule and you may well prefer some substitutions. Be daring enough to make changes if you find a vegetable dish with the lamb menu that you would like to use with your beef main course.

Outdoor cooking and eating can become habit-forming. With the excellent weather we have year-round, there's some time in every month of the year that meals can be cooked outdoors. So use our menus as we have suggested, or make substitutions and combinations for your own special pleasure. Whatever your choice, we hope we will have had a part in making your outdoor meals more creative and more enjoyable.

Roast beef is a universal favorite. Try our menu for Rolled Rib Roast on Spit, with our suggested recipes for vegetables and salad; menu on page 4.

Rolled Rib Roast on Spit

Dinner for Eight

Rolled Rib Roast on Spit
Grilled Rice with Olives
Okra-Tomato Casserole
Fresh Spinach-Mushroom Salad
Grilled Biscuits
Fresh Peach Ice Cream

Rolled Rib Roast on Spit

1 (3- to 4-pound) boneless rolled rib roast
¼ cup port wine
½ teaspoon dry mustard
1 teaspoon brown sugar
¼ teaspoon black pepper
Dash garlic powder
2 tablespoons salad oil
¼ cup catsup
1 tablespoon Worcestershire sauce
1 teaspoon freshly squeezed lemon juice
Dash paprika

Have roast tied tightly at meat counter. Center securely on spit of rotisserie and place over low heat of grill. Cook slowly for 30 minutes. Combine other ingredients in small saucepan; heat just to boiling point. And then brush on roast every 15 minutes. Use a meat thermometer to cook meat to desired doneness. It will take about 1 to 1½ hours to reach the rare stage. Yield: 8 servings.

Grilled Rice with Olives

2⅔ cups cooked rice
2⅔ cups water
4 tablespoons minced onion
1 teaspoon salt
¼ teaspoon pepper
2 teaspoons prepared mustard
½ teaspoon Tabasco sauce, or 2 teaspoons Worcestershire sauce
4 tablespoons chili sauce
4 tablespoons butter
6 tablespoons water
½ cup sliced stuffed olives

Double a large sheet of heavy-duty aluminum foil; fit foil into 2-quart dish to form a pouch. Combine all ingredients in foil except olives. Seal tightly and remove foil from dish. Place on grill over hot coals. Cook for approximately 20 minutes. Open foil and toss rice with fork just before serving. Add olives and stir. Yield: 8 servings.

Okra-Tomato Casserole

2 cups okra, cut into ½-inch pieces
4 to 5 tomatoes, peeled and cut into small wedges; or 1½ cups drained canned tomatoes
1 pod green hot pepper, minced (optional)
½ cup water (omit water if using canned tomatoes)
Salt and pepper to taste
1 large onion, chopped
1 tablespoon butter or margarine

Combine all ingredients and cook over medium heat until vegetables are tender. Serve hot. Yield: 8 servings.

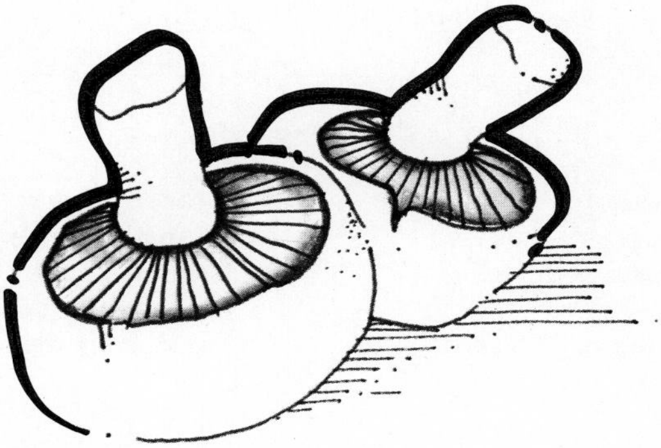

Fresh Spinach-Mushroom Salad

1 pound fresh spinach
½ pound fresh mushrooms
Grated rind of 1 lemon
¼ cup salad oil
Juice of 1 large lemon

Tear well-washed spinach into bite-size pieces and put in a large bowl. Wash mushrooms, cut in halves and slice; add to spinach. Combine grated lemon rind, salad oil, and lemon juice. Just before serving, pour over spinach-mushroom mixture and toss gently to coat. Yield: 8 servings.

Grilled Biscuits

(see Index)

Fresh Peach Ice Cream

(see Index)

Your Guest List

When making a guest list, a thoughtful hostess should include persons that have something in common, people she feels will be compatible even though they may not know each other well. If views of a certain person are distasteful to the group as a whole, it would be wise to exclude him from a small gathering. He will probably feel more comfortable invited to a larger party where the guest list would be varied.

Churrasco Dinner

Dinner for Six

Churrasco

Celery Amandine

Summertime Garden Vegetable Casserole

Zesty Salad

Pumpkin Pudding

Churrasco

1¼ cups butter, divided
¼ teaspoon rosemary
1 (3-inch thick) sirloin steak or chuck roast
2 cups finely chopped green onions
1½ teaspoons salt
1 tablespoon freshly ground black pepper
1 cup white wine
½ cup wine vinegar

Combine 3 tablespoons melted butter and rosemary; baste steak once or twice with this mixture while broiling it. (Broil steak to desired degree of doneness.) Melt remaining butter and sauté green onions until just soft. Add rest of ingredients; bring to boil, then lower heat and simmer 5 minutes. Cut steak into diagonal slices and let stand in sauce for a few minutes before serving. Yield: 6 servings.

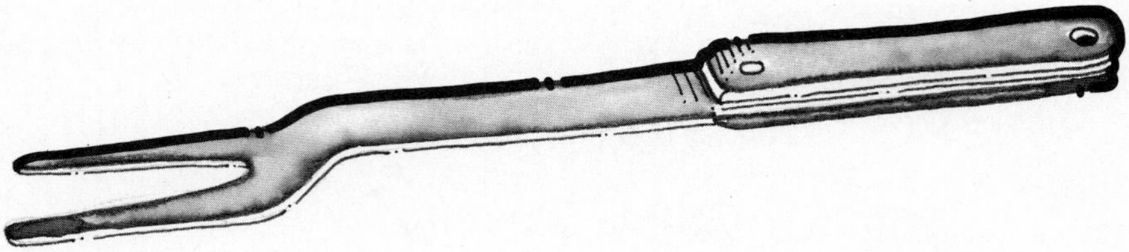

Celery Amandine

½ cup butter, divided
4 cups celery, diced
Salt and pepper to taste
2 tablespoons finely chopped fresh chives
2 tablespoons grated onion
1 cup blanched, chopped almonds
½ teaspoon finely chopped garlic (optional)
2 tablespoons dry white wine

Melt ¼ cup butter in saucepan; add celery, salt, and pepper and blend well. Cover pan and cook over low heat until celery is tender. Stir frequently while cooking to prevent scorching; add chives and onion. Melt remaining butter in a heavy pan; add blanched almonds and cook over medium heat until brown. Add garlic and wine; cook for 1 minute. Pour over celery and serve immediately. Yield: 6 servings.

Fat, juicy sirloins are mouth-watering starters for a Churrasco Dinner by the pool.

Summertime Garden Vegetable Casserole

- ½ cup butter
- 1 cup sliced onions
- 1 clove garlic, minced
- 2 yellow squash, cut into ½-inch pieces
- 1 medium eggplant, peeled and cut into ½-inch pieces
- ½ cup all-purpose flour
- 2 green peppers, chopped
- 2 tomatoes, cut into wedges
- 1 teaspoon salt
- ¼ teaspoon oregano
- ⅛ teaspoon celery salt
- ⅛ teaspoon pepper

Melt butter in large skillet; sauté onion and garlic until tender. Dredge squash and eggplant in flour to coat lightly. Add squash, eggplant, and green pepper to onions. Cover and simmer for 30 minutes. Add tomatoes, salt, oregano, celery salt, and pepper. Simmer an additional 20 minutes. Yield: 6 to 8 servings.

Zesty Salad

- 1 onion, thinly sliced and separated into rings
- 4 well-ripened tomatoes, sliced ½-inch thick
- ½ teaspoon salt
- ¼ teaspoon sugar
- Fresh ground black pepper
- 1 tablespoon chives
- 1 tablespoon basil
- 1 tablespoon dill
- 1 teaspoon celery seed
- ¼ cup commercial French dressing

Place onion rings and tomato slices on large platter. Sprinkle each slice with salt, sugar, pepper, chives, basil, dill, and celery seed. Top with French dressing. Cover salad with foil and refrigerate about 3 hours to blend flavors. Yield: 6 servings.

Pumpkin Pudding

- 1½ cups milk
- ½ cup brown sugar, firmly packed
- ¼ teaspoon freshly grated orange peel
- ¼ teaspoon ground ginger
- ½ teaspoon ground cinnamon
- ½ teaspoon salt
- 3 eggs, slightly beaten
- 1 cup cooked puréed pumpkin or canned pumpkin

Combine milk, brown sugar, orange peel, ginger, cinnamon, and salt. Stir thoroughly and add eggs and puréed pumpkin; blend well. Beat vigorously until mixture is smooth. Pour into a greased, shallow 1½-quart baking dish. Place the dish in a large pan in the middle of the oven; pour enough boiling water into the pan to come halfway up the sides of the baking dish. Bake at 350° for about 1¼ hours, or until a knife inserted in the center of the pudding comes out clean. Remove the baking dish from the water; cool the pudding to room temperature before serving or refrigerate at least 3 hours, or until thoroughly chilled. Pudding may be made in six 4-ounce individual glass molds. If cooked in molds, bake at 350° for about 40 minutes, or until firm. Yield: 6 servings.

How To Save Refrigerator Space

Use insulated ice chests to keep bottled drinks and other items cold. This saves refrigerator space. Have plenty of ice on hand!

Pool Party Dinner

Dinner for Eight

Charley-bobs
Oven-Cooked French-Fried Potatoes
Grilled Vegetables
Tossed Salad with French Dressing
Garlic Toast
Chocolate Supreme

Charley-bobs

4 pounds sirloin steak, 2 inches thick
3 pound slice center-cut ham, 2 inches thick

Cut sirloin steak and ham into 2-inch cubes. Alternate the two meats on metal skewers, and cook on grill over medium heat to desired doneness. Yield: 8 servings.

Oven-Cooked French-Fried Potatoes

3 pounds frozen French-fried potatoes
3 tablespoons salt

Place potatoes in a single layer on a cookie sheet. Bake at 400° for 10 minutes, stir once, then bake 10 minutes longer. Sprinkle with salt and serve at once. Yield: 8 servings.

Grilled Vegetables

Yellow squash, cut into 2-inch slices
Small whole onions
Carrots, cut into 1- to 2-inch slices
Zucchini squash, cut into 2-inch slices
Green pepper strips, (optional)

Select the vegetables preferred by guests, or have a dish of prepared raw vegetables and let guests make and cook their selection. Put vegetables on skewers and cook over medium heat until vegetables are done.

Meat Temperature

Meat should be at room temperature before it is put on the grill or rotisserie.

Tossed Salad with French Dressing

4 to 6 cups salad greens, broken into bite-size pieces
1 cup fresh spinach, broken into bite-size pieces
1 cup chopped celery
½ cup diced carrots
½ cup onion rings
½ cup coarsely chopped green peppers
1 cup cauliflowerettes
Commercial French dressing

Prepare vegetables and dry well. Cover and chill until just before serving. When ready to serve, add desired amount of French dressing, gently toss and serve at once. Yield: 8 servings.

Garlic Toast

(see Index)

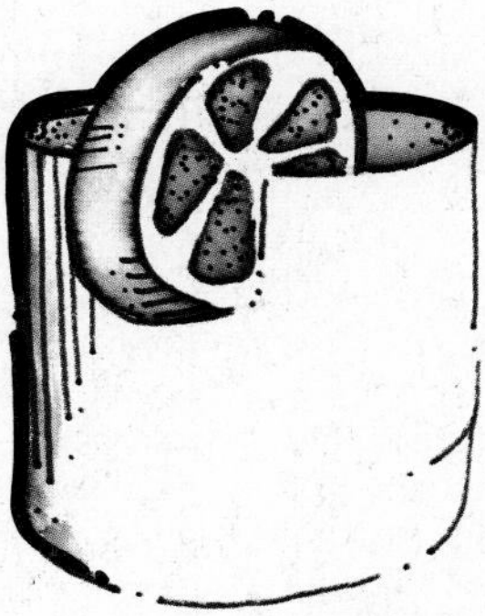

Chocolate Supreme

5 (1¼-ounce) chocolate bars
⅓ cup butter
3 egg yolks, beaten
½ cup powdered sugar
½ cup chopped nuts
3 egg whites, beaten to soft peaks
2½ cups crushed vanilla wafers
1 quart vanilla ice cream, softened

Melt chocolate bars in top of double boiler; add butter and egg yolks and let mixture come to a boil. Cool. Add powdered sugar, nuts, and beaten egg whites; stir until well-blended. Spread 1½ cups vanilla wafer crumbs in bottom of 9-inch square pan. Cover with softened vanilla ice cream. Pour cooled chocolate mixture over ice cream. Top with remaining cup of vanilla wafer crumbs. Freeze until ready to serve. Yield: 8 to 10 servings.

Watch that Grill!

When you start to barbecue, stay with it. Dripping fat from the meat can start a flame which can cremate a piece of meat very quickly. Get an easy chair, a cold drink, a bottle of water to put out flames of your charcoal fire, and settle down by the grill to keep a watchful eye on the meat as it cooks. If fire is too hot, lower the firebox or raise the grill, if they're adjustable. Move food to edge of grill away from intense heat. If fire is too cool, tap the ash off the briquettes since it acts as an insulator. Lower the grill nearer the heat, if possible.

A swimming pool, a full plate, and a teenager, equal total entertainment. The young set will especially appreciate the Charley-bobs and all the foods that go with them.

Sukiyaki Cookout

Dinner for Six to Eight

Sukiyaki
Brown Rice
Mandarin Salad
Frozen Lemon Sherbet Pie

Sukiyaki

2 pounds sirloin tip, cut into ¼- x 2-inch diagonal strips
2 onions, thinly sliced
½ cup bean curd (optional)
6 green onions including tops, chopped
6 ribs Chinese celery or cabbage
2 cups mushrooms, thinly sliced
1 pound spinach, cut into 1-inch strips
2 cups bean sprouts
3 tablespoons peanut oil
½ cup soy sauce
½ cup beef broth
3 tablespoons brown sugar
½ teaspoon monosodium glutamate

Have all ingredients at room temperature. Cut all vegetables into uniform shape and thickness. Slice green onions and celery diagonally, and cut mushrooms so each slice forms a "T". Divide all meat and vegetables into two equal portions (half of recipe fits well in skillet). Combine peanut oil, soy sauce, beef broth, brown sugar, and monosodium glutamate; blend well to make sauce in which to cook meat and vegetables. Pour half of sauce in skillet; add beef slices and cook the meat over medium heat without browning it (about 3 minutes). Push meat aside in skillet; add a vegetable and cook a short time; push this vegetable aside in pan. Continue to add a little sauce when needed in cooking remainder of vegetables. Vegetables should retain their color and crispness. Total cooking time takes about 20 minutes. This one-dish meal can be cooked at the table in an electric skillet or wok, or an iron skillet over a hibachi. Serve over brown rice. Garnish with chopped green onions. Yield: 6 to 8 servings.

Brown Rice

2 (10½-ounce) cans beef broth
3 cups water
1½ teaspoons salt
2 cups brown rice
Toasted sesame seeds

Combine beef broth, water, and salt; cook over medium heat until mixture boils. Slowly stir in rice. Cover and cook over low heat for 50 to 60 minutes. Uncover for last 5 minutes of cooking and sprinkle with sesame seeds. Yield: 6 to 8 servings.

Note: To be authentic, serve a raw egg over each plate of rice and spoon Sukiyaki over egg.

Cutting Sticky Foods

To cut sticky foods, such as marshmallows, use a pair of kitchen shears and dip them in a cup of water frequently while cutting.

Mandarin Salad

3 (11-ounce) cans mandarin orange sections, drained
3 bananas, sliced
½ cup grated coconut
Commercial Italian dressing
Toasted sesame seeds

Combine mandarin oranges, bananas, and coconut; add a small amount of Italian dressing and toss lightly. Sprinkle with sesame seeds. Yield: 6 to 8 servings.

Frozen Lemon Sherbet Pie

½ cup sugar
3 egg yolks
3 tablespoons freshly squeezed lemon juice
Pinch salt
1 tablespoon lemon rind
½ pint whipping cream, whipped
3 egg whites, stiffly beaten
Crumb Crust

Cook sugar, egg yolks, lemon juice, salt, and rind in top of double boiler until thick, stirring constantly. Cool. Fold in whipped cream and stiffly beaten egg whites. Pour mixture into cooled Crumb Crust. Freeze until ready to serve. Yield: 1 (9-inch) pie.

Avoid Collection of Fat on Fire

Make every effort to prevent a burst of flames from touching the meat being cooked on the grill. Before meat is put on the grill, trim off all excess fat. When using charcoal, be sure that all lighter fluid has burned off before putting meat on grill. If you are using a portable grill, tilt slightly to allow some of the fat drippings to run to one side. Keep a squirt bottle of water handy to put out flames when using a charcoal fire.

Barbecued Steak Dinner

Dinner for Eight

Steak à la Henry Bain
Chinese Vegetable Casserole
Mimosa Salad
Sinful Apple Pie

Steak à la Henry Bain

1 (12-ounce) bottle chili sauce
1 (14-ounce) bottle catsup
1 (10-ounce) bottle A-1 sauce
1 (10-ounce) bottle Worcestershire sauce
1 (17-ounce) bottle chutney, finely chopped or put through blender
Tabasco sauce to taste
3 to 4 pounds sirloin steak

Combine first six ingredients and mix well. This makes enough sauce for several "cookings"; it stores well in refrigerator and is better after flavors have had time to blend.

Put steak in hinged basket on grill over low heat; baste with sauce as meat cooks. Yield: 1 quart sauce; steak to serve 8.

Chinese Vegetable Casserole

1 (15-ounce) can asparagus, drained
1 (16-ounce) can tiny peas, drained
1 (16-ounce) can mixed Chinese vegetables, drained
1 (16-ounce) can bean sprouts, drained
1 (2-ounce) jar pimiento, chopped
1 (3-ounce) can French-fried onions
1 cup nuts, chopped
2 hard-cooked eggs, chopped
1 (10¾-ounce) can cream of mushroom soup
½ cup margarine, melted
Salt and pepper to taste
1 cup breadcrumbs
1 cup shredded Cheddar cheese

Combine all vegetables, nuts, eggs, and mushroom soup. Place in casserole dish. Pour margarine over mixture; add salt and pepper. Top with breadcrumbs and cheese. Bake at 350° for 30 minutes. Leftover casserole will keep in refrigerator. Yield: 8 to 10 servings.

Grilling on a Windy Day

When grilling on a windy day, use aluminum foil as a shield for grill. By using long sheets of foil, partially cover the food to speed up the cooking time.

Mimosa Salad

½ cup salad oil
2 tablespoons wine vinegar
1 teaspoon salt
Dash pepper
⅔ clove garlic, finely minced
2 quarts crisp salad greens
3 hard-cooked eggs, finely chopped

Combine oil, vinegar, salt, pepper, and garlic in jar with a tightly fitted lid. Shake and pour over greens in salad bowl. Sprinkle egg on top. Yield: 8 servings.

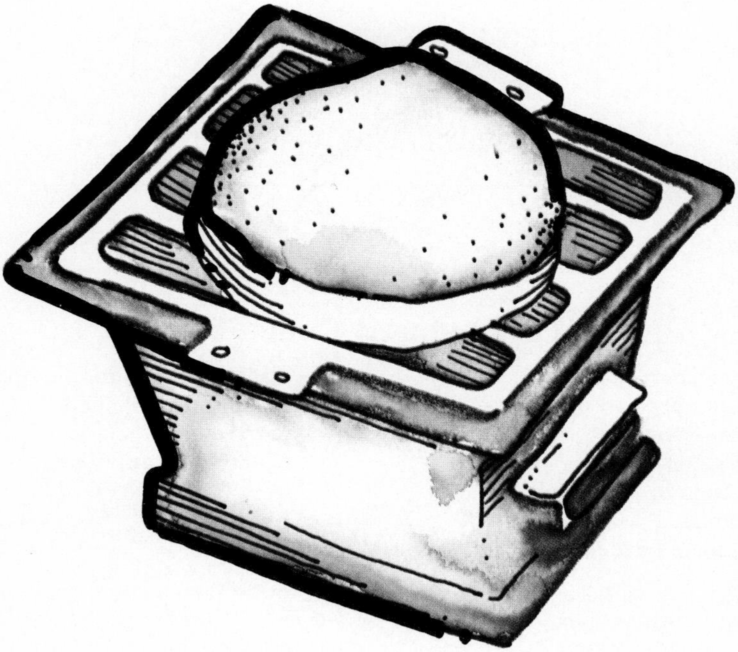

Sinful Apple Pie

¾ cup oatmeal
1 cup all-purpose flour
1 cup brown sugar
½ cup margarine, melted
4 cups apples, pared and sliced

Combine oatmeal, flour, brown sugar, and margarine; mix with apples. Put in 10-inch piepan; bake at 350° for 25 minutes. Yield: 1 (10-inch) pie.

When To Turn Steaks

The correct time to turn steaks is when droplets of red juice appear on the uncooked side. Use tongs or asbestos gloves when turning meat on the grill. Do not pierce meat with a fork, for this allows juice to run out of meat.

Chuck Roast in Deluxe Dinner

Dinner for Six to Eight

Hot Barbecued Chuck Roast
Eggplant Casserole Delight
Fresh Green Beans
Sliced Tomatoes and Green Peppers
Toasted English Muffins
Heavenly Hash Dessert

Hot Barbecued Chuck Roast

2 tablespoons salad oil
½ cup finely chopped onion
¼ cup finely chopped green pepper
2 tablespoons brown sugar
1½ cups catsup
Dash Tabasco sauce
2½ tablespoons cider vinegar
½ teaspoon garlic salt
1 teaspoon salt
1 (3- or 4-pound) chuck roast

Heat salad oil in small skillet; sauté chopped onion and green pepper until limp. Stir in brown sugar, catsup, Tabasco sauce, vinegar, garlic salt, and salt. Bring to a boil, lower heat, and simmer for 10 minutes.

Place roast in hinged basket or place on grill over low heat for 10 minutes; turn and cook 10 minutes on other side. Begin brushing sauce on roast and turn often. Use meat thermometer to cook to desired doneness. Yield: 6 to 8 servings.

Eggplant Casserole Delight

1 (1½-pound) eggplant
3 medium onions, chopped
1 cup water
2 tablespoons butter or margarine, melted
2 egg yolks, beaten
1 teaspoon salt
½ cup dry breadcrumbs
½ cup water
½ cup grated Parmesan cheese

Pare eggplant and cut in small pieces. Boil eggplant and onions in 1 cup water until tender, stirring occasionally. Drain and mash; stir in butter, egg yolks, salt, breadcrumbs, and water. Spoon mixture into a greased 1½-quart casserole dish. Bake at 350° for 20 minutes. Sprinkle grated Parmesan cheese on top and bake an additional 10 minutes. Yield: 6 servings.

Fresh Green Beans

2 pounds fresh green beans, cut-up
3 cups water
Fatback or bacon strips

Place green beans in large saucepan. Add water and fatback or bacon strips for seasoning. Cook, covered, over medium heat until beans are barely tender, about 45 minutes. Drain before serving. Yield: 8 servings.

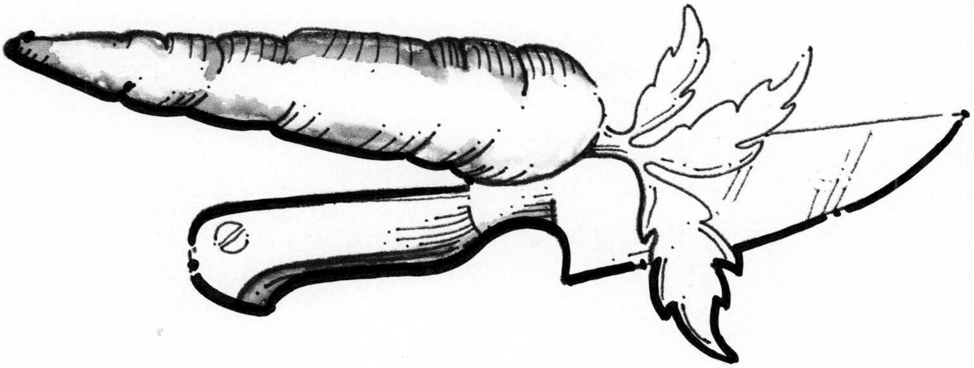

Toasted English Muffins

(see Index)

Heavenly Hash Dessert

2 apples, diced
1 (8¼-ounce) can sliced pineapple, drained and chopped
½ cup maraschino cherries
2 bananas, sliced
2 oranges, peeled, sectioned, and cut-up
½ cup chopped pecans
2 cups miniature marshmallows
1 cup sweetened whipped cream

Mix fruits, pecans, and marshmallows. Stir in whipped cream and chill thoroughly before serving in chilled dessert dishes. Yield: 10 to 12 servings.

Hostess Helper Ideas

If guests want to help you with the meal, give them the tidy jobs, such as setting tables, putting out flower arrangements, or lighting lamps. If you have done all these jobs beforehand, suggest that they just be "company" and talk with other guests or visit with you while you finish up the last-minute chores.

Cook-In, Eat-Out Patio Dinner

Dinner for Six to Eight

Gazpacho
Company Best Meatballs
Rice Casserole
or
Green Bean Casserole
Nine-Day Slaw
Corn Sticks
Pineapple-Cream Cheese Pie

Gazpacho

1 (10½-ounce) can tomato soup
5 cups water
1 cup V-8 juice
¼ cup minced green pepper
¼ cup minced celery
1 tablespoon commercial Italian dressing
1 small onion, minced
½ teaspoon salt
⅛ teaspoon black pepper
Dash garlic salt, Tabasco sauce, and Worcestershire sauce
½ medium cucumber, thinly sliced

Put soup in 3-quart saucepan; stir in water, bring to a boil, and simmer for about 5 minutes. Pour into large bowl and allow to chill. Add all other ingredients except sliced cucumber. Put into a jar, seal, and chill thoroughly. When thoroughly chilled, add cucumber slices and serve in chilled glasses or mugs. Yield: 6 to 8 servings.

Company Best Meatballs

1 egg
¾ cup milk
1½ cups breadcrumbs
1½ pounds ground chuck
2 tablespoons Worcestershire sauce
1 teaspoon salt
⅛ teaspoon pepper
⅛ teaspoon red pepper (optional)
2 tablespoons shortening
1 (10¾-ounce) can golden mushroom soup
⅔ cup water

Combine egg and milk; beat slightly. Add breadcrumbs and stir until moistened. Add meat, Worcestershire sauce, salt, and pepper. Mix well. Shape into small meatballs and brown in shortening. Pour off any accumulated fat. Combine soup and water. (Do not use cream of mushroom soup.) Pour over meatballs. Cover and simmer for 30 minutes. Yield: 24 meatballs.

Rice Casserole

½ cup margarine, melted
1 cup uncooked rice
1 (10½-ounce) can beef consommé
1 (10½-ounce) can onion soup
2 tablespoons Worcestershire sauce
⅛ to ¼ teaspoon red pepper (optional)

Combine margarine and rice in skillet; cook over low heat until rice is lightly browned. Pour into 2-quart baking dish. Add remaining ingredients. Stir lightly with a fork. Cover and bake at 350° for 1 hour. (Do not stir while baking.) Yield: 6 to 8 servings.

Green Bean Casserole

1 (10¾-ounce) can cream of mushroom soup
Dash pepper
1 teaspoon soy sauce (optional)
2 (16-ounce) cans green beans, drained
2 (3-ounce) cans French-fried onions
½ cup shredded Cheddar cheese

Combine soup, pepper, and soy sauce. Place beans in casserole dish in layers with soup mixture and 1 can onions. Cover and bake at 350° for 20 minutes. Sprinkle with remaining onions and cheese. Bake 5 minutes longer. Yield: 6 to 8 servings.

Nine-Day Slaw

1 medium cabbage, shredded
2 stems celery, diced
2 medium onions, diced
1 green pepper, diced
2 cups sugar
1 cup salad oil
1 cup cider vinegar
2 tablespoons salt
2 tablespoons sugar
Pimiento (optional)

Combine cabbage, celery, onion, and green pepper; add 2 cups sugar and blend well. Combine remaining ingredients and bring to a boil, stirring constantly. Pour dressing over cabbage mixture immediately and allow to cool. Cover and store in refrigerator. Slaw will stay fresh and crisp for 9 days. (Chill at least 1 day before serving.) Yield: 6 to 8 servings.

Don't Overcook

When cooking a combination of foods together, as in stews with assorted vegetables or a fish stew with different fish and shellfish, always add those foods that require the longest cooking time first, and add others later.

Corn Sticks

1½ cups milk
2 eggs
4 tablespoons shortening, melted
1½ cups plain cornmeal
½ cup all-purpose flour
2 teaspoons salt
1 tablespoon baking powder
2 tablespoons sugar (optional)

Combine milk and egg; beat slightly. Add shortening. Combine dry ingredients; add to milk mixture. Stir only until moistened. Pour into preheated, greased cornstick pans; bake at 450° about 10 minutes or until golden brown. (Muffin pans or skillet may be used.) Yield: 6 to 8 servings.

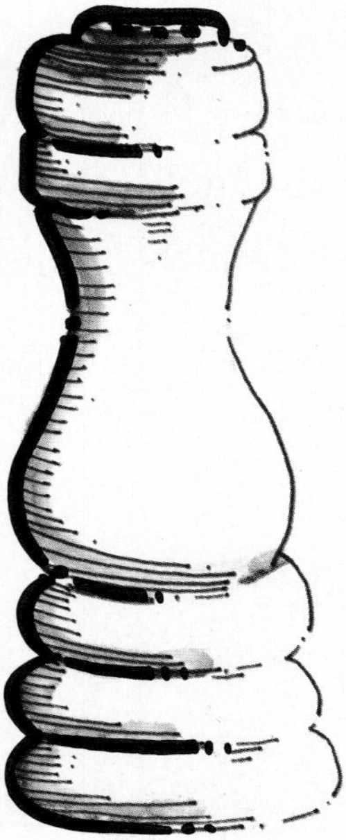

Pineapple-Cream Cheese Pie

1 (14-ounce) can condensed milk
¼ cup freshly squeezed lemon juice
1 (3-ounce) package cream cheese, softened
1 (8½-ounce) can crushed pineapple, drained
1 (9-inch) graham cracker shell

Combine condensed milk and lemon juice; add cream cheese and beat mixture until smooth. Fold in pineapple. Pour mixture into prepared crumb crust. Chill 4 to 5 hours before serving. Yield: 1 (9-inch) pie.

Organize Your Grocery List

After deciding on the menu for an outdoor party, divide the list into two parts: things to buy early and store, and the perishables that have to be purchased the day of the party.

Hamburger Specials

Dinner for Six

Hamburger Specials
Barbecued Beans
Sour Cream Cole Slaw
Hot Hamburger Buns
Frozen Lemon Sherbet Pie

Hamburger Specials

2 teaspoons salt
Dash pepper
2 pounds ground beef
6 onion slices, very thinly sliced
6 bacon slices

Mix seasonings with ground beef. Divide ground beef to make 12 patties. Make two thin patties (about 4½ inches in diameter) for each burger. Place onion slice between two patties. Seal edges of patties well. Wrap each patty with bacon slice, fastened with toothpick. Grill each side 6 to 7 minutes for rare hamburgers and 9 to 10 minutes for medium. Yield: 6 patties.

Barbecued Beans

½ cup chopped celery
2 (16-ounce) cans pork and beans
2 (4-ounce) cans Vienna sausage, drained
1 cup brown sugar
1 large onion

Spread celery in bottom of a 2½-quart casserole dish. Spoon 1 can of pork and beans over celery. Arrange sausage links on top of beans, and cover with the other can of beans. Sprinkle brown sugar over top and press onion into center of dish. Bake at 300° about 1 to 1½ hours, or cover and cook on grill for 1 hour. Yield: 6 to 8 servings.

Sour Cream Cole Slaw

1 teaspoon salt
⅛ teaspoon pepper
¼ teaspoon dry mustard
1 tablespoon sugar
2 tablespoons freshly squeezed lemon juice
½ cup commercial sour cream
3 cups finely shredded cabbage

Combine seasonings, sugar, and lemon juice with sour cream; blend well. Add to cabbage; toss lightly. Chill. Yield: 6 servings.

Frozen Lemon Sherbet Pie

(see Index)

Best Brisket Barbecue

Dinner for Four to Six

Barbecued Brisket
Stuffed Tomato Salad
Potato Casserole in Foil
Brandy Ice

Barbecued Brisket

1 (4- to 5-pound) boneless beef brisket
½ cup grated onion
½ cup vinegar
½ cup catsup
1 cup water
1 tablespoon prepared mustard
1 tablespoon sugar
1½ tablespoons Worcestershire sauce
½ teaspoon black pepper
½ teaspoon paprika
1 clove garlic, crushed

Put beef brisket in large glass or enameled dish. Combine other ingredients for marinade and pour over brisket. Refrigerate overnight. The next day, remove brisket from marinade; place on double thickness of heavy-duty aluminum foil. Pour marinade over brisket. Partially close top and place on grill over very low heat. Cook until desired doneness. Yield: 4 to 6 servings.

Alternate method: Brisket may be spread with salt, pepper, and liquid smoke and cooked directly on grill. When meat is done, slice and place in hot sauce mixture.

Stuffed Tomato Salad

1 (10-ounce) package frozen English peas
6 medium tomatoes
Lettuce leaves
Creamy commercial salad dressing

Cook peas according to package directions. Scoop out centers from tomatoes, leaving only the shell. Stuff tomatoes with peas and chill until serving time. Serve on lettuce leaves and top with your favorite dressing (onion, Green Goddess, or blue cheese). Yield: 6 servings.

Storing Charcoal

Store briquettes or charcoal in a dry place because they absorb moisture and cause the fire to kindle slowly.

Potato Casserole in Foil

6 medium potatoes, peeled and cut into ⅜-inch slices
4 medium onions, peeled and sliced
Salt and pepper to taste
8 ounces Cheddar cheese, cut into cubes
6 bacon strips, fried crisp and crumbled

Place potato and onion slices on heavy-duty aluminum foil. Season with salt and pepper. Sprinkle with cheese cubes and crumbled bacon. Wrap foil tightly. Cook about 1 hour on grill or in covered casserole dish at 375° for 1 hour. Yield: 4 to 6 servings.

Brandy Ice

1 quart vanilla ice cream, slightly thawed
3 ounces brandy
1¼ ounces crème de cacao

Combine all ingredients in blender and blend until smooth. Serve as a milk shake. Yield: 4 to 6 servings.

Locating a Portable Grill

The grill can be adapted to any location, depending on the crowd and recreational plans. The pit should be placed parallel with the wind as nearly as possible. This will give a good drawing effect, and the smoke will travel away from the cooks who are tending the meat on the grill. Avoid using a grill in an enclosed area. Fires produce carbon monoxide which can be extremely hazardous if it accumulates in closed porches or garages. Keep party decorations away from the grill.

Flank Steak Special

Dinner for Six

Barbecued Flank or Skirt Steak
Special Hot Potato Salad
Assorted Relishes
Celery Bread
Fresh Fruit
Quick Brownies

Barbecued Flank or Skirt Steak

1 (2- to 3-pound) flank or skirt steak
Salt and pepper to season
1 to 2 cloves garlic, crushed
1½ teaspoons oregano, crushed
2 tablespoons vinegar
4 tablespoons salad oil

Put steak in a flat glass baking dish. Combine salt, pepper, garlic, oregano, vinegar, and salad oil. Pour mixture over steak and let it marinate in this mixture for 1 hour. Remove from marinade and broil over high heat for 3 or 4 minutes; turn and cook on other side for 3 or 4 minutes. Carve into thin diagonal slices. Yield: 6 servings.

Special Hot Potato Salad

10 to 12 small new potatoes
6 strips bacon
1 medium onion, chopped fine
¼ cup vinegar
6 scallions or 2 green peppers, finely chopped
Salt and pepper to taste
3 hard-cooked eggs, cut into quarters

Cook potatoes in boiling salted water until just tender. Plunge into cold water, peel, and thinly slice. While potatoes are cooking, fry bacon until crisp. Remove bacon, crumble it, and set aside. Add chopped onion to bacon drippings and cook until tender. Add vinegar, scallions, salt and pepper, and blend. Pour this sauce over potatoes and mix lightly. Garnish with hard-cooked eggs. Yield: 6 servings.

Serve All Guests at One Time

To be sure all guests are served at the same time, it's better to cut a very large steak into eight pieces than to cook only four steaks at a time on the grill.

Celery Bread

⅓ to ½ cup butter or margarine, softened
½ to 1 teaspoon celery seed
⅛ teaspoon salt
1 (1-pound) loaf unsliced bread

Combine softened butter or margarine, celery seed, and salt; mix well and set aside. Remove crusts from three sides and both ends of an unsliced loaf of bread. Slice lengthwise and crosswise into 2-inch squares, not cutting through to bottom crust. Spread butter between squares and over top and side of bread. Bake at 300° for 20 to 25 minutes. Remove from oven, wrap in heavy-duty aluminum foil, and keep warm on grill. Yield: 6 to 8 servings.

Quick Brownies

(see Index)

Cooking Steaks

Turn steaks only once, always using tongs. A fork will pierce the meat and let juice escape. To prevent steak from curling, score or slit the fat on edge at about 1½-inch intervals before placing it on the grill. Be careful not to cut into the meat, or you will lose precious juice. It is not necessary to score steaks that are thicker than 1½ inches.

Meal from the Coals

Dinner for Six to Eight

Chuck Roast on Coals
Summer Squash and Corn
Spiced Peach Salad
Garlic Bread
Vanilla Ice Cream

Chuck Roast on Coals

1 (3- or 4-pound) chuck roast, 3 inches thick
2 large cloves garlic, crushed
½ cup salad oil
¼ cup Dijon mustard
1 cup ice cream salt

Spread roast with crushed garlic. Combine salad oil and mustard, and brush this mixture on roast to completely cover it. Put ice cream salt over oil-mustard mixture and press into meat to coat it. Let stand awhile, then repeat applications of oil-mustard and salt. Let roast sit for 2 hours, adding as much salt as roast will take to form a crust.

Brush gray ash from a flat bed of charcoal briquettes, and lay roast directly on coals. A piece of aluminum foil may be placed on top of roast. Cook about 20 minutes, then move to another bed of coals from which ash has been brushed. Cook 20 minutes. Check for desired doneness, and cook longer if necessary. To serve, cut in strips across the grain. Yield: 6 to 8 servings.

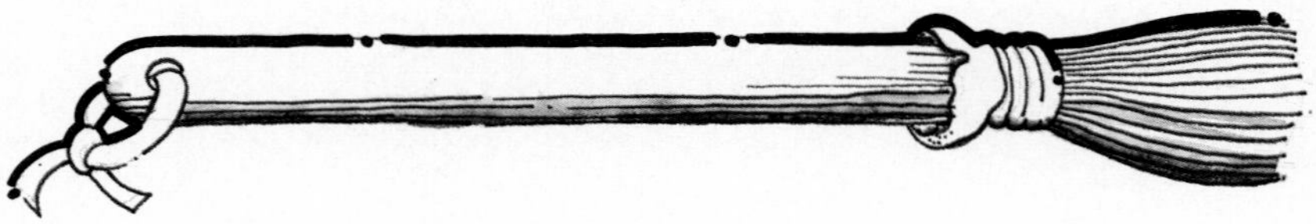

Summer Squash and Corn

¼ cup chopped onion
2 tablespoons butter or margarine, melted
Corn cut from 4 medium ears, or 1 (10-ounce) package frozen corn
3 medium tomatoes, diced
4 medium zucchini squash, thinly sliced
½ teaspoon sugar
1 teaspoon salt
¼ teaspoon ground black pepper
¾ teaspoon ground oregano

Sauté onion in melted butter or margarine. Add other ingredients, stir until mixture comes to a boil; cover saucepan and cook over low heat for 20 minutes. Adjust seasonings and serve hot. Mixture will be thick. Yield: 8 servings.

Spiced Peach Salad

- 1 teaspoon ground cinnamon
- ½ teaspoon ground cloves
- 1 teaspoon ground allspice
- ¾ cup brown sugar
- ½ cup cider vinegar
- 1 (29-ounce) can peach halves, drained
- 1 (3-ounce) package cream cheese
- Half-and-half

Mix spices, brown sugar, and vinegar with ¾ cup juice drained from peaches. Bring to a boil, reduce heat and simmer for 5 minutes. Pour mixture over peach halves while hot. Let sit for several hours or overnight. Before serving, combine cream cheese and enough half-and-half to make smooth mixture. Place a teaspoon of this mixture in center of each peach half. Yield: 7 to 8 servings.

Garlic Bread

(see Index)

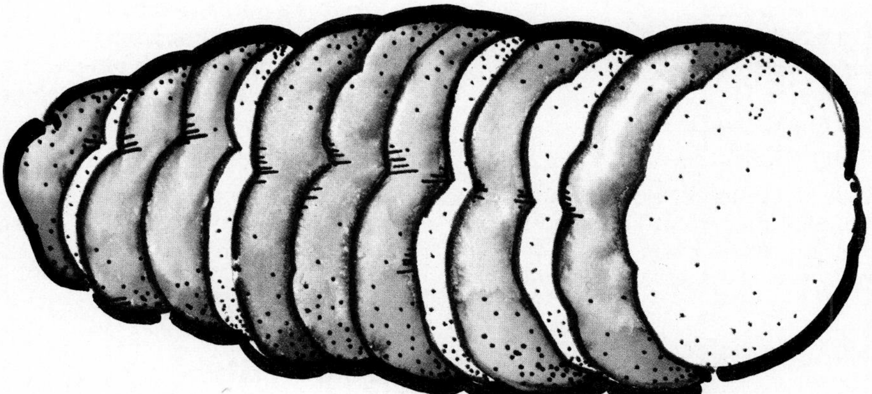

Vanilla Ice Cream

- 1½ cups milk
- ¾ cup sugar
- ⅛ teaspoon salt
- 2 or 3 egg yolks
- 1 tablespoon vanilla extract
- 1 pint whipping cream, whipped

Scald milk over low heat. Add sugar and salt; stir until dissolved. Beat egg yolks and add hot milk mixture slowly. Beat until well-blended. Cook in top of double boiler until thick and smooth. Chill and add vanilla extract. Whip cream and fold into custard mixture. Freeze in electric or hand-turned freezer. Yield: 1½ quarts.

Quick Barbecue

For a quick barbecue dinner, slice leftover cold roast beef or pork, mix your favorite barbecue sauce, and cook on the grill, basting generously with the sauce as meat cooks.

Teriyaki Beef Special

Dinner for Eight

Teriyaki Beef Sticks
Marinated Vegetable Platter
Spinach Madeleine
Garlic Toast
Peach Meringue
Marlene's Punch

Teriyaki Beef Sticks

1½ cups soy sauce
½ cup salad oil
1 cup vinegar
1 cup water
1 cup brown sugar
1 teaspoon salt
5 cloves garlic, minced
1 large onion, chopped
⅓ cup chopped fresh gingerroot, or 5 tablespoons ground ginger
3 pounds boneless beef roast or round steak

Combine all ingredients except meat to make marinade. Slice meat into 1-inch strips that are ⅛ inch thick. Skewer meat strips accordion-style on bamboo sticks, using 4 inches of meat per stick. Marinate in sauce 4 hours or overnight. Grill about 15 minutes, turning often. Yield: 8 servings.

Marinated Vegetable Platter

(see Index)

Spinach Madeleine

2 (10-ounce) packages frozen chopped spinach
2 tablespoons chopped onion
4 tablespoons butter, melted
2 tablespoons all-purpose flour
½ cup vegetable liquor
½ cup evaporated milk
½ teaspoon pepper
¾ teaspoon garlic salt
¾ teaspoon salt
1 teaspoon Worcestershire sauce
1 (6-ounce) roll of Jalapeño cheese, cut into small pieces
Buttered breadcrumbs (optional)

Cooling a Charcoal Fire

Small amounts of crushed ice will cool a charcoal fire quickly.

Cook spinach according to package directions; drain and reserve liquor. Sauté onion in butter until tender. Add flour, stirring until blended and smooth. Slowly add liquor and milk, stirring constantly; cook until smooth and thick. Add pepper, garlic salt, salt, Worcestershire sauce, and cheese; stir until cheese is melted. Combine with spinach. Put into a 2-quart casserole dish; top with breadcrumbs. Bake at 350° for about 30 minutes or until bubbly. Yield: 8 servings.

Garlic Toast

(see Index)

Peach Meringue

2 cups canned peaches, drained
1 tablespoon freshly squeezed lemon juice
1 envelope unflavored gelatin
½ cup cold water
2 egg whites
1 (4½-ounce) container whipped topping

Cut peaches into pieces and put into blender. Add lemon juice and blend 4 seconds. Soften gelatin in cold water and heat until dissolved. Add to fruit and blend 2 seconds. Let stand 5 minutes. Add 1 unbeaten egg white; blend 10 seconds. Add second egg white; blend 3 seconds. Put 2 tablespoons whipped topping into eight sherbet glasses; pour peach mixture on top. Top with another spoonful of whipped topping. Chill overnight. Yield: 8 servings.

Marlene's Punch

1 quart orange sherbet
1 (46-ounce) can pineapple juice
Gin to taste

Soften sherbet with pineapple juice, mixing slowly with a big spoon or whip. Add gin and mix slowly. Serve in chilled glasses. Yield: 8 servings.

When Stocking the Bar

For a small gathering (20 or so) ask your co-host or a friend to tend the bar for the first hour, after which time he may leave his post to join other guests, leaving bottles, ice, and mixers out so guests may help themselves to refills.

When buying liquor remember that there are seventeen 1½-ounce drinks in a fifth of liquor; roughly 200 drinks to a case (12 bottles to a case). To be on the safe side, allow three drinks per guest. Although some guests will have only one drink, it's better to have too much than not enough.

If your party is a sizeable one, you'll undoubtedly have some non-drinkers. For them, it's thoughtful to provide a large pitcher of chilled fruit juice and an assortment of carbonated drinks.

Make ice a week before the party and store the cubes in plastic bags in the freezer. If you don't have a freezer, buy the ice the afternoon before the party and keep it in a tub out of sight.

Provide plenty of napkins, olives, cherries, lemon and orange wedges, and also a tray or table for used glasses.

Lamb-on-the-Spit

Dinner for Eight

Kraut Barbecued Lamb
Fresh Tomato Salad
Corn-Stuffed Peppers
Grilled Biscuits
Fresh Summer Fruit
Picnic Lemonade

Kraut Barbecued Lamb

1 cup kraut juice
1 medium onion, sliced
2 cloves garlic, cut in halves
¼ teaspoon celery seed
¼ teaspoon ground black pepper
1 (5- to 6-pound) leg of lamb
⅓ cup honey
1 teaspoon freshly squeezed lemon juice

Combine kraut juice, onion, garlic, celery seed, and pepper. Put lamb in shallow glass dish and pour marinade over meat; cover dish and chill for 1 day, turning occasionally. Skewer lamb on rotisserie spit. Place spit about 8 inches above heat, and cook for 30 minutes per pound for medium doneness. Blend honey and lemon juice, heat and brush on lamb during the last 30 minutes of cooking time. Yield: 8 servings.

Fresh Tomato Salad

12 ripe tomatoes, chopped
4 fresh green onions, chopped
1 large green pepper, chopped
¼ cup vinegar
¼ teaspoon salt
2 teaspoons sugar
½ teaspoon basil

Combine tomatoes, onions, and pepper. Mix vinegar, salt, sugar, and basil, and stir into vegetable mixture. Cover dish and refrigerate until ready to serve. Yield: 8 to 10 servings.

Corn-Stuffed Peppers

8 medium green peppers
1½ teaspoons salt
4 cups corn, cut from cob; or frozen corn, thawed
1⅓ cups diced fresh tomatoes
1½ teaspoons instant minced onion
¼ teaspoon ground black pepper
¼ teaspoon garlic powder
1 teaspoon chili powder
4 tablespoons all-purpose flour
2 tablespoons butter or margarine, melted

Slice tops from green peppers; carefully remove seeds and membranes. Put in a saucepan with salted water; cover and boil for 5 minutes. Carefully remove from water with a slotted spoon. Combine other ingredients, and spoon into peppers. Place filled peppers in a shallow baking dish, and bake at 375° for about 25 to 35 minutes, or until done. Yield: 8 servings.

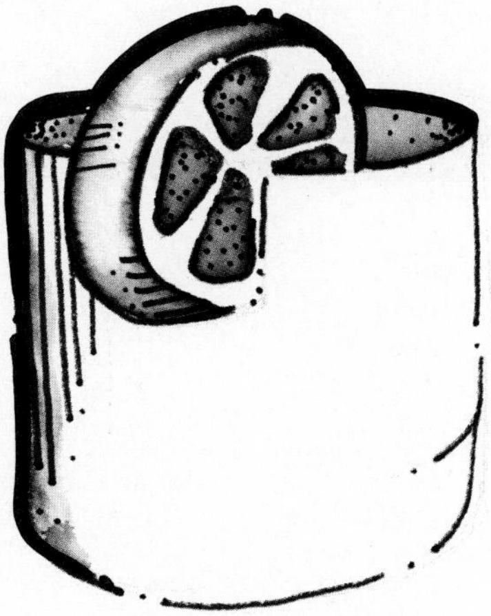

Grilled Biscuits

(see Index)

Picnic Lemonade

½ cup light corn syrup
½ cup sugar
⅔ cup water
2 tablespoons grated lemon rind
1¼ cups freshly squeezed lemon juice
7 cups water
Cherries and lemon slices

Combine corn syrup, sugar, water, and lemon rind. Bring mixture to a boil, and allow to boil for 5 minutes. Strain and cool. Place ice cubes in large pitcher; add cooled mixture, lemon juice, and water. Garnish with cherries and lemon slices. Yield: 10 servings.

No-Fuss Vegetable Tip

Frozen vegetables are delicious cooked on the grill. Remove from package, dot with butter, season, and wrap securely (while still frozen) in heavy-duty aluminum foil. Turn package once during cooking process, which takes about 30 to 35 minutes.

Lamb Kabob Dinner

Dinner for Six to Eight

Cold Avocado Soup
Lamb Kabobs
Polynesian Sweets
Marinated Vegetable Platter
Grilled Biscuits
Ice Cold Watermelon Wedges

Cold Avocado Soup

1 large avocado
1 (10½-ounce) can consommé
Several dashes Tabasco sauce
3 tablespoons freshly squeezed lemon juice
1 pint commercial sour cream
Chopped parsley or chives

Peel and pit avocado; cut into small pieces and put into blender with consommé, Tabasco sauce, and lemon juice. Blend well. Add sour cream and blend just to mix well. Chill in refrigerator for several hours and serve cold. Garnish with chopped parsley or chives. Yield: 8 (6-ounce) servings

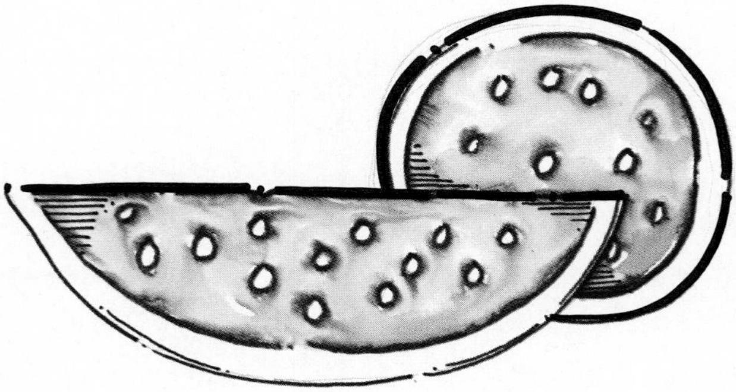

Lamb Kabobs

1 (3- to 4-pound) loin of lamb
1 cup red wine
¼ cup olive oil
3 cloves garlic, crushed
Salt and pepper to taste
Dash oregano

Cut lamb into 2-inch squares. Combine wine, olive oil, garlic, salt, pepper, and oregano for marinade and put in glass or enameled dish. Place lamb in marinade, cover, and let stand for 2 or 3 days. Remove from marinade, place on skewers and cook over low heat about 25 to 30 minutes for well-done lamb. Brush often with marinade as meat is cooking. Yield: 6 to 8 servings.

Polynesian Sweets

2 sweet potatoes, peeled and cut into ½-inch slices
2 bananas, cut diagonally into ½-inch pieces
1 cup pineapple tidbits, drained
1 cup miniature marshmallows
Margarine
Brown sugar
Almonds, diced

Place sweet potato slices on large piece of aluminum foil. Top with banana slices, pineapple, and marshmallows. Dot with margarine; sprinkle with brown sugar and diced almonds. Wrap tightly in foil. Grill 10 to 15 minutes. Yield: about 6 to 8 servings.

Marinated Vegetable Platter

6 medium carrots
1 small head cauliflower
½ cup wine vinegar
¾ cup salad oil
½ teaspoon garlic powder
½ teaspoon prepared mustard
¼ teaspoon salt
½ teaspoon basil leaves, crushed
1 tablespoon minced onion
Salad greens
Cherry tomatoes

Peel carrots and cut into halves; boil in lightly salted water until just tender. Cook cauliflower in boiling water until just tender. Remove both pans from heat, drain and chill thoroughly. Combine vinegar, salad oil, garlic powder, mustard, salt, basil leaves, and minced onion. Stir or shake to blend well. Divide dressing and pour half over the drained carrots and half over the drained cauliflower. Seal containers and let sit in refrigerator overnight.

To serve, put salad greens on outer layer of platter, place carrot strips and cherry tomatoes around next layer, and put cauliflower in center of platter. Serve with remaining marinade. Yield: 6 to 8 servings.

Grilled Biscuits

2 cups all-purpose flour
3 teaspoons baking powder
1 teaspoon salt
⅓ cup shortening
About ⅔ cup milk
4 tablespoons margarine, melted

Combine flour, baking powder, and salt in large bowl. Cut in shortening with two knives or a pastry blender until mixture resembles coarse cornmeal. Add milk and mix lightly. Turn out onto lightly floured board or pastry cloth, and roll to ½-inch thickness. Cut with a 2-inch biscuit cutter. Brush tops with melted margarine, and place biscuits directly on grill over low heat. Cover with a sheet of aluminum foil. Bake about 10 minutes, or until biscuits are browned. If you prefer the tops browned, turn biscuits once. Yield: 16 (2-inch) biscuits.

Using Skewers

Select long, sturdy skewers that reach completely across the grill. Place foods on skewers with some space between them to allow for heat penetration and thorough basting. Unless some vegetables are parboiled, they may require a longer cooking time than meat cubes; therefore you may want to put them on separate skewers. When using bacon strips, string in and out, along chunks of food on skewer. Unpainted wire coat hangers or small green sticks make handy skewers.

Lamplighter Luau

Dinner for Eight

Rumaki
Roast Leg of Lamb
Buttermilk Rice
Easy Cole Slaw
Carrot Sticks
Celery Bread
Watermelon
Tropical Treat Cubes

Rumaki

10 canned water chestnuts, halved
5 chicken livers, cut into quarters
10 slices bacon, halved
¼ cup soy sauce
2 tablespoons brown sugar

Wrap a piece of water chestnut and chicken liver in a half slice of bacon; fasten with a toothpick. Combine soy sauce and brown sugar; chill appetizers in this mixture for ½ hour. Spoon marinade over appetizers occasionally; drain. Broil 3 inches from heat until bacon is crisp, turning once. Yield: 20 appetizers.

Roast Leg of Lamb

1 (4- to 5-pound) boned leg of lamb
1 (10-ounce) package frozen asparagus, thawed
½ cup chopped parsley
½ cup finely chopped celery
½ cup lime juice, divided
1 tablespoon dry white wine
½ teaspoon salt
⅛ teaspoon pepper
¼ teaspoon garlic powder
18 fresh mint leaves, chopped
Salt
3 tablespoons créme de menthe liqueur
½ cup salad oil

Remove all fell (tissue-like covering) from lamb. Thaw asparagus and combine it with parsley, celery, 1 tablespoon lime juice, wine, salt, pepper, garlic powder, and 9 chopped mint leaves. Spread stuffing mixture on lamb and roll up, tying every 2 inches with strong string. With a sharp knife, make incisions in lamb and insert remainder of mint leaves. Rub some salt on surface. Place lamb securely on rotisserie; cook over medium heat 2 hours for well-done lamb. During last 15 minutes of cooking, baste meat with mixture of remaining lime juice, créme de menthe, and salad oil. Remove to hot platter and let set 10 minutes before carving. Drizzle some of basting sauce on slices after carving. Yield: 8 to 10 servings.

Buttermilk Rice

- **1½ cups cooked rice**
- **½ cup cornmeal**
- **3 cups buttermilk**
- **¾ teaspoon soda**
- **1 teaspoon salt**
- **3 eggs, slightly beaten**
- **3 tablespoons margarine, melted**
- **¼ to ½ cup sugar (optional)**

Combine all ingredients in large bowl in order given. Pour into greased, shallow 2-quart casserole dish and bake at 350° for 30 minutes, or cook in foil. Cut eight pieces of heavy-duty aluminum foil into 12-inch squares. Place a square of foil in small bowl, patting it into shape of bowl. Place a serving of rice mixture in each foil packet and seal tightly. Place foil packets on low-heat part of grill. Cook until slightly firm, about 30 minutes, moving packets about occasionally. Fold back foil and use as individual serving dishes. Yield: 8 servings.

Easy Cole Slaw

- **3 cups finely shredded cabbage**
- **¼ cup chopped green pepper**

Toss shredded cabbage with ice cubes; refrigerate until ready to serve. Remove ice and drain. Add green pepper. Toss with Slaw Dressing. Yield: 8 servings.

Slaw Dressing

- **⅓ cup salad dressing**
- **1 tablespoon wine vinegar**
- **2 tablespoons peanut oil**
- **1 teaspoon salt**
- **½ teaspoon celery seed**

Combine salad dressing, vinegar, peanut oil, salt, and celery seed. Mix well and pour over Cole Slaw. Yield: ½ cup.

Celery Bread

(see Index)

Tropical Treat Cubes

- **2 bananas, mashed**
- **1 (6-ounce) can orange juice**
- **1 (6-ounce) can pineapple juice**
- **Juice of 1 lime**
- **Juice of 1 lemon**
- **⅔ cup sugar**
- **Mint leaves**

Combine mashed bananas, orange, pineapple, lime, and lemon juices with sugar. Mixture can be well-blended in blender. Pour mixture into refrigerator tray and freeze into cubes. Serve in sherbet glasses and garnish with mint leaves, or serve on tray, piercing each cube with a toothpick. Yield: 8 servings.

Deluxe Lamb Steak Dinner

Dinner for Four

Pepper Lamb Steaks
Herbed Vegetable Kabobs
Curried Fruit
Garlic-Dill French Bread
Pineapple Sherbet
Mint Punch

Pepper Lamb Steaks

4 lamb steaks, cut ½-inch thick
Unseasoned meat tenderizer
Seasoned salt
1 tablespoon peppercorns

Moisten lamb and sprinkle with meat tenderizer, following label directions. Sprinkle lightly with seasoned salt. Place peppercorns in a plastic bag and crush with a rolling pin. Press onto each side of steaks. Place steaks on grill about 6 inches above hot coals. Grill, turning once; cook 12 minutes for medium doneness or cook until meat reaches desired degree of doneness. Yield: 4 servings.

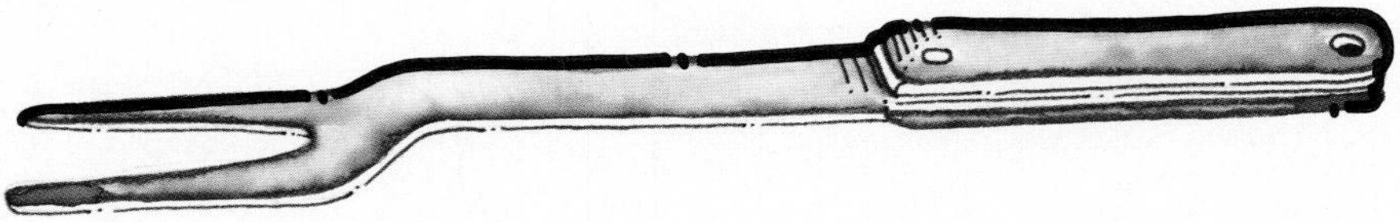

Herbed Vegetable Kabobs

8 small new potatoes
2 medium zucchini squash
2 medium yellow squash
8 large fresh mushrooms
2 large tomatoes
1 large green pepper
¼ cup butter, melted
2 teaspoons herb seasoning

Scrub potatoes and cut off a band of skin around the middle of each. Trim zucchini and yellow squash but do not pare; cut each into 1-inch thick slices. Parboil potatoes in boiling salted water for 15 minutes; drain. Combine zucchini and yellow squash and parboil in boiling salted water for 5 minutes; drain. Wash mushrooms and cut into halves lengthwise. Cut each tomato into 8 wedges. Cut pepper into ¼-inch thick slices. Thread potatoes and squash alternately onto four long skewers; thread mushrooms, tomato wedges, and green pepper strips, alternately, onto four more long skewers. Combine butter and seasoning; brush part of mixture over vegetables. Place potato-squash skewers on grill about 6 inches above heat. Grill, turning and brushing several times with butter mixture, for 10 minutes. Place mushroom-tomato skewers on grill. Continue grilling for 10 minutes or until potatoes and squash are tender and mushrooms and tomatoes are heated through. Yield: 4 servings.

Curried Fruit

1 (17-ounce) can mixed fruit, drained
1 (8½-ounce) can pineapple tidbits, drained
1 (8¾-ounce) can apricot halves, drained
¼ cup margarine, melted
¾ cup brown sugar
1 tablespoon curry powder

Place drained fruit in shallow casserole dish. Combine margarine, brown sugar, and curry powder; pour over fruit. Bake at 300° for 30 minutes. Serve hot. Yield: 4 to 6 servings.

Garlic-Dill French Bread

(see Index)

Pineapple Sherbet

1 quart milk
1½ cups sugar
½ cup freshly squeezed lemon juice
1 cup crushed pineapple

Scald milk. Cool. Add sugar, lemon juice, and pineapple. Freeze in freezer section of refrigerator or in electric or hand-turned freezer. Yield: 2 quarts.

Mint Punch

18 to 20 sprigs fresh mint
1 cup sugar
1 quart boiling water
1 cup plus 2 tablespoons frozen lemonade concentrate
1 quart orange juice
1⅓ cups pineapple juice
2 cups club soda
2 cups ginger ale
12 sprigs mint
½ cup thin lemon slices

Wash 18 to 20 sprigs mint; put into large saucepan with 1 cup sugar and 1 quart boiling water. Simmer, uncovered, for 10 minutes. Chill. When ready to serve, strain mint syrup and add chilled lemonade, orange juice, pineapple juice, club soda, and ginger ale. Serve with mint sprigs and lemon slices. Yield: 4 to 6 servings.

When Using Mushrooms

If your grocer does not stock fresh mushrooms, here's a guide for substituting canned ones:

1 (6- or 8-ounce) can is the equivalent of 1 pound fresh.

1 (3- or 4-ounce) can is the equivalent of ½ pound fresh.

Should a recipe call for fresh mushrooms by measure instead of by weight, here's your guide:

For 1 quart (or 20 to 24 medium mushroom caps), substitute 1 (6- to 8-ounce) can.

For 1 pint (or 10 to 12 medium mushroom caps), substitute 1 (3- to 4-ounce) can.

Chicken Surprise Dinner

Dinner for Eight to Ten

Chicken Surprise
Shirley's Potato Salad
Asparagus Deluxe
Fresh Peach Ice Cream

Chicken Surprise

4 chickens, cut into halves
½ cup olive oil
Salt and pepper to taste
Paprika
Juice of 8 large lemons
1¾ cups wine vinegar
4 teaspoons light brown sugar
2 large pieces candied ginger, minced
3 tablespoons candied orange peel, minced
4 teaspoons rosemary

Rub chicken with olive oil; sprinkle with salt, pepper, and paprika. Combine remaining ingredients and mix well; use sauce to baste chicken frequently while cooking over medium heat. Turn chicken and continue to baste often. Yield: 8 to 10 servings.

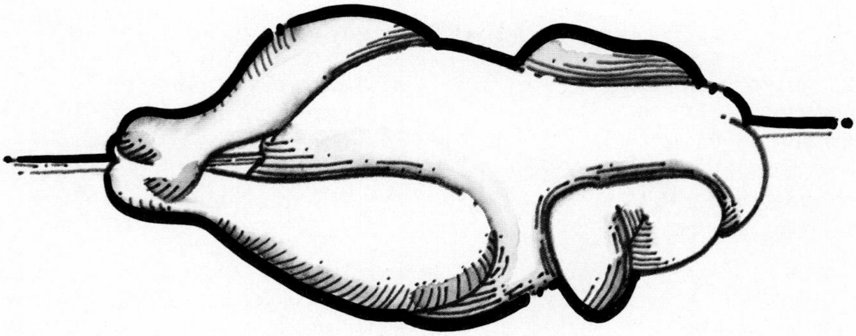

Shirley's Potato Salad

8 medium potatoes
2 tablespoons wine vinegar
4 tablespoons olive oil
1 tablespoon salt (or to taste)
2 teaspoons white pepper (or to taste)
1 cup chopped celery
1 small purple onion, chopped
4 hard-cooked eggs
10 small Spanish olives, sliced
8 dark olives, sliced
¾ cup mayonnaise

Cook potatoes until tender. While still hot, dice and coat potatoes with the vinegar and olive oil. Add salt and pepper. Allow to cool. Stir in the celery, onion, eggs, and olives. Add mayonnaise. Cover and allow flavors to blend. Yield: 8 to 10 servings.

Asparagus Deluxe

6 tablespoons butter, melted
6 tablespoons cornstarch
2 (10½-ounce) cans asparagus spears
Milk
4 hard-cooked eggs, thinly sliced
2 cups shredded Cheddar cheese
Buttered breadcrumbs

Combine butter and cornstarch; stir over medium heat until mixture is smooth and bubbly. Drain asparagus and reserve juice; add enough milk to reserved juice to make 3 cups. Add milk mixture to sauce; cook, stirring constantly, until mixture begins to thicken. Layer asparagus, eggs, cheese, and sauce in a greased 1½-quart casserole dish. Repeat layers. Top with buttered breadcrumbs. Bake at 325° for 30 minutes. Yield: 8 to 10 servings.

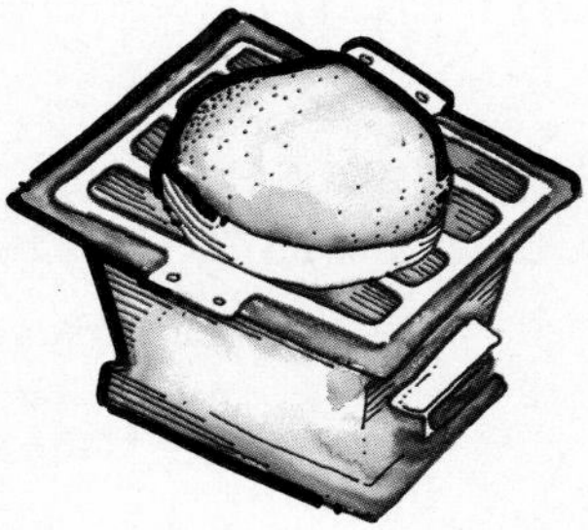

Fresh Peach Ice Cream

1½ cups sugar
2 tablespoons all-purpose flour
½ teaspoon salt
3 eggs, beaten
1 quart whole milk, divided
½ pint whipping cream
1 tablespoon vanilla extract
6 cups mashed fresh peaches
1 cup sugar

Combine the 1½ cups sugar, flour, and salt; add eggs and blend well. Add 1 pint of the milk and cook slowly over low heat until slightly thickened. Cool. Add the whipping cream, remainder of milk, vanilla, and peaches which have been sweetened with 1 cup sugar. Pour into electric or hand-turned freezer and freeze until firm, using 8 parts crushed ice to 1 part ice cream salt. Yield: 1 gallon.

For a Successful Chicken Barbecue

1. Organize a time schedule and follow it through for a perfect family or community chicken barbecue.
2. Allow time for all off-odors to leave the source of heat before starting to cook.
3. Remember advance insect control is a must for everyone's comfort and good sanitary practices.
4. In case of rain, have a small tarpaulin and four posts available for an emergency tent over the grill.
5. If fire becomes too hot, turn chickens more often and mop with sauce.
6. Place all chickens with skin-side up to begin cooking. Unless a hinged basket is used, be very careful to check that all chickens are turned at one time.
7. Be liberal with barbecue sauce. Be sure to have enough to serve as a side dish with the cooked chicken.
8. Barbecued chicken, packed tightly in boxes lined with heavy-duty aluminum foil will keep hot for an hour or longer.
9. Consider the serving and keep all food in a sanitary condition.
10. Careful cleaning of the grounds is a must after any serving of foods. Be sure that all fires are extinguished before leaving.

Barbecued Chicken Deluxe

Dinner for Eight

Barbecued Chicken Deluxe
Candied Sweet Potatoes
Cabbage Casserole
Garlic Toast
Rich Peach Ice Cream

Barbecued Chicken Deluxe

- **½ cup dry white wine**
- **½ cup salad oil**
- **1 teaspoon chopped chives**
- **2 tablespoons chopped parsley**
- **3 (2-pound) chickens, cut-up**
- **Tomato Wine Sauce**

Combine wine, salad oil, chives, and parsley; marinate chicken at room temperature for 1 hour in this mixture. Turn chicken in the marinade several times. Broil or grill for 30 minutes or until done, turning frequently and basting with Tomato Wine Sauce. Yield: 8 servings.

Tomato Wine Sauce

- **1 cup canned tomatoes**
- **1 cup dry white wine**
- **1 cup thinly sliced okra**
- **1½ cups beef bouillon**
- **½ cup finely chopped celery**
- **1 tablespoon freshly squeezed lemon juice**
- **¼ teaspoon Tabasco sauce**
- **2 cloves garlic, minced**
- **1 teaspoon salt**
- **1 teaspoon chili powder**
- **¼ cup Worcestershire sauce**
- **½ cup salad oil**
- **1 tablespoon sugar**
- **1 bay leaf, crumbled**
- **½ teaspoon oregano**
- **½ teaspoon basil**
- **½ cup finely chopped onion**
- **Freshly ground black pepper**

Combine all ingredients and bring to a boil. Reduce heat and simmer for 45 minutes. Strain or put through blender. Serve with barbecued chicken. This sauce is also excellent with ham, pork, or lamb. Yield: about 6 cups.

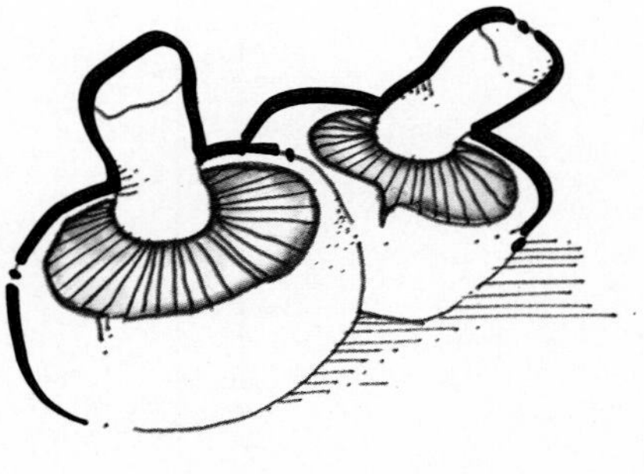

Candied Sweet Potatoes

- 4 medium sweet potatoes, unpeeled
- ⅓ cup sugar
- ⅓ cup brown sugar, firmly packed
- ¾ cup orange juice
- 1 tablespoon cornstarch
- ¼ cup butter or margarine

Cook potatoes in boiling salted water until almost tender. Remove from water and cool. Remove skin and cut potatoes in quarters; place in a flat 1½-quart baking dish. Combine other ingredients in a saucepan and bring to a boil. Pour over potatoes, cover and bake at 375° for 15 minutes. Remove cover and cook an additional 10 minutes. Yield: 8 servings.

Cabbage Casserole

- 1 medium cabbage
- 4 tablespoons butter, melted
- 4 tablespoons all-purpose flour
- ½ teaspoon salt
- ¼ teaspoon pepper
- 2 cups milk
- ½ green pepper, chopped
- ½ medium onion, chopped
- ⅔ cup shredded Cheddar cheese
- ½ cup mayonnaise
- 3 tablespoons chili sauce

Cut cabbage in wedges; boil in salted water until tender, about 15 minutes. Drain cabbage and place in 13- x 9- x 2-inch casserole dish. Combine butter and flour in saucepan over low heat; stir until smooth and bubbly. Add salt, pepper, and milk. Stir constantly over medium heat until sauce is smooth and thick. Pour sauce over cabbage in casserole dish and bake at 375° for 20 minutes. Combine green pepper, onion, cheese, mayonnaise, and chili sauce; mix well and spread over cabbage. Bake at 400° for 20 minutes. Yield: 8 to 10 servings.

Garlic Toast

- ½ cup margarine
- 1 tablespoon grated Parmesan cheese
- 1 teaspoon garlic powder
- 2 tablespoons processed Old English Sharp Cheese
- 1 (1-pound) loaf French-style bread

Combine margarine, Parmesan, garlic powder, and sharp cheese; whip until light and fluffy. Cut bread into 4-inch slices, then split slices. Toast outer crust, then spread cut-side with cheese mixture. Return to oven and toast until mixture is bubbly and edges are golden brown. Yield: 6 to 8 servings.

Rich Peach Ice Cream

- 1 quart whipping cream
- 2½ cups sugar, divided
- Pinch salt
- 3 cups crushed ripe peaches

Scald cream and half of sugar in top of double boiler. Stir well to dissolve sugar. Add salt. Mash peaches to a purée or blend well in blender. Add remaining sugar to peaches, stirring well to dissolve sugar. Place cream in electric or hand-turned freezer and freeze to a thick mush. Stir in peaches and complete freezing. Remove dasher and pack with more ice and salt. Allow ice cream to stand an hour or two before serving. Yield: 2 quarts.

Cook-Your-Dinner-at-Night

Dinner for Eight to Ten

Smoked Turkey
Orange Candied Sweet Potatoes
Tomato Piquante
Tossed Spinach-Orange Salad
Butterscotch Crunch Squares

Smoked Turkey

1 (12- to 16-pound) turkey
Seasoned salt

Rub turkey with seasoned salt. Put 10 pounds of charcoal briquettes in charcoal pan and light fire. Let fire burn 10 to 15 minutes and add 6 to 8 blocks of hickory to fire. Place water pan in smoker and fill with water. Place grill in smoker, put turkey on and cover with top. It will take 10 to 12 hours to cook. Do not peek at meat but allow it to cook slowly to perfection without being disturbed. You may wish to put the turkey in the smoker at night before you go to bed, and it will be juicy and tender the next morning. Yield: 8 to 10 servings.

Orange Candied Sweet Potatoes

4 medium sweet potatoes, unpeeled
⅓ cup brown sugar, firmly packed
⅓ cup sugar
¾ cup orange juice
Dash salt
¼ cup butter or margarine

Cook potatoes in boiling salted water until barely soft. Remove from water and cool. Remove skin and cut into quarters or ¾-inch slices. Place in a flat 1½-quart baking dish. Combine other ingredients in small saucepan and bring to a boil; pour over potatoes in baking dish. Cover dish and bake at 375° for 25 minutes; uncover dish and bake an additional 15 to 20 minutes, or until syrup has cooked down and potatoes are glazed. Yield: 8 servings.

Tomato Piquante

8 ripe tomatoes
1 cup salad oil
4 tablespoons tarragon vinegar
4 tablespoons chopped parsley
¼ cup sliced green onions
2 teaspoons chopped fresh thyme, or ½ teaspoon dry thyme
1 teaspoon salt
¼ teaspoon pepper
1 clove garlic, minced

Peel and quarter tomatoes; put into a deep bowl. Combine other ingredients in a jar and mix well. Pour over tomatoes, cover bowl, and chill several hours or overnight. When ready to serve, drain and serve tomatoes. Dressing may be stored and used again. Yield: 8 servings.

You can cook a perfect, evenly browned smoked turkey without any fuss and bother. It's delicious served with Orange Candied Sweet Potatoes, Tomato Piquante, Tossed Spinach-Orange Salad, and Butterscotch Crunch Squares.

Tossed Spinach-Orange Salad

3 cups fresh spinach, torn into small pieces
3 medium oranges, sectioned
1 tablespoon sugar
Salt to taste
¼ cup French Dressing

Combine spinach, orange sections, sugar, and salt in a large bowl. Add ¼ cup (or more, if desired) French Dressing and toss. Yield: 6 to 8 servings.

French Dressing

1 teaspoon salt
¼ teaspoon sugar
3 tablespoons freshly squeezed lemon juice
¼ cup catsup
½ cup salad oil
1 (3-ounce) package cream cheese, softened (optional)

Combine the first five ingredients in a pint jar; shake well and let sit several hours before using. The softened cream cheese may be added to dressing just before serving. Yield: 1 cup.

Butterscotch Crunch Squares

1 cup all-purpose flour
¼ cup quick-cooking oatmeal
¼ cup brown sugar, firmly packed
½ cup butter or margarine
½ cup chopped nuts
1 (12-ounce) jar butterscotch ice cream topping
1 quart vanilla ice cream, softened

Combine flour, oatmeal, and brown sugar; cut in butter until mixture resembles coarse crumbs. Stir in nuts. Pat mixture into a 13- x 9- x 2-inch baking pan. Bake at 400° for 15 minutes. Stir mixture while still warm to crumble; cool. Pat three-fourths of crumb mixture in bottom of 9-inch square pan; drizzle half of ice cream topping over crumbs in pan. Stir ice cream to soften; spoon carefully over topping mixture. Drizzle with remaining topping; sprinkle with remaining crumb mixture. Freeze. Yield: 8 to 10 servings.

Basting Tip

Food may be basted during the entire cooking time or during the last half hour, depending on the ingredients in the sauce. A small paintbrush or long handled cotton dishmop works well for basting and brushing on sauce. Sauces containing sugar (or ingredients that burn readily) should be applied during the last 15 to 30 minutes of cooking time.

Tailgate Picnic

Picnic for Twelve

Gingered Chicken
Tangy Baked Beans
Tarragon-Tuna Eggs
Crisp Relish
Prune Cake
Spiced Coffee or Lemon-Orange Drink

Gingered Chicken

1½ cups all-purpose flour
2 tablespoons ground ginger
2 teaspoons salt
3 teaspoons pepper
2 (2½-pound) chickens, cut-up
Shortening for frying

Combine flour, ginger, salt, and pepper in paper bag. Place chicken pieces in bag; shake until chicken is coated with flour. Remove chicken pieces to dry; replace in flour and shake again. Heat shortening in iron skillet and fry chicken until brown on both sides. Yield: 12 servings.

Tangy Baked Beans

1 (1-pound 15-ounce) can pork and beans, drained
1 (16-ounce) can pork and beans, drained
½ cup brown sugar, firmly packed
3 tablespoons sherry
1½ tablespoons orange-flavored instant breakfast drink
1½ teaspoons instant coffee
½ teaspoon salt

Drain beans. Add rest of ingredients and mix well. Spoon into 2-quart casserole dish. Bake at 350° for about 45 minutes. Yield: 12 servings.

Tarragon-Tuna Eggs

12 hard-cooked eggs
1 (7-ounce) can tuna
½ cup mayonnaise
1 teaspoon vinegar
½ teaspoon crushed tarragon leaves
½ teaspoon salt

Cut eggs in halves lengthwise. Remove yolks to small bowl and mash well. Drain and flake tuna; mix with egg yolks. Add other ingredients and mix well. Stuff tuna mixture into whites. Refrigerate until time to serve. Yield: 12 servings.

Crisp Relish

4 cups chopped cabbage
1 small onion, chopped
1 medium green pepper, chopped
1 teaspoon turmeric
1 cup vinegar
1 teaspoon salt
1 teaspoon celery seed
1 cup sugar

Combine cabbage, onion, green pepper, and turmeric; mix well. Mix vinegar, salt, celery seed, and sugar; boil for 5 minutes. Pour over the vegetables and mix well. Cool and refrigerate. Yield: 12 servings.

Prune Cake

1 (16-ounce) package dried prunes
1 (18½-ounce) package spiced cake mix
½ cup chopped walnuts
Orange Icing

Cook prunes as directed on package (omit any sugar). Drain and reserve liquid. Chop prunes finely. Make cake as directed, using prune juice in place of water. Fold in 1 cup prunes and walnuts with cake batter. Pour into greased 13- x 9- x 2-inch pan. Bake at 350° for 30 to 40 minutes or until cake tests done. Cool completely. Frost with Orange Icing. Yield: 12 to 15 servings.

Orange Icing

1 (8-ounce) package cream cheese, softened
1½ tablespoons orange-flavored instant breakfast drink
½ cup powdered sugar
1 tablespoon water
Cooked prunes

Combine all ingredients except prunes and mix well. Fold in remainder of chopped prunes. Mix well. Yield: enough icing to cover a 13- x 9- x 2-inch cake.

Spiced Coffee

Hot strong coffee
Grated sweet chocolate
Sweetened whipped cream
Cinnamon stick

Brew coffee to double strength and have other ingredients in small bowls. For each cup, use: 1 soup spoon chocolate and 1 heaping spoon whipped cream. Stir with cinnamon stick and serve in mugs.

Lemon-Orange Drink

3 (6-ounce) cans frozen orange juice concentrate
Cold water
1½ cups fresh or bottled lemon juice
Cracked ice
Lemon slices
Maraschino cherries

Combine concentrate with ½ can less water than called for in directions on can. Add ½ cup lemon juice, mixing well. Pour into glasses filled with cracked ice. Garnish each glass with a lemon slice and a maraschino cherry. Yield: 12 servings.

A sunny summer picnic and romance naturally go together. The old-fashioned picnic is far from being outdated as it remains one of the most popular ways to eat outdoors.

Easy Barbecued Chicken Dinner

Dinner for Eight

Easy Barbecued Chicken
Onion-Bean Bake
Zucchini and Corn Casserole
Garlic Toast
Five-Cup Salad

Easy Barbecued Chicken

4 (2- to 2½-pound) fryers, cut into halves
2 to 3 cups commercial barbecue sauce

Wash chicken halves and drain well. Place on barbecue grill over low heat with meat-side down; turn after 10 minutes and begin brushing with barbecue sauce. Keep a close watch on chicken so that it does not burn. Baste often and turn often. It will take about 30 to 45 minutes to cook chicken. Yield: 8 servings.

Onion-Bean Bake

4 wieners, sliced
2 (1-pound) cans pork and beans
1 cup shredded Cheddar cheese
2 tablespoons brown sugar
2 teaspoons parsley flakes
½ teaspoon seasoned salt
1 (3-ounce) can French-fried onion rings

Combine wieners, beans, cheese, brown sugar, parsley flakes, and seasoned salt. Stir in ½ can of onion rings. Spoon mixture into a greased 1½-quart casserole dish. Bake at 350° for 25 minutes. Sprinkle top with remaining onion rings, and bake 5 minutes longer.

Using the Meat Thermometer

A meat thermometer inserted so that the bulb doesn't touch bone or fat is the most accurate way to test doneness of meat. For a roast, insert thermometer in the center. Beef will be rare when the internal temperature is 140°, medium at 160°, and well-done at 170°. For poultry, the thermometer should be inserted in the thickest part of the thigh, close to the body. For ham, place thermometer in the middle of the thickest part of meat. Fresh pork should always be cooked to well-done stage, or 185°.

Zucchini and Corn Casserole

6 medium zucchini squash, sliced
½ cup diced onion
2 tablespoons butter or margarine, melted
1 cup cooked cream-style corn
Dash ground cumin
Dash garlic salt
¼ teaspoon black pepper
¾ teaspoon salt
Dash paprika
¼ cup seasoned croutons
½ cup shredded Cheddar cheese

Sauté squash and onion in melted butter or margarine until tender, stirring constantly. Stir in corn, cumin, garlic salt, pepper, salt, and paprika. Mix well and spoon mixture into a 1½-quart casserole dish. Sprinkle top with seasoned croutons and sprinkle shredded cheese on top. Bake at 300° for 30 minutes. Yield: 6 to 8 servings.

Garlic Toast

(see Index)

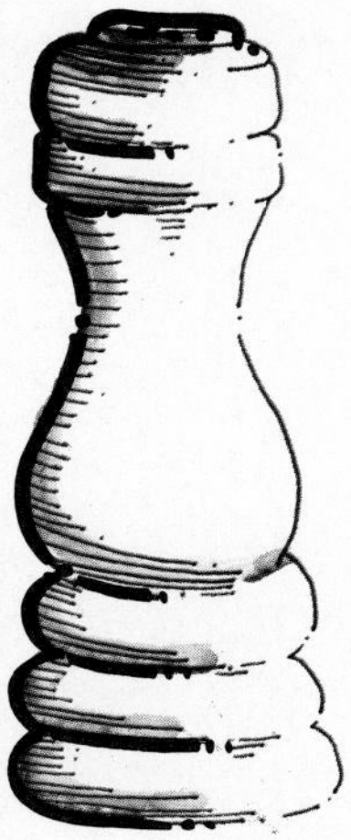

Five-Cup Salad

1 cup drained mandarin oranges
1 cup drained pineapple chunks
1 cup miniature marshmallows
1 cup flaked coconut
1 cup commercial sour cream

Combine all ingredients in a large bowl, and stir gently to blend. Cover and place in refrigerator for 3 hours before serving. Yield: 8 servings.

When Is the Chicken Done?

It's easy to tell if chicken is done by twisting the drumstick. If the joint twists out of the socket easily, the meat is done. Be sure to serve the chicken while it is hot, and try to have extra sauce to serve alongside the barbecued chicken.

A Picnic Packed for Two

Crudités
Chicken Liver Pâté
French Bread
Roasted Rock Cornish Hens
Ham and Tomato Open-Faced Sandwiches
Fresh Fruit and Assorted Cheese
Smaland Twists and Chocolate Diagonals
Rhine Wine and Bordeaux Wine

Crudités

1 carrot
1 stalk celery
Cauliflower
Green pepper

Clean and peel the carrot. Slice into sticks. Clean and slice celery into sticks. Break several cauliflower buds from the head. Clean the interior of a green pepper, then slice in rounds. Crisp the raw vegetables in cold water in the refrigerator overnight or several hours before packing for the picnic. Pack in a plastic container or plastic bag for carrying. Yield: 2 servings.

Chicken Liver Pâté

1 pound fresh chicken livers
½ cup sherry wine
½ cup butter
Salt, pepper, rosemary, and thyme to taste

Put the fresh chicken livers in a saucepan and add sherry to just cover the livers. Simmer over low heat until done, but not tough. Put in the blender, add butter and seasonings. Blend and pour into ramekins for serving. Yield: about 3 cups.

Roasted Rock Cornish Hens

2 rock Cornish hens
Rock salt
Brown paper
Salad oil

Clean the hens. Fill the bottom of an earthenware Dutch oven with the rock salt. Place the hens in the Dutch oven and cover with the brown paper which has been greased with the salad oil. Bake at 300° about 1 hour, or until done. Yield: 2 to 4 servings.

One of the best things about a bicycle is that it can take you to a picnic. You are sure to have an appetite when you get there.

Ham and Tomato Open-Faced Sandwiches

- **1 (½-pound) small loaf brown-and-serve bread**
- **½ cup butter or margarine, softened**
- **About 32 cherry tomatoes**
- **1 (14½-ounce) can asparagus spears**
- **¼ cup mayonnaise**
- **6 slices baked ham, thinly sliced**

Cook the small loaf of bread according to the directions on the package. When cool, slice as thin as possible and spread with the softened butter. Refrigerate. The hardened butter keeps a moist sandwich topping from making the bread soggy. When the butter has hardened remove from the refrigerator and proceed with the sandwiches.

Using half the loaf of buttered bread, cover each slice with a layer of sliced cherry tomatoes. Lay a spear or two of asparagus across each sandwich. Put the mayonnaise in a plastic container and carry on the picnic. Just before serving, drop a teaspoon on each sandwich. Yield: about 6 to 8 small sandwiches.

Using the remaining buttered bread, roll each ham slice into a cornucopia and place seam-side down on a bread slice. Put a piece of parsley in the end of the ham cornucopia. Yield: 6 small sandwiches.

Smaland Twists

- **1 cup butter**
- **½ cup sugar**
- **1 cup commercial sour cream**
- **1 teaspoon soda**
- **3 cups all-purpose flour**

Work butter and sugar until smooth. Gradually add sour cream. Add soda mixed with small amount of flour. Gradually work in remaining flour. Turn dough onto floured board and work until smooth. Divide dough into 40 equal parts and roll out each piece into a string. Shape into twists. Dip in sugar and bake on greased baking sheet at 475° for about 10 minutes or until light golden. Serve soft; or dry twists at 250°. Yield: 40 twists.

Chocolate Diagonals

- **1 cup butter or margarine**
- **1 cup sugar**
- **1 egg**
- **⅓ cup cocoa**
- **½ teaspoon vanilla extract**
- **¼ teaspoon soda**
- **2 cups all-purpose flour**
- **½ egg, slightly beaten**
- **¼ cup slivered almonds**

Cream butter and sugar; add egg, cocoa, and vanilla extract. Sift soda and flour together and gradually add to butter mixture. Work dough until smooth. Divide dough into three parts. Roll out each part into ½-inch thick strand. Place on buttered cookie sheet. Brush strands with egg and sprinkle with almonds. Bake at 350° about 10 minutes. Cut strands into ¾-inch diagonals while still hot. Yield: 35 to 40 cookies.

How Many Ice Cubes?

To eliminate the bothersome task of filling and refilling ice trays, make your ice cubes ahead of time and store them in a plastic bag in the freezer. Count on 350 cubes for 50 people, or 7 cubes per person.

Teriyaki Meal From the Grill

Dinner for Four

Chicken Teriyaki
Corn-Okra Special
Island Fruit Salad
Skewered Bread Chunks
Lemon Sherbet

Chicken Teriyaki

⅔ cup soy sauce
¼ cup white wine
2 tablespoons sugar
1 clove garlic, minced
1 tablespoon salad oil
½ teaspoon ground ginger
1 medium-size fryer, cut-up

Combine soy sauce, wine, sugar, garlic, salad oil, and ginger. Marinate chicken in this mixture at least 1 hour or overnight. Chicken may be baked at 325° or on outdoor grill. Baste two or three times while cooking. Yield: 4 servings.

Corn-Okra Special

1 small onion, cut in strips
1 medium green pepper, diced
3 large ears of corn
1 cup fresh okra
1 beef bouillon cube
½ cup boiling water
2 tablespoons butter or margarine
Dash garlic salt
½ teaspoon salt
Dash white pepper

Prepare onion and green pepper. Remove husks and silks from corn. Cut off kernels with a sharp knife; scrape down with back of knife to remove pulp. There should be about 1½ cups.

Slice okra into ½-inch rounds. Dissolve bouillon cube in hot water and set aside. Melt butter or margarine in 10-inch skillet. Add onion and green pepper; cook gently, stirring often, until partly tender. Add corn, okra, bouillon, garlic salt, salt, and pepper. Cover tightly and simmer, stirring several times, until corn and okra are tender, about 5 to 10 minutes. Yield: 4 servings.

Tenderizing Meat

Tenderize meat and chicken by rubbing inside and out with lemon juice.

Island Fruit Salad

1 small fresh pineapple
1 small cantaloupe
1 fresh pear
2 bananas
1 cup strawberries
2 oranges
1 cup seedless grapes
Lemon juice
Fruit Dressing

Cut pineapple into chunks, cut cantaloupe into balls, and slice pear, bananas, and strawberries. Section oranges and cut into bite-size pieces; leave grapes whole. Dip all fruits in lemon juice, combine fruits and chill in covered container. Pour dressing over fruit, blend well and serve cold. Yield: 4 generous servings.

Fruit Dressing

½ to ¾ cup orange juice
¼ cup salad oil
1 tablespoon sugar
½ teaspoon salt
½ teaspoon paprika
¼ teaspoon celery seed
½ clove garlic, crushed

Combine all ingredients in jar; shake gently to blend, cover and allow to sit several hours in refrigerator before serving on fruit salad. Yield: 1¼ cups.

Skewered Bread Chunks

1 or 2 cloves garlic, crushed
½ cup butter or margarine, melted
2 tablespoons minced fresh parsley
1 (1-pound) loaf French bread
3 to 6 tablespoons grated Parmesan cheese

Combine garlic, butter, and parsley. Cut French bread in half lengthwise, then crosswise in 2-inch slices. Spread butter on bread and sprinkle with Parmesan cheese. Spear bread on skewers and grill about 5 inches above heated grill for about 5 minutes, or until lightly toasted. Yield: 4 to 6 servings.

Lemon Sherbet

2 (6-ounce) cans frozen lemonade concentrate
1¾ cups sugar
¼ teaspoon salt
2 tablespoons grated lemon rind
6 cups evaporated milk

Put lemonade concentrate, sugar, salt, and lemon rind in a large bowl. Beat together until well-blended. Slowly stir in evaporated milk and mix well. Pour mixture into 1-gallon freezer can. Freeze in electric or hand-turned freezer, using a mixture of 8 parts crushed ice to 1 part ice cream salt. When ice cream is frozen, tip freezer to drain off water.

Before opening can, wipe lid carefully. Scrape ice cream off dasher and pack firmly in can. Cover with double thickness of waxed paper and replace lid (fitted with cork or paper plug). Repack with a mixture of 4 parts crushed ice to 1 part ice cream salt. Cover with paper or heavy cloth. Let stand 1½ to 2 hours to ripen. Yield: 1 gallon.

Deluxe Cornish Hen Dinner

Dinner for Six

Stuffed Cornish Hens
Mushroom Potatoes
Pickled Eggs
Wilted Endive Salad
Cheesecake

Stuffed Cornish Hens

6 Cornish hens
½ lemon
3 teaspoons salt
2 teaspoons pepper
12 chicken livers
3 tablespoons butter, melted
6 medium mushrooms, sliced
2 tablespoons butter, melted
½ cup chopped ham
¼ cup chopped toasted almonds
¼ cup butter, melted
¼ cup dry white wine
2 tablespoons red currant jelly

Wash hens; rub cavities with lemon, salt, and pepper. Sauté chicken livers in 3 tablespoons butter; remove from heat and chop very fine. Sauté mushrooms in 2 tablespoons butter; combine livers, mushrooms, ham, and almonds to make dressing. Stuff hens lightly with dressing; skewer the openings and tie legs together. Combine ¼ cup melted butter, wine, and jelly; baste hens with this mixture. Place hens in shallow pan and put in smoker or bake in oven at 350°. Cook until fork-tender, about 45 minutes to an hour, basting frequently. Yield: 6 servings.

Mushroom Potatoes

3 to 4 potatoes, peeled and thinly sliced
1 (10¾-ounce) can cream of mushroom soup
Salt and pepper to taste
Butter
Grated Parmesan cheese

Boil sliced potatoes until about half done. Layer in shallow, buttered casserole dish with mushroom soup; sprinkle lightly with salt and pepper and dot with butter. Top with Parmesan cheese. Bake at 350° for about 30 minutes, or until potatoes are done and soup is bubbly. Yield: 6 servings.

Pickled Eggs

1 (16-ounce) jar pickled beets
6 hard-cooked eggs, peeled

Drain beets and reserve juice. Place beets and eggs in clean glass jar. Heat beet juice and pour over beets and eggs. Cover and let sit overnight. Yield: 6 servings.

Wilted Endive Salad

1 large head endive
5 slices bacon, fried crisp and crumbled
1 onion, thinly sliced
¼ cup bacon fat
½ cup sugar (less if desired)
1 teaspoon salt
¼ cup vinegar
Water (optional)

Separate endive and wash thoroughly. Toss with bacon bits and onion slices. Combine bacon fat, sugar, salt, vinegar, and water; heat until it bubbles and sugar is dissolved. Pour hot dressing over salad greens. Toss thoroughly so greens are wilted. Serve immediately. Yield: 6 servings.

Cheesecake

1 (8-ounce) carton ricotta or cottage cheese, drained
½ (8-ounce) package cream cheese, softened
1 tablespoon commercial sour cream
2 tablespoons all-purpose flour
¼ teaspoon salt
½ teaspoon vanilla extract
Rind of ½ lemon, grated
2 egg yolks, beaten
2 egg whites
½ cup sugar
1 (8½-ounce) can crushed pineapple, drained
Pastry

Put drained ricotta in blender and blend until smooth. Add cream cheese, sour cream, flour, salt, vanilla extract, lemon rind, and egg yolks to ricotta in blender. Blend until smooth. Beat egg whites with sugar until soft peaks form; fold into cheese mixture. Put crushed pineapple in bottom of baked pastry shell; fill shell with cheese mixture. Bake at 300° for 30 to 45 minutes until cheese sets. Chill before serving. Yield: 6 servings.

Pastry

10 tablespoons all-purpose flour
3 tablespoons sugar
6 tablespoons butter
1 egg, slightly beaten

Combine flour and sugar. Cut in butter with pastry blender until mixture resembles coarse meal. Gradually add egg to dry mixture. Dough will be quite soft. Line bottom and sides of greased 9-inch piepan with pastry. Bake at 300° for 15 minutes. Cool before filling shell. Yield: 1 (9-inch) pie.

Tip for Serving French Bread

Here is a tip for the hostess who has watched guests tugging at French bread trying to break slices away from the bottom, uncut crust.

After preparing the loaf in the usual manner, butter between slices and complete the slicing all the way through the bottom crust. Hold the loaf into shape with your hands. Taking a long skewer, stick it through the loaf, lengthwise, thus holding the loaf firmly in place. Keep the skewer in the loaf throughout the heating process, and just before serving time, slide the slices off the skewer into a basket or onto a platter.

North of the Border Meal

Dinner for Four

Chili con Queso with Corn Chips
Tequila and Tonic
Pollo Rollenas
(Chicken Rolls)
Patatas Mantequilla
(Potatoes in Butter)
Ensalada Mexicana
(Mexican Salad)
Dulce Paraíso
(Paradise Dessert)

Chili con Queso with Corn Chips

3 tablespoons butter
3 tablespoons all-purpose flour
1½ cups milk
1½ cups shredded Cheddar cheese
1 to 2 (4-ounce) cans green chiles, finely chopped*
Dash black pepper
½ teaspoon salt
Dash paprika
¼ teaspoon Tabasco sauce (optional)
Corn chips

Melt butter in 1-quart saucepan over low heat. Add flour and stir until smooth. Cook a few minutes; add milk slowly, stirring to keep mixture free from lumps. Cook and stir until mixture thickens.

Add cheese and chopped chiles (add 1 can and taste before adding second can). Mix well. Remove from heat as soon as cheese melts. Add pepper, salt, paprika, and Tabasco sauce. Serve hot with corn chips. Yield: 2½ cups.

*This sauce is fairly hot with 2 cans of chiles. For those guests too far north of the border, reduce the fire by adding ½ teaspoon sugar.

Note: If by chance there is any left over, this makes a delicious topping over baked potatoes, vegetables, or as a sandwich spread.

Tequila and Tonic

1 jigger tequila
2 ice cubes
Quinine water
Lemon slices (optional)

Put tequila and ice cubes in a 6- or 8-ounce glass. Fill glass with quinine water and serve with a slice of lemon if desired. Yield: 1 serving.

Pollo Rollenas

(Chicken Rolls)

4 whole chicken breasts
2 tablespoons shortening
1 small onion, chopped
2 cloves garlic, minced
3 fresh tomatoes, chopped
3 eggs, beaten
1 cup toasted almonds
1 teaspoon chopped parsley
Salt to taste
½ cup salad oil
Juice of 1 lemon
¼ cup water

Remove bones from chicken breasts, leaving each breast in one piece. Set aside. Melt shortening in skillet; sauté onion and garlic until lightly browned. Add chopped tomatoes; stir in eggs and cook until eggs coagulate. Add almonds, parsley, and salt. Remove from heat and cool slightly. Stuff chicken breasts with this mixture; fasten with skewers. Broil over hot coals for 30 minutes, or until chicken is tender, turning frequently. During the last 15 minutes of cooking time, brush chicken with basting sauce made by combining salad oil, lemon juice, and water. Yield: 4 servings.

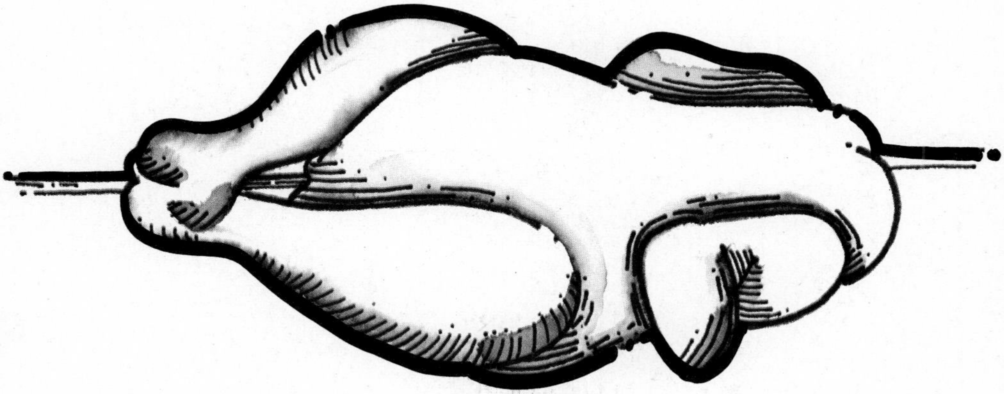

Patatas Mantequilla

(Potatoes in Butter)

4 medium potatoes
4 tablespoons butter or margarine
Salt and pepper

Pare and slice each potato onto a double 12-inch square of heavy-duty aluminum foil. Add 1 tablespoon butter to each packet; sprinkle with salt and pepper. Wrap securely. Cook over hot coals about 1 hour, turning packets frequently. Yield: 4 servings.

Plan Meal Around Meat

Plan your menus to include three or four simple dishes, and think of the entire meal rather than just the meat. Serve vegetables and salads that are compatible with the meat. Desserts may be served, but make them simple. Since most barbecue meals are rather heavy, many guests do not want dessert; make it a "take your choice" or "take it or not" type dessert.

A delightful patio dinner with sausages, grilled chicken, and ribs is deliciously basted with colorful Sweet 'n Sour Sauce (page 128) or our Bang-Up Barbecue Sauce (page 126).

Ensalada Mexicana

(Mexican Salad)

3 large green peppers
1 medium onion
4 medium, ripe tomatoes
4 slices bacon
1 teaspoon chili powder
½ cup vinegar
Lettuce leaves

Thinly slice peppers, onion, and tomatoes in a large bowl; mix gently. Cut bacon into 1-inch pieces; cook until crisp in a hot skillet. Stir in chili powder and vinegar. Bring quickly to a boil and pour over vegetables. Toss gently and serve on lettuce leaves. Yield: 4 servings.

Dulce Paraíso

(Paradise Dessert)

½ cup sugar
½ cup water
1 ounce liqueur (any flavor)
12 ladyfingers
2 cups milk
2 tablespoons cornstarch
3 eggs, beaten
¾ cup sugar
¼ pound blanched almonds, ground
Ground cinnamon

Boil ½ cup sugar and ½ cup water for 10 minutes. Remove from heat and add liqueur. Place ladyfingers in a 1½-quart glass platter and cover with syrup.

Combine ⅓ cup milk with cornstarch; stir in beaten eggs, mix well and set aside. Heat ¾ cup sugar and the remainder of the milk; stir in the egg-cornstarch mixture and mix well. Cook slowly, stirring constantly, until mixture thickens. Add ground almonds, remove from heat, cool slightly, then pour over ladyfingers. Sprinkle with ground cinnamon and chill. Yield: 4 to 6 servings.

Disposable Pans

Make disposable pans from heavy-duty aluminum foil for heating vegetables, buns, and other foods on top of grill. Turn up edges for 1½- to 2-inch sides; pinch corners so "pan" won't leak.

Barbecued Chicken Special

Dinner for Six to Eight

Peppered Barbecue Chicken
Cheesy Zucchini Casserole
Rice Salad
Hot Curried Fruit in Foil
Raspberry Delight

Peppered Barbecue Chicken

1 cup salad oil
2 cups freshly squeezed lemon juice or vinegar
1 cup water
4 tablespoons white pepper
2 to 3 (2½-pound) fryers, cut-up

Combine salad oil, lemon juice, water, and pepper in a large flat dish. Lay chicken pieces in marinade and let sit for at least 2 hours. Remove chicken from marinade and drain carefully. Place in hinged basket on grill over low heat; cook until meat is done, brushing often with marinade, and turning basket often to keep chicken from burning. Chicken should cook about 25 minutes. Yield: 6 to 8 servings.

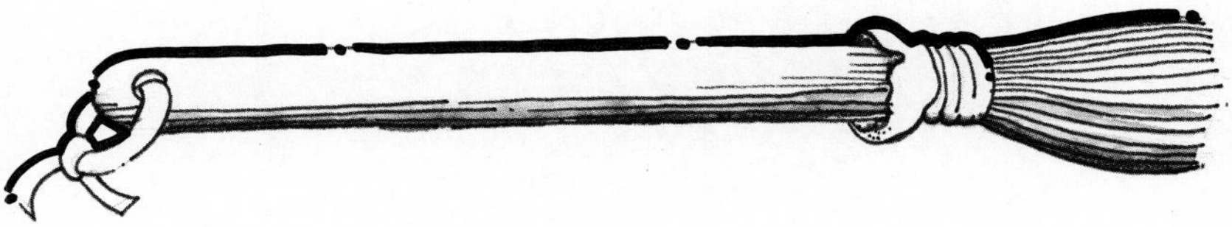

Cheesy Zucchini Casserole

4 to 6 tender zucchini squash
2 hard-cooked eggs, sliced
2 tablespoons butter or margarine
2 tablespoons all-purpose flour
¼ teaspoon salt
1 cup milk
½ cup shredded Cheddar cheese
Cayenne pepper to taste
4 to 6 tablespoons buttered breadcrumbs
¼ cup grated Parmesan or Romano cheese

Wash squash well; split each lengthwise into three pieces; boil in salted water for 5 minutes. Drain well and place in a shallow baking dish; place sliced eggs over squash. Melt butter over low heat; stir in flour and salt until well-blended. Add milk and cook, stirring constantly, until mixture thickens. Add shredded Cheddar cheese and stir until cheese is melted. Pour over squash and eggs. Taste and adjust salt; add cayenne pepper. Top with a mixture of buttered breadcrumbs and sprinkle grated cheese over top. Bake at 375° for 25 to 30 minutes, or until mixture is bubbly and brown. Yield: 6 to 8 servings.

Rice Salad

- 3 cups cooked rice
- 6 hard-cooked eggs, chopped
- ½ cup chopped green pepper
- 1 bunch green onions, chopped
- 1 (2-ounce) jar pimientos, chopped
- 1 stalk celery, finely chopped
- 1 tablespoon freshly squeezed lemon juice
- Salad dressing or mayonnaise
- Salt and pepper to taste

Combine rice, eggs, green pepper, onions, pimientos, and celery in a large bowl. Combine lemon juice with just enough salad dressing or mayonnaise to moisten and hold salad together. Add salt and pepper to taste. Yield: 6 to 8 servings.

Hot Curried Fruit in Foil

- 6 slices canned pineapple, drained
- 1 cup sliced strawberries or drained canned whole blueberries
- 3 tablespoons butter or margarine, melted
- 1½ teaspoons curry powder

Cut 12 (8-inch) squares of heavy-duty aluminum foil. Make a double thickness. Put a slice of pineapple on each of the six packets. Put strawberries or blueberries on top of pineapple slices. Combine melted butter and curry powder and spoon over berries. Wrap packets securely, and place on coolest part of the grill to cook for about 15 minutes, turning packets several times. Yield: 6 servings.

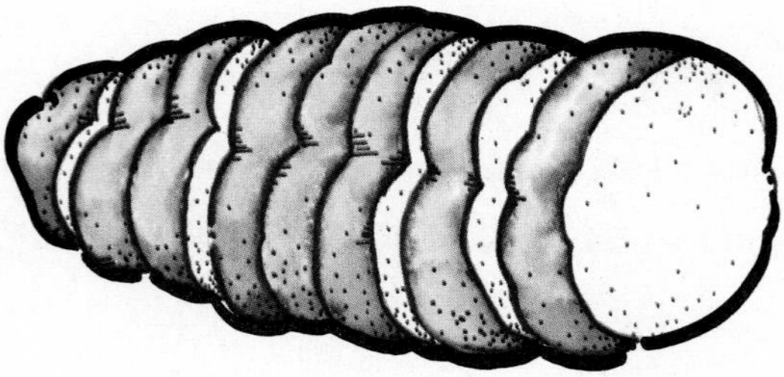

Raspberry Delight

- 1 (6-ounce) can frozen pink lemonade concentrate
- Cold water
- 1 pint raspberry sherbet
- Whipped topping
- Cherries

Mix lemonade with cold water as directed on can and chill until very cold. Spoon one or two scoops raspberry sherbet in tall glasses and pour lemonade over. Just before serving, add whipped topping, and top with a cherry. (Serve with a straw and a parfait spoon.) Yield: 4 servings; double the recipe to serve 8.

Onion Juice in a Hurry

When you need just a few drops of onion juice for flavor, sprinkle a little salt on a slice of onion and scrape the salted surface with a knife or spoon to obtain the juice.

Oriental Chicken Dinner

Dinner for Eight

Chicken Oriental

Grilled Rice with Olives

Mixed Vegetable Casserole

Sliced Tomatoes

Twenty-Four Hour Salad or Dessert

Chicken Oriental

8 chicken breast halves
½ cup soy sauce
½ cup dry white wine
Juice of 2 limes or 1 lemon
1 clove garlic, crushed
2 teaspoons curry powder
1 teaspoon ground ginger
1 teaspoon minced onion

Wash chicken and dry with paper towels. Combine all other ingredients for marinade sauce. Put chicken in large, flat, glass or enameled dish; cover with marinade and allow to sit overnight, turning chicken several times. Drain and cook on grill about 15 minutes; turn and cook an additional 15 minutes, or until chicken is done, basting often with sauce. Yield: 8 servings.

Grilled Rice with Olives

(see Index)

Using Rack or Grill

Do not put rack or grill over heat until ready to start cooking.

Mixed Vegetable Casserole

2 (10-ounce) packages frozen mixed vegetables
1 (10½-ounce) can asparagus spears
4 hard-cooked eggs
1 cup mayonnaise
1 small onion, chopped
1 teaspoon dry mustard
1 teaspoon Worcestershire sauce
½ to 1 teaspoon Tabasco sauce

Cook frozen mixed vegetables according to package directions. Cut asparagus spears into small pieces; cook over medium heat until thoroughly heated. Separate cooked egg whites and yolks. Chop cooked egg whites and combine with mayonnaise, onion, mustard, Worcestershire sauce, and Tabasco sauce; blend sauce well and combine with drained vegetables. Put into a greased, flat 2-quart casserole dish and heat at 350° until mixture begins to bubble. Garnish with crumbled egg yolks and serve hot. Yield: 8 servings.

Twenty-Four Hour Salad or Dessert

1 (20-ounce) can pineapple tidbits
1 (1-pound) can pitted white cherries
3 egg yolks
2 tablespoons vinegar
2 tablespoons sugar
Dash salt
1 tablespoon butter or margarine
2 medium oranges, peeled and diced
2 cups miniature marshmallows
¼ cup maraschino cherries, halved
1 cup whipping cream, whipped

Drain pineapple, reserving 2 tablespoons juice. Drain white cherries and set aside. Beat egg yolks slightly in top of double boiler; add reserved pineapple juice, vinegar, sugar, salt, and butter. Cook over hot, not boiling, water for 12 minutes or until mixture thickens, stirring constantly. Remove from heat and cool. Combine well-drained oranges, pineapple, white cherries, marshmallows, and maraschino cherries; add cooled cooked mixture. Mix gently; fold in whipped cream. Pour into a serving bowl, cover, and refrigerate for 24 hours. Yield: 8 servings.

When Grilling Chicken

For outdoor grilling, place bony or rib-cage side of chicken down next to heat first. The bones act as an insulator and prevent chicken from browning too fast.

Chicken Breast Dinner From the Grill

Dinner for Four

Barbecued Chicken Breasts
Deluxe Broccoli with Shrimp Sauce
Sliced Tomatoes
Sour Cream-Dill Potato Salad
Walnut-Butterscotch Pie

Barbecued Chicken Breasts

2 chicken breasts, cut into halves
1 clove garlic, crushed
¼ cup olive oil
½ teaspoon thyme
½ teaspoon dry mustard
¼ cup wine vinegar

Clean and wash chicken breasts; set aside. Combine crushed garlic, olive oil, thyme, mustard, and vinegar to make a basting sauce. Place chicken breasts on grill over medium heat. Cook about 10 minutes on each side before beginning to baste with sauce. Continue cooking, basting, and turning chicken until done, about 30 minutes. Yield: 4 servings.

Deluxe Broccoli with Shrimp Sauce

2 (10-ounce) packages frozen broccoli
¼ cup chive cream cheese
¼ cup milk
1 (10½-ounce) can condensed cream of shrimp soup
2 tablespoons freshly squeezed lemon juice
2 tablespoons toasted slivered almonds

Cook broccoli according to package directions. Drain and set aside. Blend cream cheese and milk in small saucepan; add soup and mix well. Cook and stir until mixture is hot. Add lemon juice and mix well. Spread broccoli in bottom of 11- x 8-inch flat casserole dish. Pour sauce over top of broccoli and sprinkle with almonds. Bake at 350° about 10 minutes, or until mixture is bubbly. Yield: 6 to 8 servings.

Need a Flat Plate?

A cookie sheet placed on top of the grill makes an acceptable flat plate.

Sour Cream-Dill Potato Salad

- 4 cups cooked, diced potatoes
- ¼ cup olive oil
- 1 cup diced celery
- 1 small purple onion, grated
- 3 tablespoons wine vinegar
- 1 teaspoon salt
- ¼ teaspoon black pepper
- ½ teaspoon dry dill weed
- ¾ to 1 cup commercial sour cream

Combine potatoes and olive oil while potatoes are still warm. Combine other ingredients in a small bowl; pour over potatoes and toss gently. Cover and refrigerate several hours for flavors to blend. Yield: 6 servings.

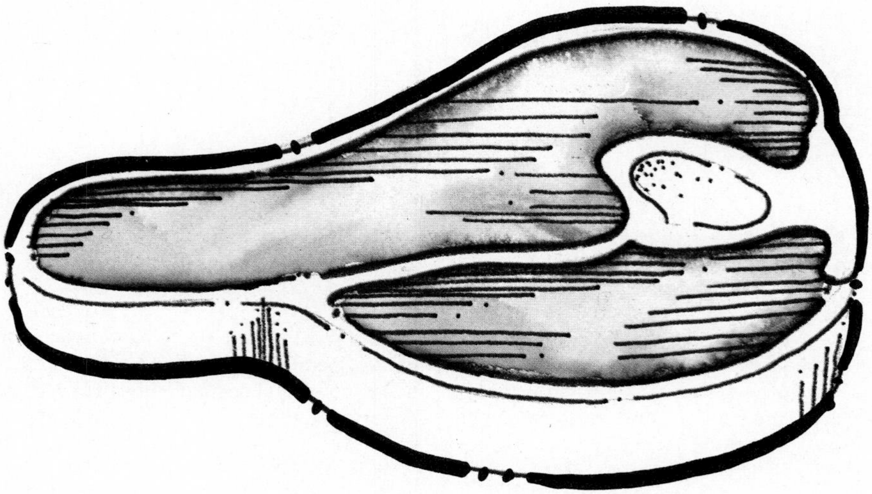

Walnut-Butterscotch Pie

- 3 eggs
- 1 cup dark corn syrup
- ⅔ cup sugar
- 1 tablespoon margarine, melted
- ¼ teaspoon salt
- 1 teaspoon vanilla extract or 3 tablespoons bourbon
- 1½ cups chopped walnuts
- 1 (10- or 11-inch) unbaked pie shell

Beat eggs slightly; add corn syrup, sugar, margarine, salt, vanilla or bourbon, and chopped walnuts. Spoon mixture into prepared pie shell and bake at 450° about 8 minutes; reduce heat to 350° and bake an additional 30 minutes, or until filling is set. Insert a knife in center of filling; if blade comes out clean, pie is done. Yield: 1 (10- or 11-inch) pie.

Tip for a Perfect Pie Shell

When baking an empty pie shell, prick it thoroughly along the bottom with a fork. Cut a piece of aluminum foil to fit bottom of shell, place it in pan, and fill pan with dried beans or rice to prevent pie crust from bubbling.

Barbecued Pork Loin

Dinner for Six to Eight

Sangría Southern
Barbecued Pork Loin
Creamy Eggplant Custard
Hot Potato Salad
Blueberry Coupe

Sangría Southern

1 lemon, thinly sliced
1 orange, thinly sliced
1 lime, thinly sliced
1 to 2 tablespoons sugar
1 jigger Triple Sec or orange liqueur
1 (4/5 quart) bottle dry red wine
½ cup chilled club soda

Remove seeds from sliced lemon, orange, and lime; place slices in glass pitcher and add sugar to taste. Do not add too much sugar until after wine has been added. Allow to stand a few minutes; add Triple Sec and stir with wooden spoon, bruising fruit to extract juices. Add wine and chill until time to serve.

Add ice cubes and chilled club soda to pitcher. Serve in punch cups with an ice cube and some fruit slices in each. Yield: about 12 servings.

Barbecued Pork Loin

1 (5- to 8-pound) pork loin
2 (18-ounce) cans pineapple juice
½ cup Worcestershire sauce
¼ cup soy sauce
1 teaspoon Tabasco sauce
1 cup cooked, pitted prunes
Ice cream salt
1 tablespoon black peppercorns

Have butcher remove shin bone and tie roast at 3- to 4-inch intervals. Slash pork fat in several places in diamond shape.

Combine pineapple juice, Worcestershire, soy, and Tabasco sauces. Place roast into an enameled pan and put prunes around roast. Pour marinade mixture over all, and let marinate overnight.

The next day, remove roast from pan, reserving marinade. Pierce loin from both ends with spit of rotisserie. Stuff slashes of roast with prunes. Rub ice cream salt onto roast, and press peppercorns into meat.

Place rotisserie on grill over low heat. Baste often as meat cooks. Cook until meat reaches the well-done stage. Remove from spit and place on wooden platter; pour 1 cup of marinade over loin, and allow to rest 5 minutes. Carve and serve. Yield: 6 to 8 servings.

Creamy Eggplant Custard

1 large eggplant (approximately 1½ pounds)
Salted water
4 eggs, beaten
1 cup half-and-half
¼ cup butter or margarine, melted
½ teaspoon salt
¼ teaspoon black pepper
⅛ teaspoon dill weed
¼ cup finely chopped fresh parsley

Peel eggplant and cut into ¼-inch cubes. Heat about 2½ cups salted water in a 4-quart saucepan; add eggplant and cook until fully tender. Stir occasionally, and cook for about 8 minutes. Remove from water and drain well.

Put eggplant into a large bowl and mash until very smooth. You should have about 2 cups mashed eggplant. Add the beaten eggs, half-and-half, butter or margarine, salt, pepper, dill weed, and chopped parsley. Beat mixture until light and fluffy. Pour mixture into a greased, shallow 1½-quart baking dish that can be taken to barbecue table. Bake, uncovered, at 325° for about 35 minutes, or until mixture is set when knife inserted in center comes out clean. Serve hot. Yield: 6 to 8 servings.

Hot Potato Salad

6 medium potatoes (about 2 pounds)
8 slices bacon
¼ cup bacon drippings
1½ tablespoons all-purpose flour
1 cup water
⅓ cup vinegar
1¾ teaspoons salt
⅛ teaspoon black pepper
1 tablespoon sugar
2 stalks celery, sliced
1 small head romaine lettuce, broken into bite-size pieces
1 pared cucumber, sliced
2 small onions, sliced
6 radishes, sliced

This is best cooked in an electric skillet close by the barbecue table, since it is served directly from the pan it is cooked in. It can be cooking while loin is on the rotisserie.

Cook potatoes in salted water in an electric skillet; cool, slice, and set aside. Cook bacon until crumbly; drain on paper towels, crumble and set aside. Measure ¼ cup bacon drippings; add flour, water, vinegar, salt, pepper, and sugar. Stir well, and cook slowly until mixture thickens.

When sauce thickens, add layer of potatoes, celery, romaine, cucumber, and onion; repeat layers until all has been used. Toss gently. Top with crumbled bacon and sliced radishes. Serve hot. Yield: 6 to 8 servings.

Blueberry Coupe

1½ cups red port wine
½ cup brown sugar
3 tablespoons cornstarch
¾ teaspoon grated lemon peel
¾ cup blueberries, fresh or frozen
6 to 8 scoops vanilla ice cream

The sauce for this dessert can be made in advance and kept warm. Spoon ice cream into serving dishes and keep in freezer until ready to serve.

Combine wine, brown sugar, cornstarch, and lemon peel in saucepan. Heat until sugar dissolves; add blueberries and continue heating until blueberries are warm through. Spoon sauce over ice cream and serve. Yield: 6 to 8 servings.

Beachcomber Party

Dinner for Eight to Ten

Hawaiian Grilled Spareribs
Blender Potato Casserole
Cold Vegetable Platter
Curried Compote
Ginger Pick-Up

Hawaiian Grilled Spareribs

4 racks of ribs
Garlic salt to taste
Pepper to taste
4 cups orange juice
1 cup Champale
½ cup brown sugar, firmly packed
½ cup soy sauce
4 tablespoons instant minced onion

Sprinkle ribs with garlic salt and pepper. Put ribs in shallow glass or enameled pan. Combine orange juice, Champale, brown sugar, soy sauce, and onion; pour over ribs. Marinate for 1 to 2 hours. Drain ribs; save marinade. Grill ribs on rack about 6 inches above hot coals. Cook 15 to 20 minutes on one side; turn ribs and cook 15 to 20 minutes longer. Brush with marinade every few minutes. Continue to cook ribs until done. Cut into serving pieces. Yield: 10 servings.

Blender Potato Casserole

1 cup milk
3 eggs
1½ teaspoons salt
¼ teaspoon pepper
2 tablespoons butter or margarine
1 cup cubed Cheddar cheese
½ green pepper, diced
1 small onion, quartered
4 medium uncooked potatoes, peeled and cubed

Combine all ingredients in a blender container in the order listed; cover and blend on high speed just until potatoes go through the blades (do not overblend). Pour the mixture into a greased 1½-quart casserole dish, and bake uncovered at 350° for 50 minutes to 1 hour. Yield: 8 to 10 servings.

Precook Spareribs

Precooking spareribs in the kitchen cuts down on cooking time on the grill. Boiling in a small amount of water, or baking at 350° helps to remove some of the fat and eliminates "flare-ups" on the grill. Drain well before putting on grill, and brush on marinade as ribs cook.

Cold Vegetable Platter

- 1 quart salad greens
- 2 carrots, sliced
- 1 cucumber, sliced
- 2 small red onions, sliced
- ½ head cauliflower, cut into flowerettes
- ⅛ pound mushrooms, trimmed and sliced
- 1 cup sliced radishes
- 1½ cups sliced celery
- 2 tomatoes, cut into wedges
- Beer Dressing

Wash salad greens and tear into bite-size pieces. Fill salad bowl with greens. Arrange vegetables in layers starting with carrots and continuing with remainder of vegetables. Serve with Beer Dressing. Yield: 10 servings.

Beer Dressing

- ¾ cup salad oil
- ½ cup beer
- 1½ teaspoons Worcestershire sauce
- 1 (10½-ounce) can tomato soup
- ½ small onion, minced
- ½ clove garlic, crushed
- 1½ teaspoons sugar
- 1 teaspoon salt
- 1½ teaspoons prepared horseradish

Put all ingredients in blender and blend until smooth. Chill until ready to serve. (It may be necessary to whirl in blender again before serving.) Yield: 3½ cups.

Curried Compote

- 1 (16-ounce) can apricot halves, drained
- 1 (16-ounce) can purple plums, drained
- 1 (16-ounce) can peach halves, drained
- 3 or 4 thin orange slices, cut into halves
- ½ cup orange juice or ½ cup Champale
- ¼ cup brown sugar
- ½ teaspoon freshly grated lemon peel
- 4 teaspoons curry powder
- 2 tablespoons butter, melted

Arrange drained fruit in shallow baking dish. Combine orange juice, brown sugar, lemon peel, and curry powder; mix well and pour over fruit. Drizzle butter over fruit. Put on back of grill and simmer for 15 to 20 minutes. Serve warm. Yield: 10 servings.

Ginger Pick-Up

- 1 cup orange-flavored instant breakfast drink
- 1½ cups pineapple juice
- 1 (1-pint 12-ounce) bottle ginger ale

Combine orange-flavored instant breakfast drink, pineapple juice, and ginger ale; stir well to dissolve. Pour over ice cubes to serve. Yield: 8 to 10 servings.

Ham-on-the-Rotisserie

Dinner for Eight

Ham with Port Wine
Peas Supreme
Grits Soufflé
Sliced Tomatoes
Shakertown Lemon Pie

Ham with Port Wine

1 (4- to 5-pound) precooked ham
1 cup port wine
½ teaspoon ground cinnamon
1 (12-ounce) can apricot nectar

Pierce ham in several places with a meat fork, and place in a glass bowl. Combine wine, cinnamon, and apricot nectar; pour over ham, and allow ham to remain in marinade for several hours, turning frequently. Remove ham from marinade and place on rotisserie. Grill over medium heat about 1 hour, basting often with marinade. Yield: 8 servings.

Peas Supreme

2 (10-ounce) packages frozen green peas
1 (4-ounce) can mushroom pieces, drained
1 tablespoon diced pimiento
1 tablespoon butter or margarine, melted

Cook peas according to package directions. Sauté mushroom pieces and pimiento in melted butter for about 3 minutes; add to hot, cooked and drained peas. Serve hot. Yield: 8 servings.

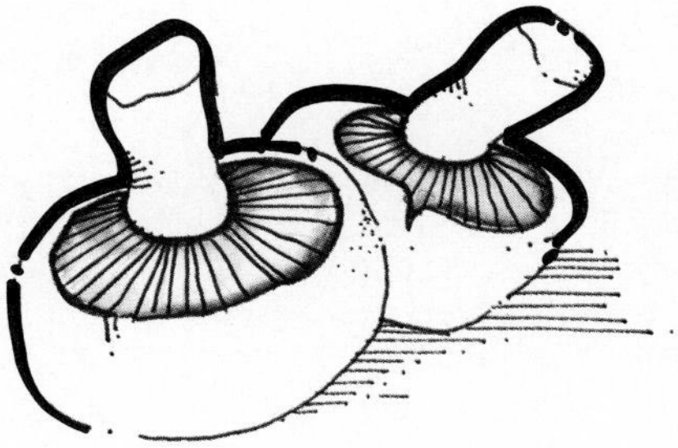

Quick Baked Potatoes

To bake potatoes in half the usual time, let them stand in boiling water for 15 minutes before baking in a very hot ove

Grits Soufflé

5 cups cold water
1 cup uncooked regular grits
½ cup margarine, softened
2 eggs, beaten
½ teaspoon cayenne pepper
Dash salt
Dash Tabasco sauce
½ pound sharp Cheddar cheese, shredded

Bring water to a boil in large saucepan; add grits and cook until mixture thickens. Add other ingredients and mix well. Spoon mixture into a greased 2-quart casserole dish. Bake at 350° for 1 hour. This may be prepared ahead of time and refrigerated until time to bake. Yield: 8 servings.

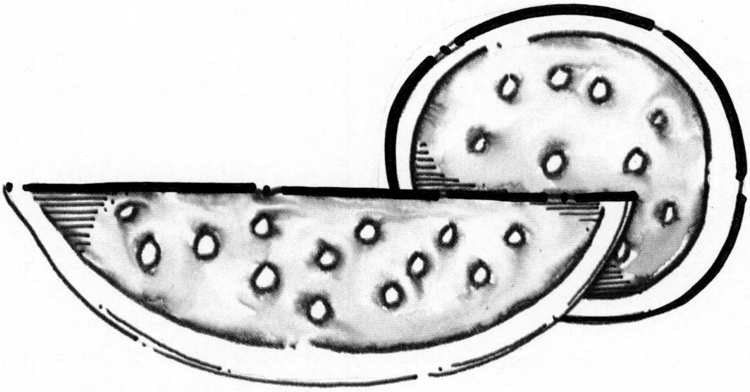

Shakertown Lemon Pie

2 lemons
2 cups sugar
4 eggs, beaten well
1 (9-inch) unbaked double crust pastry

Slice lemons into paper-thin slices. Remove seeds and place lemon slices in a bowl. Add sugar, stir well, and let stand for at least 2 hours. Add beaten eggs to lemon-sugar mixture and spoon into unbaked pie shell. Roll out top crust, put top on pie, and cut slits in top for steam to escape. Bake at 450° for 15 minutes; reduce heat to 350° and bake an additional 35 minutes. Test with a silver knife; pie is done when knife inserted in center comes out clean. Yield: 1 (9-inch) pie.

Seasoning the Meat

Most meats cooked on the grill need little or no seasoning at the beginning of the cooking period. Some cooks prefer to cook the meat without sauce and serve sauce on the side. At any rate, use sauce only during the last half of cooking time.

Ham-on-the-Grill

Dinner for Six to Eight

Sour Cream Dip with Carrot and Celery Sticks
Sangría Blanca
Glazed Grilled Ham
Green Chile Hominy Casserole
Grilled Zucchini
Toasted English Muffins
Coconut Pound Cake

Sour Cream Dip

2 cups commercial sour cream (use low-calorie if possible)
1/8 teaspoon fresh basil
1/8 teaspoon thyme
1/8 teaspoon marjoram
1/4 teaspoon onion salt
1/2 teaspoon seasoned salt
Carrot sticks
Celery sticks

Combine sour cream, basil, thyme, marjoram, onion salt, and seasoned salt in bowl; mix well, taste, and add more seasoning if desired. Store in a covered container in refrigerator at least 6 hours before serving.

Place bowl on table; arrange carrot and celery sticks on plate for dipping into sour cream dip. Yield: 8 servings.

Sangría Blanca

1 bottle Riesling white wine
1 (6-ounce) can frozen lemonade concentrate
1 cup club soda
Lime slices

Combine wine and lemonade concentrate; mix well. Add club soda and stir. Serve over ice cubes. Garnish with lime slices. Yield: 6 to 8 servings.

Glazed Grilled Ham

1 (3- or 4-pound) precooked boneless ham
1/2 cup dark corn syrup
1/2 cup pineapple juice

Slice ham into 1/2-inch slices. Tie securely into its original shape as nearly as possible. Cook at low heat on a covered grill about 1 hour. Combine corn syrup and pineapple juice and baste ham at 15-minute intervals. Yield: 8 servings.

Green Chile Hominy Casserole

2 (16-ounce) cans hominy, drained
3 tablespoons margarine, melted
3 tablespoons all-purpose flour
1 (8-ounce) can green chiles (use less if desired)
Milk
1 tablespoon chopped pimiento
1½ cups shredded sharp Cheddar cheese

Place hominy in oblong, buttered casserole dish; set aside. Combine margarine and flour in saucepan; heat and stir until smooth. Drain juice from chiles and add enough milk to make 2 cups; add liquid to flour mixture. Continue to stir over low heat until well-blended. Add chiles and pimiento. Pour sauce over hominy; sprinkle with cheese. Bake at 350° for 30 minutes. (Chiles make this casserole very hot.) Yield: 8 servings.

Grilled Zucchini

3 tablespoons salad oil
1½ teaspoons basil
8 zucchini squash, sliced lengthwise

Combine salad oil and basil. Brush zucchini with marinade and allow to marinate 1 hour. Place zucchini on grill on low heat; turn frequently. Yield: 6 to 8 servings.

Toasted English Muffins

8 to 10 English muffins, split in halves
½ cup butter or margarine, softened

After all food has been removed from grill, spread softened butter on muffin halves and place on grill to toast. Serve hot. Yield: 8 servings.

Coconut Pound Cake

1 cup butter or margarine
½ cup vegetable shortening
3 cups sugar
6 eggs
½ teaspoon almond extract
1 teaspoon coconut flavoring
3 cups all-purpose flour
1 cup milk
1 (3½-ounce) can flaked coconut

Cream butter, shortening, and sugar until light and fluffy. Add eggs, one at a time, beating well after each addition. Add flavorings and mix well. Alternately add flour and milk, beating after each addition. Stir in coconut. Spoon batter into a 10-inch greased tubepan or Bundt pan. Bake at 350° for 1 hour and 15 minutes. Yield: 1 (10-inch) cake.

Preventing Runovers

To keep vegetables, spaghetti, or rice from boiling over the sides of saucepan, rub butter around edge of pan.

Pork Chop Special

Dinner for Eight

Herb-Flavored Pork Chops
Cucumbers with Sour Cream
Roasted Seasoned Corn
Sliced Tomatoes
Garlic Bread
Pineapple Fluff

Herb-Flavored Pork Chops

8 (1-inch thick) loin pork chops
2 (12-ounce) cans tomato juice
1 teaspoon salt
½ teaspoon pepper
1 to 2 tablespoons basil

Put loin chops in flat container. Combine tomato juice, salt, pepper, and basil and pour over chops. Marinate for several hours. Remove chops carefully from marinade so that basil clings to chops. Cook over low heat on grill until meat is done, basting as meat cooks. Turn chops often. Yield: 8 servings.

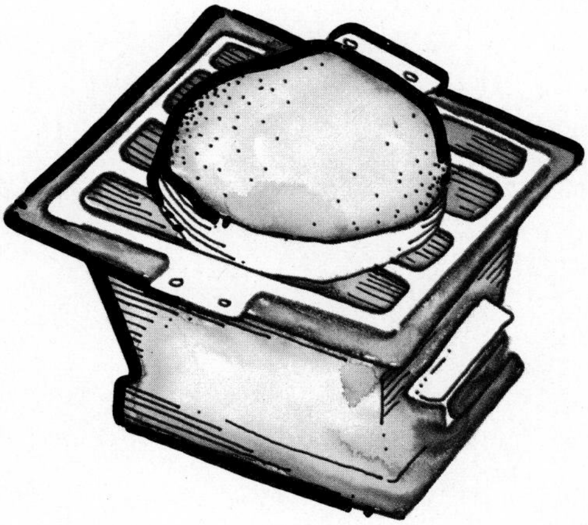

Cucumbers with Sour Cream

6 medium cucumbers
3 teaspoons salt
¼ teaspoon black pepper
6 tablespoons minced chives
2 cups commercial sour cream
4 tablespoons freshly squeezed lemon juice

Pare and slice cucumbers. Combine other ingredients and pour over cucumbers. Cover dish and let stand in refrigerator for several hours before serving. Yield: 8 to 10 servings.

Roasted Seasoned Corn

8 ears corn, fresh or frozen
½ cup butter or margarine, melted
1 tablespoon minced parsley
Dash paprika
1 teaspoon salt
Dash fresh ground pepper

Remove husks and silks from fresh corn, or thaw frozen ears. Combine melted butter, parsley, paprika, salt, and black pepper and spread liberally over each ear of corn. Wrap each ear of corn in a square of heavy-duty aluminum foil. Bake on grill for about 15 to 20 minutes, turning two or three times. Serve hot directly from foil. Yield: 8 servings.

Garlic Bread

(see Index)

Pineapple Fluff

1 fresh pineapple
¼ cup sugar
2 cups miniature marshmallows
½ pint whipping cream, whipped
Sliced maraschino cherries

Pare and cut pineapple into small pieces. Place a layer in a bowl, sprinkle with sugar and marshmallows; continue until all has been placed in bowl. Cover bowl and let stand for several hours. To serve, fold in whipped cream and spoon into serving dishes. Garnish with cherries. Yield: 8 servings.

Balance Meat on Rotisserie

If you are using the rotisserie with your barbecue grill, be sure that the rotisserie rod is inserted in the center of the meat, lengthwise, and the spit forks tightened so that meat will be well-balanced and rotisserie will turn evenly. Then insert meat thermometer so that it reaches the center of the meat, being careful that it does not touch a bone or the rod itself. Large cuts of meat are successfully cooked on the rotisserie.

Polynesian-on-Your-Grill

Dinner for Four to Six

Artichoke Appetizer with Lemon Sauce
Hickory-Smoked Peppered Pork Chops
Hot Applesauce
Almond Rice
Pineapple Paradise

Artichoke Appetizer with Lemon Sauce

4 to 6 artichokes
3 cloves
4 slices lemon
⅓ cup butter or margarine
½ teaspoon salt
½ teaspoon black pepper
¼ cup freshly squeezed lemon juice

Wash artichokes (allow one per person) in cold water. Place artichokes in boiling salted water to which garlic and lemon slices have been added. Cover and simmer for 25 to 30 minutes, or until leaves can be removed easily. Drain.

Combine butter, salt, pepper, and lemon juice in a saucepan. Heat about 1 minute. Serve with hot artichokes. Yield: 4 to 6 servings.

Note: To eat, tear off one leaf at a time, dunk in sauce, turn leaf upside-down, bite and peel. Disregard center of fuzzy choke and use a fork for eating the heart.

Hickory-Smoked Peppered Pork Chops

Buy a center cut pork loin, allowing ¾-to 1-pound per person. Have the butcher slice the loin into ¾- to 1-inch thick chop portions. Bring the pork to room temperature and cover with packaged, coarsely ground lemon-pepper marinade, 1 tablespoon per chop. Let stand while preparing fire.

For charcoal grill: Soak hickory chips in water for about 20 minutes. Using about 15 charcoal briquettes, light with a match; arrange briquettes to cover bottom of grill evenly. Put a few of the hickory chips on after fire has burned down some. Place meat on grill, and close hood if the grill has one; if it does not have a lid, cover with a new garbage can lid. Add more soaked chips if needed. Cook until meat is white inside, about 45 minutes to 1 hour.

For gas grill: Turn gas on high and light; turn heat to medium. Place dampened hickory chips onto ceramic briquettes. Put chops on grill and close lid. Cook about 45 minutes to 1 hour, turning chops once. For the most accurate guide, use a meat thermometer; it should register 190° when meat is done.

If you have become over-zealous on the quantity prepared, leftovers can be frozen. Wrap securely in heavy-duty aluminum foil, label, and freeze immediately.

Hot Applesauce

2 cups applesauce
½-inch stick cinnamon
1 whole clove
1 tablespoon prepared horseradish

Combine all ingredients in saucepan; heat quickly and serve hot. If your menu lacks color, add 2 drops of red food coloring. Yield: 4 to 6 servings.

Almond Rice

2 tablespoons salad oil
1 small onion, chopped
½ green pepper, chopped
¼ teaspoon garlic salt
¼ teaspoon black pepper
2 cups cooked rice
2 teaspoons soy sauce
½ cup slivered blanched almonds

Heat oil in heavy skillet. Add onion, pepper, garlic salt, and black pepper; sauté about 5 minutes over medium heat. Add rice, soy sauce, and almonds; mix well. Cook about 10 minutes, or until mixture is thoroughly heated. Yield: 4 servings.

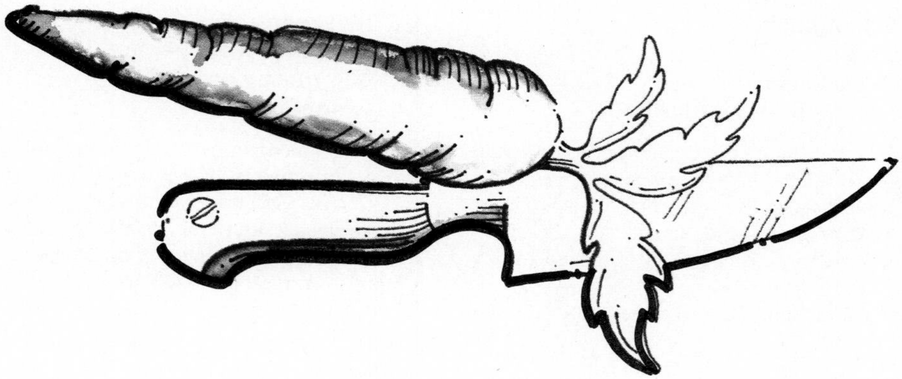

Pineapple Paradise

1 medium fresh pineapple
8 tablespoons honey
4 teaspoons brandy (optional)

Cut pineapple into eight lengthwise wedges. Place each wedge on a double thickness of heavy-duty aluminum foil. Pour 1 tablespoon honey over each wedge. One-half teaspoon brandy may be poured over each wedge. Wrap securely in foil and place on grill set at medium setting. Cook about 20 minutes on gas or electric grill, or 15 minutes on charcoal briquettes. Yield: 8 servings.

Utensils for the Outdoor Chef

Handy outdoor utensils: Large salt and pepper shakers, roll of heavy-duty aluminum foil, asbestos mitts or potholders, long-handled fork and tongs, paintbrush for basting, and a meat thermometer for checking doneness of large pieces of meat.

Luau Spareribs

Dinner for Four to Six

Luau Spareribs
Hawaiian-Style Baked Beans
Sweet Potato Casserole
Crisp Relish
Fresh Fruit with Poppy Seed Dressing
Lime Sparkle

Luau Spareribs

2 (4½-ounce) jars strained peaches (baby food)
⅓ cup catsup
⅓ cup vinegar
2 tablespoons soy sauce
½ cup brown sugar
1 clove garlic, minced
2 teaspoons ground ginger
1 teaspoon salt
Dash pepper
4 pounds meaty spareribs
Salt and pepper

Mix all ingredients except ribs for sauce. Heat well over medium heat. Rub ribs with salt and pepper. Place bone-side down on grill over low heat. Grill about 20 minutes; turn meat-side down and grill until browned, about 10 minutes. Turn meat-side up again and brush with sauce and grill without turning, about 30 minutes, or until meat is well-done. Brush frequently with sauce. Yield: 4 to 6 servings.

Hawaiian-Style Baked Beans

2 (1-pound) cans pork and beans
¼ pound cooked ham, diced
½ teaspoon dry mustard
¼ cup brown sugar, firmly packed
2 tablespoons finely chopped onion
1 cup drained pineapple chunks
¼ cup pineapple juice

Grease a 1½-quart baking dish. Spoon a can of pork and beans in bottom of dish. Combine ham, mustard, brown sugar, onion, pineapple, and pineapple juice; spoon over layer of beans, and top with the other can of pork and beans. Cover and bake at 350° for 1 hour. Yield: 5 to 6 servings.

Allow Enough Meat

For the average appetite allow: ¼ to ½ pound ground meat per person; ⅓ to ½ pound of meat, if boneless; ¾ to 1 pound of meat, bone in, depending on size of bone; and ¼ of a chicken per person. For hearty appetites, allow more.

Sweet Potato Casserole

½ cup brown sugar, divided
⅔ cup orange juice, divided
⅓ cup margarine, melted and divided
2 (1-pound) cans sweet potatoes, drained
2 eggs
1 teaspoon salt
¼ teaspoon cloves
1 teaspoon ground cinnamon
1 cup pecans, chopped

Combine ¼ cup brown sugar, 2 teaspoons orange juice, and 2 teaspoons butter; mix and set aside to use for glaze topping. Whip potatoes until smooth; beat in eggs. Add remaining sugar, orange juice, and butter. Add salt, cloves, and cinnamon; mix well and pour into a 1½-quart casserole dish. Sprinkle pecans on top. Pour glaze topping over pecans. Bake at 350° for 40 minutes. Yield: 6 servings.

Crisp Relish

(see Index)

Fresh Fruit with Poppy Seed Dressing

(see Index)

Lime Sparkle

2 (6-ounce) cans frozen lime juice concentrate
Soda water
Watermelon juice
Small wedges of peeled watermelon
Orange slices

Reconstitute lime juice concentrate according to directions on can, substituting soda water for tap water. Sweeten with a little watermelon juice (a piece of watermelon on a pieplate is easily "juiced" with a potato masher—then strain). A small wedge of peeled watermelon in the drink and an orange slice on each glass completes the picture. Yield: 6 servings.

Note: Watermelon juice is extremely sweet, so add it sparingly until sweet enough to suit your own family.

Let Ice Do a Cool Job for You

If you want ice that is not clouded or honeycombed with air pockets, use distilled water. Syphon into refrigerator molds by holding syphon tube against bottom of mold and pour slowly. If you do not have distilled water handy, use water that has been boiled and cooled slightly.

Soy Sauced Pork Chops

Dinner for Six

Barbecued Soy Sauced Pork Chops
Zucchini Casserole
Pan Browned Rice
Shredded Lettuce with Vinegar and Oil Dressing
Crusty Commercial French Bread
Raspberry Dream

Barbecued Soy Sauced Pork Chops

1 cup soy sauce
1 clove garlic, crushed
Dash pepper
6 (1-inch thick) pork chops
Barbecue sauce

Combine soy sauce, garlic, and pepper; marinate pork chops in glass bowl for 1 hour in marinade. Drain. Grill 30 minutes on each side, basting often with your favorite barbecue sauce. Yield: 6 servings.

Zucchini Casserole

8 small zucchini squash, sliced lengthwise
2 tomatoes, cut into eighths
½ green pepper, cut into thin strips
¾ cup chopped onion
½ teaspoon salt
½ teaspoon Beau Monde Seasoning
¼ teaspoon pepper
¼ cup grated Parmesan cheese
½ teaspoon sugar
¼ cup butter, melted

Place zucchini slices in buttered, oblong casserole dish. Place tomatoes, green pepper, and onion between zucchini slices. Sprinkle salt, seasoning, pepper, cheese, and sugar on top. Drizzle butter evenly over top. Bake, uncovered, at 350° for 45 minutes to 1 hour. Yield: 6 servings.

Don't Serve Cloudy Tea

Make your tea ahead of time, but do not put it in the refrigerator or it will turn cloudy. In making tea to be served on ice, use 50 percent more tea to allow for melting ice. Let steeped tea cool to room temperature, then pour over ice cubes.

Pan Browned Rice

1 small onion, chopped
½ medium green pepper
½ stick butter or margarine
1½ cups regular rice
2 (10½-ounce) cans beef broth
1 (8¼-ounce) can pineapple tidbits, drained
1 tablespoon soy sauce
½ teaspoon ground allspice

Sauté onion and green pepper in melted butter or margarine until both are limp but not browned. Stir in rice and sauté until rice turns yellow. Stir in other ingredients; cover skillet and cook until rice is tender and all liquid has been absorbed. Yield: 6 servings.

Raspberry Dream

1 envelope unflavored gelatin
¼ cup cold water
1 (8-ounce) package cream cheese, softened
½ cup sugar
½ teaspoon almond extract
Dash salt
1 cup milk
½ pint whipping cream, whipped
Raspberry Sauce

Soften gelatin in water and heat until dissolved; set aside. Combine cream cheese, sugar, almond extract, and salt; blend until smooth. Gradually add milk and gelatin; fold in whipped cream. Pour into eight small molds or a 1-quart mold. Refrigerate until set. (This can be frozen and thawed when ready to use.) Yield: 8 servings.

Raspberry Sauce

1 (10-ounce) package frozen raspberries
1 tablespoon cornstarch
2 tablespoons sherry wine

Thaw and drain raspberries. Combine raspberry syrup, cornstarch, and sherry; cook over low heat until thick. Add raspberries; blend well. Refrigerate and serve over molds. Yield: 1 cup.

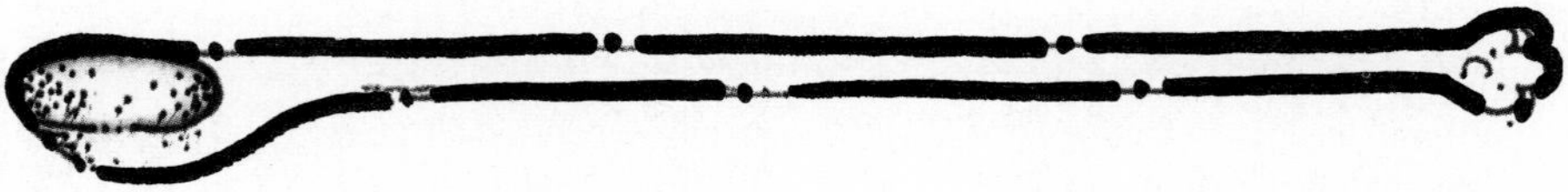

Containers for Marinating Meats

Glass or enameled dishes are preferred for marinating meats. Marinades containing soy sauce should always be put in enamel or glass; other marinades may be put in plastic containers.

Glazed Pork Loin Special

Dinner for Six to Eight

Glazed Pork Loin
Baked Cheese Grits
Broccoli with Shrimp Sauce
Special Cole Slaw
Bacon-Onion French Bread
Watermelon Boat

Glazed Pork Loin

1 (6- to 8-pound) pork loin
Salt and pepper
¼ cup soy sauce
¼ cup freshly squeezed lemon juice
2 tablespoons sugar
1 teaspoon dry mustard
¼ teaspoon ground cloves
1 teaspoon ground ginger
2 tablespoons commercial steak sauce

Salt and pepper loin; put on rotisserie over low heat for 1 hour. Combine all other ingredients; heat to boiling point. Brush sauce on loin and continue to cook for at least another hour (or longer depending on size of loin). Continue to baste with sauce. Yield: 6 to 8 servings.

Baked Cheese Grits

1½ cups regular grits
6 cups boiling salted water
½ cup butter or margarine
1 (6-ounce) roll garlic cheese
3 tablespoons cooking sherry
3 tablespoons Worcestershire sauce
½ teaspoon Tabasco sauce
3 eggs, beaten

Cook grits in boiling salted water about 2 or 3 minutes. Blend in butter or margarine, cheese, sherry, and sauces; stir in beaten eggs and mix well. Spoon mixture into a 2-quart baking dish and bake at 300° about 1 hour. Serve hot. Yield: 6 to 8 servings.

Is the Grill Ready?

Allow about 30 minutes for charcoal briquettes to turn ash-gray before putting food on grill. To make fire building easier, carry charcoal briquettes in milk cartons, and burn cartons and briquettes together. When using gas or electric heat, preheat the grill.

Broccoli with Shrimp Sauce

2 (10-ounce) packages frozen broccoli
1 (10½-ounce) can undiluted cream of shrimp soup
½ cup diced almonds

Cook broccoli according to package directions. Drain and place in a 1½-quart casserole dish. Spoon shrimp soup over broccoli, and sprinkle almonds on top. Bake at 300° for about 15 minutes. Yield: 6 to 8 servings.

Special Cole Slaw

1 medium head cabbage, chopped fine
1 (8¼-ounce) can pineapple tidbits
2 carrots, chopped fine
1 small green pepper, diced
1 large apple, unpeeled and chopped fine
½ cup flaked coconut
½ cup miniature marshmallows
7 tablespoons evaporated milk
7 tablespoons sugar
7 tablespoons vinegar
½ teaspoon celery salt
½ teaspoon onion salt

Combine first seven ingredients in large bowl. Put evaporated milk, sugar, vinegar, celery and onion salt in a pint jar and shake well to make dressing. Add to cabbage mixture and toss. Cover bowl and chill until time to serve. Yield: 6 to 8 servings.

Bacon-Onion French Bread

1 (1-pound) loaf French bread
½ (1⅜-ounce) package onion soup mix
6 or 8 slices crisp bacon, crumbled
½ cup butter or margarine

Slice bread in 1-inch slices almost through loaf. Combine soup mix, crumbled bacon, and butter or margarine. Melt and mix well. Spread on slices. Wrap loaf in aluminum foil and heat on grill. Yield: 6 to 8 servings.

Watermelon Boat

Select a nicely shaped oval watermelon and remove top third lengthwise. Use a melon ball cutter and scoop out nice little balls from the large portion. Chill. Combine melon balls with chunks of fresh pineapple, green grapes, cantaloupe balls, and peach slices, if desired. Put fruit into melon boat, garnish with mint leaves, and cover with plastic wrap. Chill until ready to serve.

Meat Roasting Tip

Slow, even heat is the key to successful roasting of meat. The meat will not be charred and will cook evenly and shrink less.

Southern Spareribs Specialty

Dinner for Four

Barbecued Spareribs
Sauerkraut in Wine
Grilled or Boiled Corn-on-the-Cob
Garlic Bread
Buttermilk Sherbet

Barbecued Spareribs

1 cup catsup
½ cup dark corn syrup
½ cup cider vinegar
¼ cup Worcestershire sauce
¼ cup Dijon mustard
1 to 2 tablespoons chili powder
2 teaspoons salt
¼ teaspoon Tabasco sauce
4 pounds spareribs, cut in 1 or 2 rib pieces

Blend catsup, corn syrup, vinegar, Worcestershire sauce, mustard, chili powder, salt, and Tabasco; set aside. Tear off four sheets of 18-inch wide heavy-duty aluminum foil. Each sheet should be 22 inches long. Place two sheets together to make two double 18- x 22-inch sheets.

Arrange half the spareribs on double sheet so that there are no more than two layers deep. Lift up edges of foil slightly and pour half the sauce over ribs. Close package by using a double fold down center and at ends.

Repeat packaging for second half of ribs. Place on grill over very low heat and cook for about 1 hour. Cut packages open with a knife or scissors. Yield: 4 servings.

Sauerkraut in Wine

1 (27-ounce) can sauerkraut
2 cloves garlic, crushed
1 teaspoon freshly ground pepper
2 cups dry white wine

Combine sauerkraut with crushed garlic, black pepper, and wine in a 2-quart casserole dish or in an electric skillet. Cover and simmer for 30 to 45 minutes. Add more wine if necessary. Serve hot. Yield: 4 servings.

For a Browner Barbecue

Add more catsup or tomato paste to your barbecue sauce during the last stages of cooking for a browner, crustier piece of meat.

Grilled Corn-on-the-Cob

4 to 6 ears corn
Softened butter
Salt and pepper

Get young tender corn as fresh from the field as possible. You may want to cook two ears per person, or at least two for the heartiest eaters.

Remove large outer husks from young tender corn; turn back inner husks and remove silk. Spread corn generously with softened butter. Pull husks back over ears, and tie with a heavy twine. Some cooks dip ears of corn in cold water at this point. Roast on grill for about 10 to 20 minutes, turning frequently. Serve at once with salt, pepper, and additional softened butter. Yield: 4 to 6 servings.

Boiled Corn-on-the-Cob

4 to 6 ears fresh sweet corn
Boiling salted water
Butter or margarine
Salt

Remove husks and silks from fresh young ears of corn. Put into a large saucepan and cover with boiling salted water. Boil for 5 to 8 minutes, depending on size of ears. Remove from water, drain, and serve hot with butter or margarine and salt. Yield: 4 to 6 servings.

Garlic Bread

1 stick butter or margarine
1 clove garlic, crushed
1 (1-pound) loaf French bread

Melt butter or margarine, and stir in crushed garlic. Slice bread and spread each slice with butter. Wrap the loaf in aluminum foil and place on the back of the grill. Turn the loaf often; serve hot. Yield: 4 servings.

Buttermilk Sherbet

2 cups fresh buttermilk
¾ cup sugar
1 (8¼-ounce) can crushed pineapple, undrained
Grated rind of 1 lemon
2 to 3 tablespoons freshly squeezed lemon juice
Few drops green food coloring
2 envelopes unflavored gelatin
2 tablespoons cold water
1 egg white, stiffly beaten

Combine buttermilk, sugar, pineapple and juice, rind and juice of lemon, and food coloring. Soften gelatin in cold water; dissolve over boiling water and add to buttermilk mixture. Pour into refrigerator trays and freeze until firm.

Remove trays from freezer and put mixture in large bowl. Break mixture with a fork, then beat until light and fluffy. Fold in egg white; return to refrigerator trays and freeze until firm. This mixture may be frozen in a half-gallon electric or hand-turned ice cream freezer. Yield: 4 to 6 servings.

Saucy Sparerib Dinner

Dinner for Four

Saucy Barbecued Spareribs
Corn Pudding
Grilled Tomatoes
Savory Green Bean Salad
Grilled Cinnamon Apples

Saucy Barbecued Spareribs

1 tablespoon celery seed
1 tablespoon chili powder
½ cup brown sugar
1 tablespoon salt
1 teaspoon paprika
2½ pounds meaty pork ribs
1 (8-ounce) can tomato sauce
¼ cup vinegar

Combine celery seed, chili powder, sugar, salt, and paprika. Rub a third of the mixture on ribs. Add tomato sauce and vinegar to remaining mixture. Cook ribs over low heat about 1 hour, basting occasionally with the sauce. Yield: 4 servings.

Corn Pudding

2 tablespoons butter
2 tablespoons salad oil
½ medium onion, chopped fine
1 cup whole-kernel corn, canned or fresh
1 tablespoon sugar
Salt and pepper to taste
3 egg yolks, well beaten
½ cup shredded Cheddar cheese
3 egg whites, stiffly beaten

Heat butter and salad oil in skillet. Sauté onion; add corn, sugar, salt, and pepper. Cool and stir in egg yolks and shredded cheese. Fold in stiffly beaten egg whites. Spoon into a well-greased 11- x 8-inch baking dish and set in a pan of water. Bake uncovered at 350° for 1 hour. Yield: 4 servings.

Cut the Spattering

To keep lard or shortening from spattering when you are frying foods, sprinkle in a little salt.

Grilled Tomatoes

15 cherry tomatoes
2 tablespoons butter, melted
2 teaspoons sweet basil
2 teaspoons chopped parsley
Salt to taste
Cracked pepper to taste

Place tomatoes on a large piece of heavy-duty aluminum foil. Combine butter, basil, parsley, salt, and pepper; pour this mixture over tomatoes. Wrap foil tightly and cook over medium heat on grill for about 15 minutes. Yield: 3 to 4 servings.

Savory Green Bean Salad

1 (16-ounce) can green beans, drained
6 tablespoons salad oil
3 tablespoons vinegar
½ teaspoon salt
½ teaspoon pepper
1 onion, minced
4 hard-cooked eggs, chopped
2 teaspoons vinegar
3 tablespoons mayonnaise
1 teaspoon prepared mustard
4 strips bacon, fried crisp and crumbled
Lettuce

Combine beans, salad oil, 3 tablespoons vinegar, salt, pepper, and onion; mix well. Cover and chill. Combine eggs, 2 teaspoons vinegar, mayonnaise, and mustard; mix well. Cover and chill. When ready to serve, toss bacon lightly with beans. Heap in lettuce-lined bowl and top with egg mixture. Yield: 4 to 6 servings.

Grilled Cinnamon Apples

4 apples
4 tablespoons red-hot cinnamon candy
4 tablespoons raisins
Butter

Core apples and place on heavy-duty aluminum foil. Fill hole of each apple with 1 tablespoon of cinnamon candy and 1 tablespoon of raisins. Dot with butter. Bring foil up loosely over apples and twist ends together to seal. Cook over glowing coals for 30 minutes or until done. Yield: 4 servings.

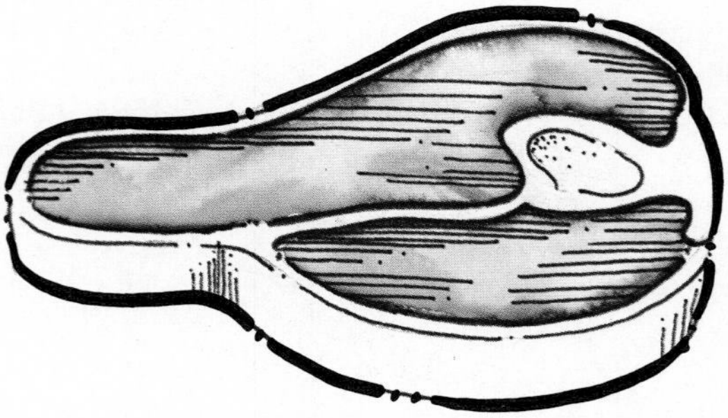

Bacon Delight

For a new bacon treat, dip bacon slices in beaten eggs, then in crushed cracker crumbs and broil.

Frankfurter Special

Dinner for Six to Eight

Cucumber Soup
Barbecued Frankfurters
Foiled French Fries
Sliced Tomatoes and Lettuce Wedges
Quick Brownies

Cucumber Soup

1 quart buttermilk
1 large cucumber, diced
½ teaspoon ground cinnamon or allspice
Salt to taste
4 or 5 leaves of mint, crushed

Combine all ingredients and put in covered container in refrigerator to chill at least 2 or 3 hours. Yield: 1 quart.

Barbecued Frankfurters

1 large onion, chopped
2 cloves garlic, minced
1⅓ cups catsup
2 teaspoons chili powder
1 tablespoon dry mustard
1 teaspoon salt
¼ cup red wine vinegar
1 cup water
1 (1-pound) package frankfurters
1 (8-ounce) package elbow spaghetti, cooked

Combine onion, garlic, catsup, chili powder, mustard, salt, vinegar, and water; bring to a boil. Cover and simmer for 25 minutes. Grill frankfurters over hot coals; brown evenly. Cut into bite-size pieces. Add to barbecue sauce mixture. Arrange cooked spaghetti on platter; pour frankfurter mixture over top. Yield: 6 to 8 servings.

Use Your Corn Popper

Weiners may be cooked in a corn popper over the grill if you do not have a hinged rack or individual skewers. Give them a hearty shake occasionally, so they will cook evenly.

Foiled French Fries

1½ pounds frozen French-fried potatoes
½ cup grated Parmesan cheese
1 teaspoon salt

Thaw potatoes slightly. Divide into six equal portions and put on individual squares of heavy-duty aluminum foil. Combine Parmesan cheese and salt and sprinkle over potatoes. Seal packets and place on grill. Cook over low heat about 15 minutes, turning packets occasionally. Yield: 6 servings.

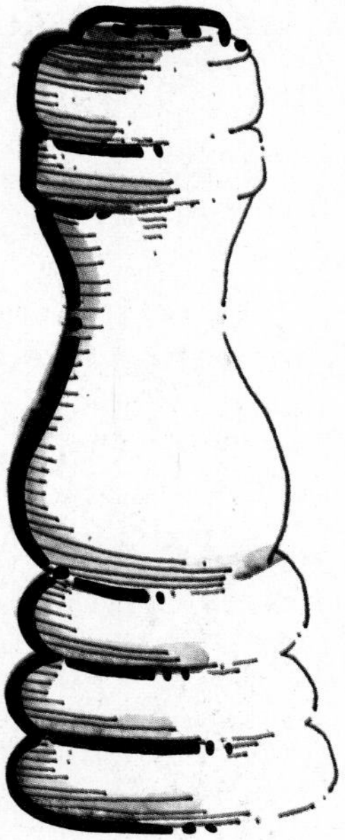

Quick Brownies

1 (22½-ounce) box fudge brownie mix
1 cup miniature marshmallows
1 (12-ounce) box quick fudge mix

Prepare brownies according to directions on package. Bake in a greased 13- x 9- x 2-inch pan. Measure marshmallows and set aside. After brownies have cooked for 15 minutes, start preparing fudge mix according to package directions. When brownies are done, remove from oven and sprinkle with marshmallows. Spread hot fudge over top of marshmallows, and allow to cool thoroughly before cutting into bars. Yield: 24 bar cookies.

Controlling the Heat

You do not need an inferno to barbecue. The most common mistake made is the use of heat that is too high. This results in cremating instead of barbecuing the meat. Place meat about 4 to 5 inches above the heat unless instructions state otherwise. Just before pieces of meat are completely done, move to outer edge of grill where they'll finish cooking and stay hot but won't cook as rapidly as when left in center of grill.

Serve chilled beverages at outdoor meals. Sure-to-please are Lemon-Orange Drink, Raspberry Delight, and Lime Sparkle. Check Index for page number of recipes.

Teen Tempter Party

Party for Six

Batter-Up Corndogs
French-Fried Onions
Cheddar Deviled Eggs
Cheesy Vegetable Salad
Colonial Apple Pie
Tangy Punch

Batter-Up Corndogs

½ cup cornmeal
½ cup all-purpose flour
1 teaspoon salt
½ teaspoon pepper
1 egg, beaten
½ cup milk
2 tablespoons salad oil
12 frankfurters
Shortening for frying

Sift dry ingredients together; add egg, milk, and salad oil. Beat until smooth. Dip wieners into batter; drain. Fry in deep fat heated to 375° for 2 to 3 minutes until golden brown. Yield: 1 dozen corndogs.

French-Fried Onions

4 large white onions, peeled
1 cup milk
2 eggs, beaten
2 cups self-rising flour
Shortening for frying
Salt

Cut peeled onions into ¼-inch slices and separate into rings. Combine milk and eggs; soak rings in milk-egg mixture for 2 hours. Drain. Dredge rings in flour and dip again in milk-egg mixture. Dredge in flour again and fry in deep fat heated to 365°. Drain on absorbent paper. Salt and serve immediately. Yield: 6 servings.

Cheddar Deviled Eggs

6 hard-cooked eggs
2 tablespoons shredded Cheddar cheese
1 tablespoon mayonnaise
1 tablespoon prepared mustard

Peel eggs and cut in half. Put yolks into small bowl and mash with a fork. Add cheese, mayonnaise, and mustard; mix well. Refill eggs with yolk mixture. Yield: 12 halves.

Cheesy Vegetable Salad

- 1 (10-ounce) package frozen baby lima beans
- 1 (10-ounce) package cut green beans
- 1 (8-ounce) package pasteurized processed cheese, cut into ¼-inch cubes
- ¾ cup diced celery
- 3 tablespoons mayonnaise
- ⅓ cup commercial sour cream
- ½ teaspoon dill weed
- ¼ teaspoon salt

Cook vegetables as directed on package; drain and chill. Add cheese and celery to vegetables and mix well. Combine mayonnaise, sour cream, dill weed, and salt; add to vegetable mixture and toss lightly. Yield: 8 servings.

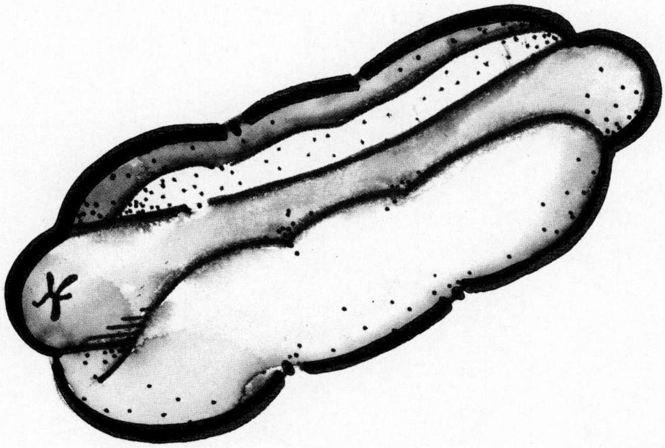

Colonial Apple Pie

- 1 cup sugar
- 1 cup unsweetened pineapple juice
- 8 medium cooking apples, pared and sliced
- 1 tablespoon cornstarch
- 2 teaspoons water
- ⅛ teaspoon salt
- ½ teaspoon vanilla extract
- 2 teaspoons butter
- 1 (9-inch) unbaked double crust pastry

Combine sugar and juice; bring to a boil over medium heat. Add apple slices; cook slowly, uncovered, until fruit is tender. Lift apples out carefully. Dissolve corn starch in water; add to syrup mixture. Cook until thick. Add salt, vanilla extract, and butter. Pour over apples in unbaked pie shell. Cover with pastry strips. Bake at 425° for 35 minutes. Yield: 1 (9-inch) pie.

Tangy Punch

- ½ cup orange-flavored instant breakfast drink
- ¼ cup instant tea
- 4 cups water
- 5 cups ginger ale

Combine instant breakfast drink, tea, and water; stir thoroughly. Add ginger ale and mix well. Yield: 6 to 8 servings.

Backyard Wiener Roast

Dinner for Four to Six

Grilled Wieners
Best Baked Beans
Pretzels
Angels' Halos
Beer

Grilled Wieners

1 (1-pound) package frankfurters
1 package frankfurter rolls
Mustard
Catsup
Pickles
Onions

Roast frankfurters on skewers, sticks, or on grill over medium hot coals. Serve on frankfurter rolls with mustard, catsup, pickles, and onions. Yield: 4 to 6 servings.

Best Baked Beans

1 (1-pound 15-ounce) can pork and beans
¼ cup catsup
3 tablespoons brown sugar
1 small onion, diced
1 tablespoon dried bacon bits
½ teaspoon chili powder
½ teaspoon dry mustard
Dash cayenne pepper
¼ teaspoon garlic salt
1 medium onion, sliced

Combine all ingredients in greased 1½-quart casserole dish. Stir well and top with onion slices. Bake at 350° for 1 hour. Yield: 4 to 6 servings.

Angels' Halos

½ dozen large glazed doughnuts
6 large marshmallows

Stick marshmallow in hole of doughnut. Run skewer or pointed green stick through doughnut and marshmallow. Toast marshmallow carefully. Yield: 4 to 6 servings.

Grilled Wieners offer an economical and easy way to entertain a large group with a minimum of preparation. Try our Backyard Wiener Roast.

Seafood Dream Dinner

Dinner for Six

Oyster Bake
Shrimp en Brochette
Grilled Corn with Bacon
Fruit Salad Delight
Lemon Pie

Oyster Bake

2 cups seasoned croutons
1 pint shucked oysters, drained
3 tablespoons butter, melted
¼ teaspoon salt
3 tablespoons freshly squeezed lemon juice
1 teaspoon Worcestershire sauce
1 teaspoon chopped parsley
⅓ cup grated Parmesan cheese

Spread croutons in a shallow, greased baking dish; place oysters over croutons. Combine butter, salt, lemon juice, and Worcestershire sauce in small fry pan; sauté parsley in this mixture. Spread over oysters. Sprinkle with Parmesan cheese. Cook in smoker or oven at 350° for about 25 to 30 minutes, or until oysters are thoroughly heated. Yield: 6 small servings.

Shrimp en Brochette

1½ pounds peeled jumbo shrimp
2 lemons, cut into wedges
Butter

Thread large, peeled shrimp on skewers, alternating every 3 or 4 shrimp with lemon wedges. Baste with melted butter. Grill about 5 minutes over hot coals, basting with butter; turn once. Yield: 6 servings.

Grilled Corn with Bacon

6 ears corn
Seasoned salt
6 strips bacon

Select corn that still has the husks on it. Strip husks back but not off; remove corn silks. Dust corn with seasoned salt and wrap a strip of bacon around ear of corn. Replace the husks and tie securely in place. Cook over charcoal for 15 to 25 minutes until done. Yield: 6 servings.

Fruit Salad Delight

- 2 bananas, thinly sliced
- Powdered sugar
- Lime, lemon, or orange juice
- 2 oranges, cut into thin slices (seeds and peel removed)
- 1 pound fresh dark cherries; or 1 (17-ounce) can dark sweet cherries, pitted
- 1 pound seedless grapes
- 1 cantaloupe, cut into chunks; or watermelon chunks
- 1 to 2 apples, sliced
- 2 cups strawberries, halved
- 1 cup flaked coconut
- ¾ cup chopped walnuts

Using a large, clear glass bowl, layer banana slices in bottom. Sprinkle lightly with powdered sugar and a squeeze of lime, lemon, or orange juice. Continue to layer all fruit in bowl; between each layer sprinkle powdered sugar and lime, lemon, or orange juice. Top salad with coconut and walnuts; garnish with some of the most colorful fruit. Yield: 6 to 8 servings.

Lemon Pie

- 1½ cups sugar
- Dash salt
- ⅓ cup cornstarch
- 1½ cups water
- 3 egg yolks, slightly beaten
- 3 tablespoons butter
- ¼ cup freshly squeezed lemon juice
- 1 tablespoon lemon rind
- 1 (9-inch) baked pie shell
- Meringue

Combine sugar, salt, and cornstarch in saucepan; gradually stir in water. Cook over moderate heat, stirring constantly until mixture boils. Boil for 1 minute or until mixture thickens. Sowly stir half the hot mixture into slightly beaten egg yolks. Blend this with remaining hot mixture. Boil for 1 minute longer, stirring constantly. Remove from heat and continue stirring until smooth. Blend in butter, lemon juice, and lemon rind. Return mixture to heat for 1 or 2 minutes, stirring constantly until firm. Pour into baked pie shell. Cover with meringue. Yield: 1 (9-inch) pie.

Meringue

- 3 egg whites
- ¼ teaspoon cream of tartar
- 6 tablespoons sugar

Beat egg whites with cream of tartar until frothy; gradually beat in sugar. Continue beating until stiff and glossy. Spread meringue over lemon filling. Seal to edge of crust to prevent shrinking. Bake at 400° until meringue is lightly browned. Yield: enough meringue for 1 (9-inch) pie.

Keep that Book!

Do keep the instruction booklets that come with your equipment, and read them carefully. If you are not sure, or have forgotten a step since you used the equipment last, re-read the suggested method.

Shrimp From the Grill

Dinner for Eight

Oysters-on-the-Rocks
Grilled Shrimp
Foiled French Fries
Cold Vegetable Platter
Double Cheddar Cornbread
Fresh Fruit with Poppy Seed Dressing
French Vanilla Ice Cream

Oysters-on-the-Rocks

Fresh oysters
Salt and pepper
Bacon
Lemon slices
Tabasco sauce

Shell and drain oysters, reserving half of shells. Season with salt and pepper. Wrap each oyster with a short strip of bacon and secure with a toothpick. Return wrapped oyster to half-shell and place in hinged wire basket. Grill quickly, turning basket often. Oysters are done when bacon is cooked to desired degree of doneness. Serve with lemon slices and Tabasco sauce.

Grilled Shrimp

2 pounds large shrimp in shell
1 cup salad oil
1 cup freshly squeezed lemon juice
2 teaspoons Italian dressing mix
2 teaspoons seasoned salt
1 teaspoon seasoned pepper
4 tablespoons brown sugar
2 tablespoons soy sauce
½ cup chopped green onions

Wash shrimp thoroughly; drain on paper towels. Mix together salad oil, lemon juice, salad dressing mix, seasoned salt, and pepper. Place shrimp in bowl and pour marinade over it. Let stand stirring occasionally.

Lift shrimp from marinade with slotted spoon and place on grill about 6 inches from hot coals (use wire basket or string shrimp on skewers). Grill for about 10 minutes, turning once and brushing with marinade.

Pour remaining marinade into pan. Stir in brown sugar, soy sauce, and chopped onions. Heat to boiling. Serve as a dip for shrimp. Yield: 8 servings.

One of the easiest meats to cook on the grill is shrimp, because there's no danger of flare-ups from fat.

Foiled French Fries

(see Index)

Cold Vegetable Platter

(see Index)

Double Cheddar Cornbread

- 1 cup yellow cornmeal
- 1 cup all-purpose flour
- 3 teaspoons baking powder
- 1 teaspoon salt
- 2 cups shredded Cheddar cheese, divided
- 1 cup milk
- ¼ cup butter, melted
- 1 egg, beaten
- ½ teaspoon dry mustard
- 4 slices bacon, fried crisp and crumbled
- 1 green pepper, cut into rings

Combine cornmeal, flour, baking powder, and salt; stir in 1 cup of cheese. Combine milk, butter, and eggs; add to dry ingredients, mixing until blended. Pour into preheated, greased 9-inch skillet. Top with remaining cheese mixed with dry mustard. Sprinkle with bacon; top with green pepper rings. Bake at 425° for 25 to 30 minutes or until golden brown. Yield: 8 to 10 servings.

Fresh Fruit with Poppy Seed Dressing

- 4 cups combined fresh and canned fruit
- ½ to 1 cup Poppy Seed Dressing

Combine fruit and Poppy Seed Dressing just before serving. Serve cold. Yield: 6 to 8 servings.

Poppy Seed Dressing

- ¼ cup sugar
- ½ cup white vinegar
- 1 teaspoon dry mustard
- 1 teaspoon salt
- 1 clove garlic, crushed
- 1 cup salad oil
- ⅓ large onion, grated
- 4 teaspoons poppy seed

Combine all ingredients in pint jar. Mix well and let sit at least 6 hours before serving. Yield: 1¼ cups.

French Vanilla Ice Cream

- 6 egg yolks
- 2 cups milk
- 1 cup sugar
- ¼ teaspoon salt
- 2 cups whipping cream
- 1 tablespoon vanilla extract

Beat egg yolks and milk with rotary beater in top of double boiler. Add sugar and salt; cook over simmering water, stirring constantly, until thickened and mixture coats a metal spoon. Let cool, then add cream and vanilla extract. Freeze in electric or hand-turned freezer. Yield: about 1½ quarts.

Hawaiian Lobster Luau

Dinner for Four

Lobster Luau
Mushroom Potatoes
Peas Oriental
Orange Lotus Blossom
Sunny Sundae
Pastel Punch

Lobster Luau

8 lobster tails
¼ cup butter or margarine, melted
1 tablespoon dry mustard
1½ teaspoons Worcestershire sauce
Juice of 2 lemons
1 (8½-ounce) can pineapple tidbits, well-drained
⅓ cup diced celery
¼ cup grated Parmesan cheese

Drop lobster tails into kettle of boiling salted water. Boil for 5 minutes. Drain water and drench with cold water; cut through undershell with scissors. Remove meat and reserve shells; cut meat into bite-size pieces. Combine butter, dry mustard, Worcestershire sauce, and lemon juice; blend well. Add pineapple, celery, and lobster. Put lobster mixture into shells and sprinkle with cheese. Wrap each lobster in a piece of heavy-duty aluminum foil. Grill over medium heat for about 15 minutes. Yield: about 4 servings.

Mushroom Potatoes

(see Index)

Peas Oriental

1 (10-ounce) package frozen peas
½ cup drained and sliced water chestnuts
Salt and pepper to taste
3 tablespoons margarine

Break frozen peas apart and combine with water chestnuts. Place on a large square of heavy-duty aluminum foil; season with salt and pepper. Dot with margarine. Wrap foil tightly and bake at 350° for 1 hour or grill over medium heat for 30 to 60 minutes, turning occasionally. Yield: 4 servings.

Orange Lotus Blossom

6 large oranges
1½ cups pitted dark sweet cherries, drained
1 (13¼-ounce) can pineapple chunks, drained
1½ cups unpeeled apricot halves, drained
⅓ cup margarine
4 tablespoons brown sugar
1 teaspoon ground curry powder
Commercial sour cream

Slice tops from oranges and remove pulp; cut edge in a zigzag pattern around top. Chop orange pulp and combine with cherries, pineapple, and apricots. Fill orange cups with mixed fruit. Combine margarine, brown sugar, and curry powder; sprinkle on top of orange cups. Place each orange on a square of heavy-duty aluminum foil and wrap securely. Grill or bake at 350° for 10 to 15 minutes. Top with sour cream and serve immediately. Yield: 6 servings.

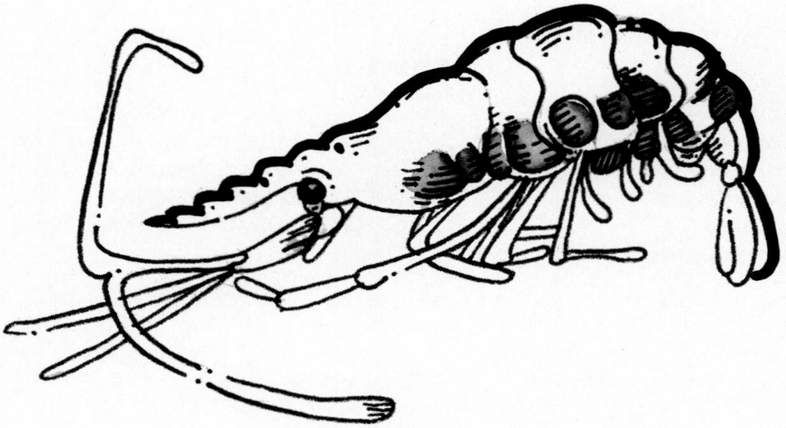

Sunny Sundae

1 pint lime sherbet
1 (8½-ounce) can pineapple tidbits, drained
1 (11-ounce) can mandarin orange sections, drained
1 cup toasted shredded coconut

Layer sherbet, pineapple, and mandarin oranges in parfait glasses. Repeat layers. Top with coconut. Serve immediately. Yield: 4 to 6 servings.

Pastel Punch

1½ tablespoons red hot cinnamon candy
2 tablespoons sugar
¼ cup water
1 pint ginger ale, chilled
3 cups pineapple juice, chilled

Combine candy, sugar, and water in saucepan; stir over low heat until candy melts. Strain and cool. Add chilled ginger ale and pineapple juice. Serve over ice. Yield: about 1½ quarts.

Almost any food can be served at a luau; just be sure it is colorful, delicious, and served with a flair.

Backyard Fish Festival

Dinner for Four to Six

Broiled Shrimp
Flounder Grilled in Foil
Dilled Yellow Squash
Sour Cream Cole Slaw
Sweet Surprise Soufflé
Corn Cakes

Broiled Shrimp

1 pound medium-sized fresh shrimp
1 pound bacon

Peel shrimp and keep on ice. Cut strips of bacon into four parts, each 2½ inches long. Wrap each shrimp with piece of bacon and secure with a toothpick. Arrange bacon-wrapped shrimp on rack in shallow broiling pan. Broil for 5 to 8 minutes until bacon begins to crisp. Pour off bacon fat from broiling pan. Turn each shrimp over and broil on other side. Serve immediately. Yield: 4 to 6 servings.

Flounder Grilled in Foil

4 to 6 pounds flounder*
¼ cup freshly squeezed lemon juice
½ cup thinly sliced onion
4 to 6 stalks celery, chopped
6 medium, ripe tomatoes, sliced
1 large green pepper, cut into strips
4 carrots, very thinly sliced
4 tablespoons freshly squeezed lemon juice
4 to 6 lemon wedges
Butter or margarine
Salt to taste

Cut four to six squares heavy-duty aluminum foil. Sprinkle lemon over flounder; then cut fish into four to six serving-size pieces. Put a serving of fish on each square of aluminum foil. On each piece of fish put sliced onion, chopped celery, sliced tomato, pepper strips, sliced carrots, lemon juice, and lemon wedges. Put a dot of butter on each stack, and add salt to taste. Seal packets securely. Lay on grill over medium heat. Turn packets every 15 minutes, and cook until fish flakes easily, about 35 minutes. Yield: 4 to 6 servings.

* Other types of fish may be used, such as trout, turbot, fish fillets of any kind, mackerel, or red snapper.

Dilled Yellow Squash

1 to 1½ pounds yellow crookneck squash
1 large onion, thinly sliced
Salt and pepper
1 teaspoon snipped fresh dill or dill weed
Butter or margarine

Slice fresh, tender young squash into ½-inch slices, and place on four to six squares of heavy-duty aluminum foil. Place onion slices on top of squash. Season with salt and pepper and a sprinkling of snipped fresh dill or packaged dill weed. Dot with butter. Seal foil packets and cook over low heat on grill for about 20 minutes, turning often. Yield: 4 to 6 servings.

Sour Cream Cole Slaw

(see Index)

Sweet Surprise Soufflé

2½ cups miniature marshmallows
½ cup milk
3 egg yolks, beaten
2 cups cooked, mashed sweet potatoes
2 tablespoons margarine, melted
½ teaspoon salt
½ teaspoon ground nutmeg
3 egg whites, stiffly beaten

Melt marshmallows with milk in top of double boiler; stir until smooth. Gradually add beaten egg yolks; stir and cook for 5 minutes. Combine potatoes, margarine, salt, and nutmeg in a large bowl; add marshmallow mixture, and stir well. Fold in stiffly beaten egg whites. Spoon mixture into 1-cup soufflé dishes or into muffin pans, filling pans half full. Bake at 325° for 30 to 35 minutes. Serve at once. Yield: 4 to 6 servings.

Corn Cakes

1¼ cups regular cornmeal
1 tablespoon all-purpose flour
½ teaspoon salt
½ teaspoon baking powder
½ teaspoon soda
1 egg, slightly beaten
1 cup buttermilk

Combine cornmeal, flour, salt, baking powder, and soda and mix well. Add slightly beaten egg to buttermilk, then stir into cornmeal mixture. Stir just until mixture is well-blended. Drop by spoonfuls onto a hot, well-greased griddle. Cook until mixture bubbles, then turn and cook on other side. Yield: 4 to 6 servings.

Protect the Bottom of Grill

Suggested materials to be used for insulating and preventing soil in the base of the charcoal cooker: first line the bottom with heavy-duty aluminum foil, then place on the foil a layer of oyster shells, non-organic kitty litter, clean sand, or small gravel.

Fish in Foil

Dinner for Six

Grilled Fish Fold-Overs
Onioned Potatoes
Green Bean Casserole
Sliced Fresh Tomatoes or Potato-Cheese Salad
Georgia Hush Puppies
Self-Ice Cake

Grilled Fish Fold-Overs

6 fish fillets
American cheese
Margarine, melted
Salt and pepper

Use sole or other thin fish fillets, fresh or thawed frozen. Make a once-over fold in each fillet, tucking a thin slice of cheese into fold. Brush outside with margarine and sprinkle with salt and pepper. Arrange in close-meshed wire basket and grill quickly over hot coals, turning frequently and brushing with more butter until done. Yield: 6 servings.

Onioned Potatoes

6 medium baking potatoes
½ cup butter or margarine, softened
1 (1⅜-ounce) package onion soup mix

Scrub potatoes, but do not pare. Cut each potato into three or four lengthwise slices. Blend butter or margarine and soup mix; spread on slices of potatoes and reassemble potatoes to original shape. Wrap each potato in a square of heavy-duty aluminum foil, overlapping ends. Place on grill over low heat and bake for 45 to 60 minutes, turning occasionally. Yield: 6 servings.

Green Bean Casserole

(see Index)

You may not have a gazebo, but you can serve some of these desserts when entertaining out of doors: watermelon, French Vanilla Ice Cream, or Coconut Pound Cake. See Index for page number of recipes.

Potato-Cheese Salad

- 3 cups cooked, diced potatoes
- 3 hard-cooked eggs, chopped
- 1½ teaspoons salt
- ¾ cup chopped celery
- 3 tablespoons grated onion
- 2 cups diced Cheddar cheese
- 1 cup commercial sour cream
- ¼ cup sweet pickle juice
- Lettuce

Combine all ingredients except lettuce in given order. Gently toss to combine. Cover and chill for at least 30 minutes for flavors to blend. Serve on lettuce. Yield: 6 servings.

Georgia Hush Puppies

- 2 cups regular cornmeal
- 1 tablespoon all-purpose flour
- ½ teaspoon soda
- 1 teaspoon baking powder
- 1 teaspoon salt
- 1 egg, slightly beaten
- 3 tablespoons minced onion
- 1 cup buttermilk
- Hot shortening

Combine cornmeal, flour, soda, baking powder, and salt in a large bowl. Mix beaten egg, minced onion, and buttermilk together and add to cornmeal mixture; stir well. Drop by spoonfuls into deep hot shortening. Fry until brown; remove from shortening and drain on paper towels. Yield: 6 servings.

Self-Ice Cake

- 1 cup chopped dates
- 1 cup boiling water
- 1 teaspoon soda
- ½ cup shortening
- 1 cup sugar
- 2 eggs
- 2 teaspoons cocoa
- 1 teaspoon vanilla extract
- 1¾ cups all-purpose flour
- ½ teaspoon salt
- ½ teaspoon cream of tartar
- 1 (6-ounce) package chocolate chips
- ¾ cup chopped nuts

Combine dates, water, and soda; let stand until cool. Cream shortening and sugar; add eggs and beat well. Add cocoa and vanilla extract; blend well. Slowly add flour, salt, and cream of tartar; stir until well-blended. Pour into 13- x 9- x 2-inch pan. Sprinkle chocolate chips and nuts over top of cake. Bake at 350° for 30 minutes. Keep cake covered in pan to store. Yield: 1 (13- x 9- x 2-inch) cake.

Cooking Time Varies

Cooking time for meat will vary with cut, shape, thickness, temperature when placed over coals, temperature of charcoal and distance of meat from charcoal, weather conditions, and degree of doneness desired. Test meat for doneness before taking it off the grill.

Fish Barbecue

Dinner for Eight

Barbecued Stuffed Trout or Whitefish
Roast Corn with Spiced Butter
Mushroom Salad
Garlic-Dill French Bread
Buttermilk Sherbet

Barbecued Stuffed Trout or Whitefish

2 cups soft breadcrumbs
2 cups peeled, chopped cucumbers, squeezed to remove liquid
2 eggs, beaten
½ cup chopped onion
4 tablespoons butter or margarine, melted
½ teaspoon salt
½ teaspoon pepper
1 (4- to 6-pound) trout or whitefish, cleaned and boned
Commercial barbecue sauce
8 slices pineapple, drained
Ripe olives

Combine breadcrumbs, cucumbers, eggs, onion, melted butter or margarine, salt, and pepper; mix well. Stuff the fish and skewer or lace together. Place on a large piece of heavy-duty aluminum foil and brush generously with barbecue sauce. Wrap well and grill over low heat for an hour or longer. Open foil, if fish flakes easily, it is done. Garnish with pineapple slices and ripe olives. Yield: 8 servings.

Roast Corn with Spiced Butter

8 ears corn
½ cup butter, melted
1½ teaspoons salt
⅛ teaspoon ground allspice

Pull husks of corn down; remove silk and rinse corn in cold water. Pull husks back up and tie to secure. Put corn on the grill and cook 15 to 20 minutes, turning once or twice. Season butter with salt and allspice; serve with corn. Yield: 8 servings.

Flavoring Olives

Spark up the flavor of ripe olives by soaking them overnight in olive oil to which a small clove of garlic has been added. Make green olives tastier by pouring off the brine, adding 2 tablespoons olive oil, then let stand 30 minutes before using.

Mushroom Salad

- 1 pound fresh mushrooms
- ¼ cup freshly squeezed lemon juice
- 6 tablespoons olive oil
- 1 teaspoon salt
- 2 teaspoons freshly ground black pepper
- 1 tablespoon chopped parsley

Trim mushroom stems and wipe caps with a damp cloth. Cut mushrooms into thin T-shaped slices. Combine mushrooms, lemon juice, oil, salt, and pepper. Mix well; marinate at room temperature for 1 hour; cover and refrigerate for 1 hour before serving. Sprinkle with parsley and serve. Yield: 8 servings.

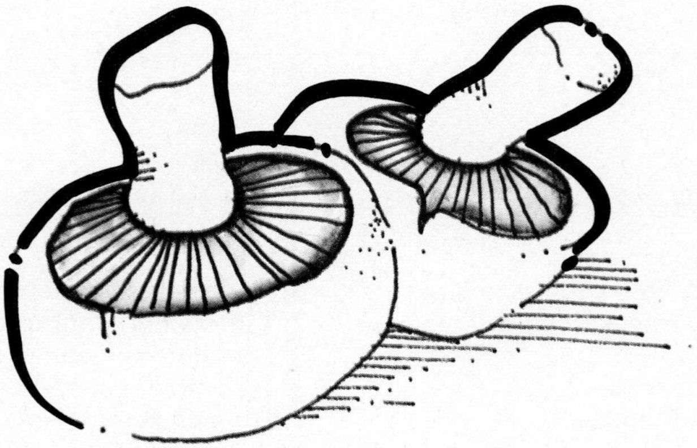

Garlic-Dill French Bread

- ½ cup butter or margarine, softened
- 1 large clove garlic, crushed
- 1 teaspoon dried parsley flakes
- ¼ teaspoon oregano
- ½ teaspoon dill weed, crushed
- 1 (1-pound) loaf French bread

Combine butter, garlic, parsley flakes, oregano, and dill weed; mix and allow to set overnight to improve flavor. Put in covered container and refrigerate. Remove from refrigerator and allow to soften for 1 hour before spreading on bread. Cut bread into ¾-inch slices, but not quite through the bottom crust. Spread butter mixture generously between slices. Wrap loosely in aluminum foil and heat on grill for 15 minutes. Yield: 8 servings.

Buttermilk Sherbet

(see Index)

To Remove Fish Odor

To remove odor from a pan after frying fish, fill pan with vinegar and let come to a boil. Discard vinegar and wash pan in hot soapy water and rinse well.

Barbecued Shrimp Special

Dinner for Eight

Barbecued Shrimp
Potatoes Deluxe
French Cold Vegetable Dish
Foil-Baked Tomatoes with Onion
Chocolate Ice Cream

Barbecued Shrimp

6 large cloves garlic, minced
⅔ cup butter or margarine, melted
2 pounds cleaned fresh shrimp
Salt and pepper to taste
2 lemons, thinly sliced
½ cup chopped parsley

Sauté garlic in butter for 2 or 3 minutes. Put layer of shrimp in bottom of a foil pan; season with salt and pepper. Put lemon slices over shrimp; drizzle with garlic butter and sprinkle with parsley. Cook over hot coals for 8 to 10 minutes or until done. Turn shrimp frequently. Yield: 8 servings.

Potatoes Deluxe

1 (8-ounce) carton commercial sour cream
¾ cup milk
1 (1¼-ounce) package sour cream sauce mix
3 cups boiled, diced potatoes
Salt and pepper to taste
½ cup buttered breadcrumbs
¼ cup grated Parmesan cheese

Heat (do not boil) sour cream; combine milk and sour cream sauce mix, and blend well with sour cream. Layer diced potatoes and sour cream mixture in greased 1½-quart casserole dish; repeat layers. Sprinkle with salt and pepper, cover with buttered breadcrumbs, and top with Parmesan cheese. Bake at 350° for 30 minutes or until crumbs are brown and casserole is bubbly. Yield: 8 servings.

To Keep Food Warm

If you don't have an electric serving tray for keeping food hot, nest bowls of sauces, casseroles, or meat in heated rock salt to keep them warm until serving time.

French Cold Vegetable Dish

1 (16-ounce) can French-style green beans, drained
1 (16-ounce) can tiny peas, drained
1 small onion, minced
½ green pepper, chopped
1 pimiento, chopped
2 stalks celery, diced
1 teaspoon paprika
Salt and pepper to taste
1 cup vinegar
½ cup salad oil
1¼ cups sugar
1 (16-ounce) can tiny whole beets, drained
1 cup shredded cabbage

Combine beans, peas, onion, green pepper, pimiento, celery, paprika, salt and pepper; mix well and set aside. Combine vinegar, salad oil, and sugar to make dressing; place over low heat, stirring constantly until sugar is dissolved. Marinate bean-pea mixture in 1½ cups dressing and use remaining dressing to marinate beets in a separate bowl. Chill both bowls of vegetables overnight. Before serving, drain all vegetables and mix with cabbage. Yield: 8 to 10 servings.

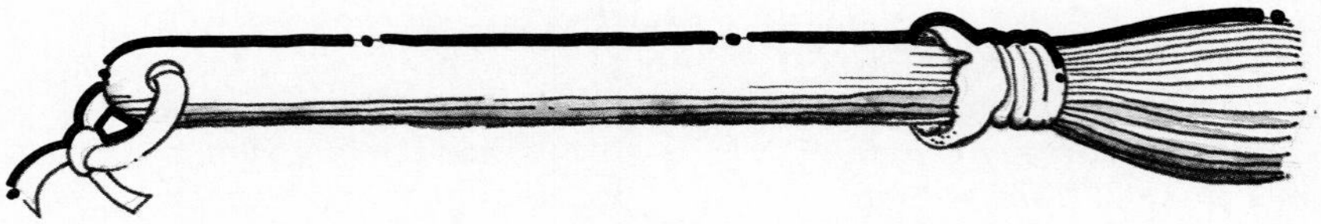

Foil-Baked Tomatoes with Onion

Tomatoes
Salt and pepper
Onion

Select medium, firm tomatoes (one tomato per person). Cut each tomato in half crosswise; sprinkle cut surfaces with salt and pepper and put together again, placing a thin slice of onion between tomato halves. Use a toothpick to hold the reassembled tomato intact. Wrap each tomato in a 6-inch square of heavy-duty aluminum foil. Cook at edge of grill for 15 to 20 minutes.

Chocolate Ice Cream

1¼ cups sugar
8 egg yolks, beaten
4 ounces sweet chocolate, grated
1 quart milk, scalded
1 teaspoon vanilla extract
1 cup whipping cream

Combine sugar, egg yolks, and chocolate in top of double boiler. Add scalded milk and cook, stirring constantly, about 3 to 5 minutes. Cool. Add vanilla extract and cream. Chill. Pour into chilled freezer container and freeze. Yield: ½ gallon.

Good Potato Salad

Potato salad is better if you marinate the potatoes with French or Italian dressing, onions, and green peppers for several hours before adding mayonnaise. You might add pimiento, hard-cooked eggs, or other seasonings to marinade. Add mayonnaise just before serving.

Southern Seafare Spread

Dinner for Eight

Cheese-Stuffed Fish Fillets
Garden Row Casserole
Harvest Slaw
Skillet Corn Cakes
Lemon Ripple

Cheese-Stuffed Fish Fillets

1 (4-pound) or 2 (2-pound) fish, cleaned and boned
½ cup butter or margarine, divided
½ cup chopped onion
¼ cup chopped green pepper
1 teaspoon salt
Dash pepper
2 cups dry breadcrumbs
6 tablespoons shredded American cheese

Cut fish into eight pieces. Melt ⅓ cup butter. Sauté onion and green pepper in butter until tender; add seasonings and breadcrumbs. Cut eight squares of heavy-duty aluminum foil. Spread center of each foil square with remaining butter and sprinkle with 1 tablespoon cheese. Place a piece of fish on cheese, skin-side down; cover with ¼ cup stuffing. Wrap fish in a tight foil packet. Grill 3 to 4 inches above medium heat for 10 to 12 minutes; turn and cook an additional 10 to 12 minutes. Serve from foil. Yield: 8 servings.

Garden Row Casserole

1 (10½-ounce) can cream of chicken soup
1 cup shredded American cheese
¼ teaspoon salt
½ cup milk
2 (16-ounce) cans tiny whole potatoes, drained
2 (16-ounce) bottles whole onions, drained
1 (16-ounce) can green peas, drained
1 cup buttered breadcrumbs

Combine soup, cheese, salt, and milk; stir over low heat until well-blended. Add vegetables and mix well. Pour into greased 3-quart casserole dish. Top with breadcrumbs. Bake at 350° for 25 minutes or until bubbly. Yield: 8 to 10 servings.

Protect Your Pans

If you are using a pan directly on heat, rub outside generously with soap before placing over the fire.

Harvest Slaw

1 medium head cabbage, shredded
2 carrots, shredded
1 green pepper, finely diced
1 medium onion, finely diced
Dressing for Slaw

Combine cabbage, carrots, green pepper, and onion in large bowl. Toss with dressing. Cover and refrigerate; slaw keeps well in refrigerator for several days. Yield: 10 to 12 servings.

Dressing for Slaw

1¼ cups vinegar
1 cup sugar
¾ teaspoon mustard seed
½ teaspoon turmeric
¾ teaspoon salt

Heat vinegar; add sugar, mustard seed, turmeric, and salt. Stir over low heat until mixture is dissolved. Cool dressing and pour over slaw. Yield: about 2 cups.

Skillet Corn Cakes

1 cup salad oil
1½ cups cornmeal
⅓ cup all-purpose flour
2 teaspoons baking powder
½ teaspoon salt
½ cup milk
1 egg, beaten
1 cup cream-style corn

Heat salad oil in heavy skillet. Combine cornmeal, flour, baking powder, and salt; add milk, egg, and corn. Mix well. Fry heaping tablespoons of batter in hot oil until golden brown, adding more oil if needed. Serve hot. Yield: about 2 dozen cakes.

Lemon Ripple

2 cups graham cracker crumbs
2 tablespoons sugar
3 tablespoons butter or margarine, softened
1 (6-ounce) can frozen lemonade concentrate, partially thawed
1 quart vanilla ice cream, slightly softened

Combine graham cracker crumbs, sugar, and butter; mix well and press crumbs evenly and firmly in bottom of 9-inch square pan, reserving 2 tablespoons of crumb mixture for topping. Chill crust. Ripple lemonade concentrate through ice cream. Spoon into chilled crumb crust. Top with reserved crumbs and freeze until firm. Cut into squares. Yield: 8 to 10 servings.

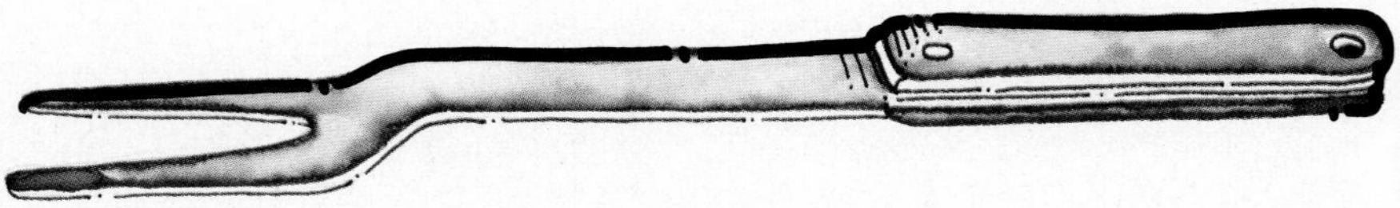

Douse That Flame!

A clothes sprinkler or a squirt bottle sold for catsup or mustard makes a good water holder for squirting on flames that flare up from fat cooking on the charcoal fire.

Crowd Pleasers

There are many occasions in the life of a Southerner that call for feeding a crowd: when the kinfolks come for a family reunion, when there's a political rally, a food festival, or special meals to celebrate Independence Day or Labor Day.

The food on these occasions varies according to the locality. Texans may serve chili or barbecue beef; Louisiana celebrants may serve Jambalaya or Shrimp Creole; Georgians favor Brunswick Stew; and folks in Kentucky may ladle up Kentucky Burgoo.

No matter what the entree, kitchen utensils are never large enough. As Southerners say, "We'll put the big pot in the little one," and they rely on black washpots for cooking the Burgoo or Jambalaya, and they dig a deep pit for barbecuing a whole pig or a beef quarter.

Along with large quantities of food for main dishes, there must be an equally ample supply of vegetables and salad; not a great variety, but plenty of the kind you do serve.

An ideal dessert is homemade ice cream or sliced watermelons which have been chilled in washtubs filled with ice.

Chili con Carne

5 pounds ground beef
2½ tablespoons salt
½ teaspoon black pepper
⅓ cup salad oil
2½ cups chopped onions
6 (1-pound) cans kidney beans
3 (2-ounce) cans tomatoes
5 tablespoons chili powder
12 cups cooked rice
1½ cups coarsely shredded Cheddar cheese

Season meat with salt and pepper; sauté about one pound of meat at a time in one tablespoon oil in a large skillet. Place meat in large pan. Sauté onions in drippings in skillet until tender but not browned. Add to meat. Add remaining ingredients except cheese and stir well. Bring to a boil, cover, reduce heat, and simmer for at least 45 minutes. Serve in soup bowls over hot rice. Sprinkle with shredded cheese. Yield: 24 (1-cup) servings.

Texas Chili

12 pounds chuck roast
½ cup salad oil
15 to 20 cloves garlic, crushed
8 large onions, chopped
12 cups hot water
¾ to 1 cup chili powder
1 tablespoon cumin
2 tablespoons oregano, crushed
8 tablespoons salt
1 (4-ounce) can green chiles, chopped
2 tablespoons all-purpose flour
½ cup cold water

Cut meat into small cubes, removing most of the fat and all of the gristle. Sauté in hot oil in a large skillet until meat turns white. Add garlic, onion, and hot water; cover pot and simmer for 1 hour, or until meat is tender.

Add chili powder, cumin, oregano, and salt. Cook slowly for another hour, stirring occasionally. Add additional water if needed. Add chopped chiles; taste and add more seasoning if needed. Stir flour into ½ cup cold water; add to chili mixture, and stir and cook until mixture is clear. Serve hot. Yield: 16 to 20 servings.

Kentucky Burgoo

2 pounds beef shank
2 pounds pork shank
2 pounds veal shank
1 (3- to 6-pound) hen, cut into serving-size pieces
2 or 3 squirrels, cut into serving-size pieces (optional)
1 (3-pound) breast of lamb
2 gallons cold water
1½ pounds onions, chopped
2 pounds potatoes, chopped
4 raw carrots, chopped
2 cups chopped celery
4 green peppers, chopped
4 cups chopped tomatoes
2 cups whole corn, canned or fresh
2 cups butterbeans or lima beans
2 pods red pepper
6 teaspoons Worcestershire sauce
Salt and pepper to taste
Tabasco sauce to taste

Put the meats and water into a 4-gallon kettle and bring slowly to a boil. Simmer until meat is tender enough to fall off the bones. Remove meat from stock and cool. Separate meat from bones, and chop into fairly large pieces. Return chopped meat to stock. Add onions, potatoes, carrots, celery, green peppers, tomatoes, corn, butterbeans, and red pepper to the stock. Cook until vegetables are tender and mixture is thick. Mixture should cook slowly for several hours and be stirred often to keep it from sticking to kettle. After mixture has thickened, add Worcestershire sauce and stir well. Add salt, pepper, and Tabasco to taste. Yield: 3 gallons.

Pit-Cooked Pig

Preparation of a pit: A hole is dug in a cleared spot about 2 feet deep and up to 6 feet in diameter. Put dried wood into the hole with hickory wood forming the top layer, just like a campfire. Place a thick wooden pole in the center and build stones around so that the wood is completely covered by the rocks. Remove the pole and push a potato bag into the hole left by the pole. If possible, push the bag all the way down so that it is touching the wood. Next pour kerosene onto the bag, saturating it well and setting it on fire. There should be sufficient wood in the pit to keep a fire burning for about 2 hours; thus insuring that the rocks are hot before adding the pig.

Preparation of the pig: The pig is dressed and the shoulders cut wide open to allow one hot stone to be placed inside each shoulder. The back legs are cut crisscross from the outside almost to the bone to allow the heat to penetrate. Three or four hot stones should be placed inside the belly.

Green leaves from non-poisonous trees are placed on top of the hot rocks in the pit. Cover pig with chicken wire and place on top of these leaves. Cover the pig with leaves on the outside. Then the whole pig and pit is completely covered with soaked, wet, gunny sacks. Put a large canvas cover over the whole pit. To finish, seal off every spot to prevent any escape of steam or heat.

Depending on the size of the pig, allow four to five hours to cook. After this amount of time, the pig is well-cooked and will fall apart very easily. When the pig is cooked, canvas and gunny sacks are removed. The pig is lifted out by means of the chicken wire and placed on a hardwood board of appropriate size.

The pig is then carried to the kitchen on the board and cut into small bite-size pieces including the skin. Before serving, the pig is seasoned with salt.

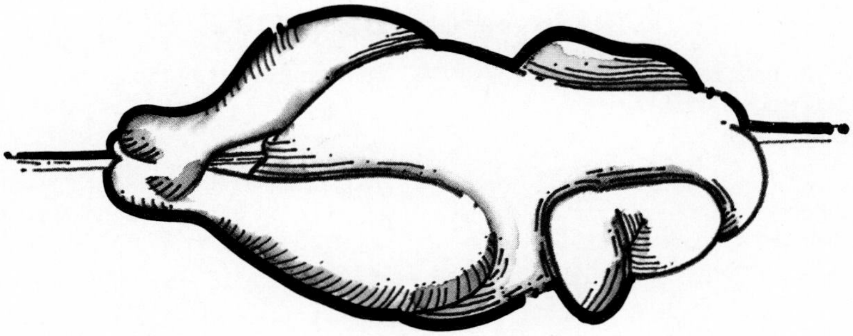

Brunswick Stew

3 (4- to 5-pound) hens
1 (3- to 4-pound) chuck roast
2 pounds beef liver
5 pounds potatoes, diced
12 large onions, finely chopped
2 gallons canned tomatoes
2 gallons canned corn
1 gallon chicken stock
2 quarts milk
2 pounds butter or margarine
2 (11½-ounce) bottles chili sauce
Worcestershire sauce to taste
Tabasco sauce to taste
Salt and pepper to taste

Put hens in a large saucepan, cover with water; cook until meat is tender and falls off the bone. Remove from stock, cool, and separate meat from bones. Shred and set aside. Save stock. Cook roast in a small amount of water in a covered utensil until meat is tender. Remove from water and cut into small pieces. Boil liver in meat stock and put through food grinder. Put chicken, beef, and liver in large iron pot. Add potatoes, onions, tomatoes, corn, chicken stock, milk, and butter or margarine. Bring stew to a simmer and cook very slowly for at least 6 hours, stirring often. Add chili sauce, mix well; taste and add Worcestershire sauce, Tabasco sauce, and salt and pepper to taste. Yield: 40 servings.

Country Captain

- 1 (3½- to 4-pound) young, tender hen
- All-purpose flour
- Salt
- Black pepper
- Shortening
- 2 onions, finely chopped
- 2 green peppers, chopped
- 1 small clove garlic, minced
- 1½ teaspoons salt
- ½ teaspoon white pepper
- 3 teaspoons curry powder
- 2 (1-pound) cans tomatoes
- ½ cup chopped parsley
- ½ teaspoon powdered thyme
- ¼ pound blanched, toasted almonds
- 3 heaping tablespoons currants
- 2 cups cooked rice
- Parsley

Cut chicken into serving-size pieces. Remove skin and coat pieces with mixture of flour, salt, and pepper. Brown in hot shortening. Remove chicken from pan, but keep it hot. Add onions, peppers, and garlic to hot shortening and cook very slowly, stirring constantly, until vegetables are limp. Season with salt, pepper and curry powder (add more curry, if desired). Add tomatoes, ½ cup chopped parsley, and thyme.

Put chicken in a large Dutch oven and pour tomato mixture over it. Cover and bake at 350° for 45 minutes, or until chicken is tender.

Place chicken in center of a large platter and pile rice around it. Drop currants into sauce mixture in Dutch oven, and pour over the rice. Sprinkle almonds over the top, and garnish with parsley. Yield: 6 to 8 servings.

Carolina Pork Barbecue

- 1 (6-pound) pork roast
- 3 to 4 cups commercial barbecue sauce
- 18 hamburger buns

Cook pork roast on a rotisserie or by open pit cooking about 3 to 4 hours, or until meat registers well-done on meat thermometer. Remove from heat and shred meat into a large bowl or saucepan. Add barbecue sauce and mix well. Heat mixture thoroughly. Spread on hamburger buns and serve hot. Yield: 18 barbecue sandwiches.

Spanish Rice Pronto

- 8 slices bacon, diced
- 4 pounds ground beef
- 2 cups chopped green peppers
- 2 cups chopped onions
- 1 cup diced celery
- 5 (28-ounce) cans tomatoes
- 1 quart water
- 2 cups firmly packed brown sugar
- 2 tablespoons salt
- 2 tablespoons prepared mustard
- 2 teaspoons basil
- ¼ teaspoon black pepper
- 2 (14-ounce) packages pre-cooked rice
- 2 cups shredded Cheddar cheese

Sauté bacon until crisp in a large, heavy skillet; remove from skillet and place bacon in a large pan, leaving drippings in skillet. Brown 2 pounds of the beef at one time in bacon drippings; add to bacon. Sauté peppers, onions, and celery in remaining drippings until golden brown; add to meat. Add all other ingredients except rice and cheese; mix well. Bring to a boil, cover and simmer for 30 minutes. Put rice in a large shallow baking pan and pour hot mixture over rice. Stir well, cover pan tightly and bake at 450° for 15 to 20 minutes. Fluff with a fork before serving. Sprinkle shredded cheese on each serving. Yield: 30 (1-cup) servings.

Chicken Jambalaya

12½ pounds frying-size chickens, cut into serving-size pieces
1 cup salad oil
3 pounds onions, coarsely chopped
6 cloves garlic, crushed
1 bunch green onions, chopped
1 large green pepper, chopped
Water (2 parts water to 1 part rice)
Salt and pepper to taste
Worcestershire sauce to taste
6 pounds regular rice

Fry chicken pieces in hot oil. Remove most of the fat from skillet or pot after chicken has been fried. Add chopped onion, garlic, green onion, and green pepper; cook until lightly browned. Add water and boil vigorously for 15 minutes. Add salt, pepper, and Worcestershire sauce. Stir in rice. Stir mixture once; cover pot tightly and let mixture cook until all water has been absorbed and rice is tender. If water boils out before rice is tender, add more boiling water. Serve hot. Yield: 25 servings.

Shrimp, a mixture of seafood, or wild game may be substituted for the chicken in this recipe.

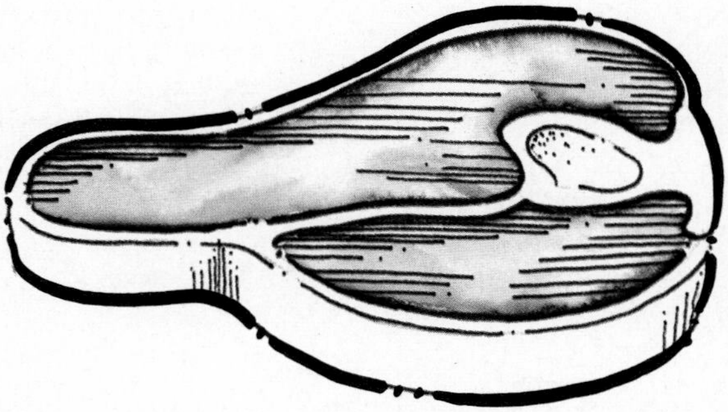

Baked Beans for 25

4 cups pinto or kidney beans
1 pound salt pork, cut in small pieces
4 small onions, chopped
½ cup molasses
2 teaspoons salt
½ teaspoon black pepper
1 teaspoon powdered mustard

Soak beans overnight in water to cover. Drain, cover with fresh water and simmer gently until beans are ready to burst their skins. Drain. Add salt pork and onions and mix well. Mix molasses, salt, pepper, and mustard in a cup and fill with boiling water. Pour this over the beans, then add enough boiling water to cover beans. Cover pans and bake at 300° for 6 to 8 hours. Pan may be uncovered the last hour of baking. Yield: 25 servings.

Roast Corn Deluxe

36 ears fresh corn in husks
4 cups melted margarine
1 cup diced green pepper

Carefully peel back corn husks. Remove all silk. Blend margarine with diced green pepper, and spread generously on ears of corn. Fold husks back over ears. Wrap each ear tightly in aluminum foil. Place on grill and cook, turning frequently, for about 20 to 30 minutes. Yield: 25 servings.

Golden Glow Salad

4 (3-ounce) packages lemon-flavored gelatin
2 teaspoons salt
6 cups boiling water
2⅔ cups drained, crushed pineapple
1⅓ cups pineapple juice
4 tablespoons freshly squeezed lemon juice
4 cups coarsely grated raw carrots
1⅓ cups chopped pecans
Crisp lettuce

Dissolve gelatin and salt in boiling water. Add crushed pineapple and juice, and lemon juice. Chill until slightly thickened. Fold in carrots and nuts. Pour into a 4-quart mold or four 1-quart molds. Chill until firm. Unmold on crisp lettuce and garnish as desired. Yield: 24 servings.

Potato Salad for a Crowd

5 pounds potatoes
½ cup French dressing
4 hard-cooked eggs, diced
6 tablespoons chopped green pepper
½ cup finely chopped pimiento
3 cups sliced celery
¼ to ½ cup finely chopped onion
2 cups mayonnaise
¼ cup prepared mustard
1½ teaspoons paprika
2 tablespoons salt
1 teaspoon white pepper

Cook potatoes in jackets; cool, peel, and dice Pour French dressing over warm potatoes and let marinate until completely cooled. Add eggs, green pepper, pimiento, celery, and onion.

Combine mayonnaise, prepared mustard, paprika, salt, and white pepper. Add to potato mixture and stir until just blended. Chill thoroughly and keep chilled until time to serve. Yield: 25 servings.

Sweet and Sour Coleslaw for a Crowd

4½ cups evaporated milk
2¼ cups sugar
2¼ teaspoons salt
¾ teaspoon black pepper
2¼ cups cider vinegar
2½ gallons finely cut, lightly packed cabbage (about 7 pounds cabbage as purchased)

Measure evaporated milk into a large bowl. Add sugar, salt, and pepper; let stand about 5 minutes, stirring occasionally to dissolve sugar. Gradually blend in vinegar to make dressing. Mixture may appear slightly curdled, but this does not affect finished salad. Chill thoroughly.

Chill cabbage before adding dressing. Stir dressing well, and add to cut cabbage. Toss to coat just before serving. Salad should be kept cool at all times. Keep leftover salad in refrigerator. Yield: 50 servings.

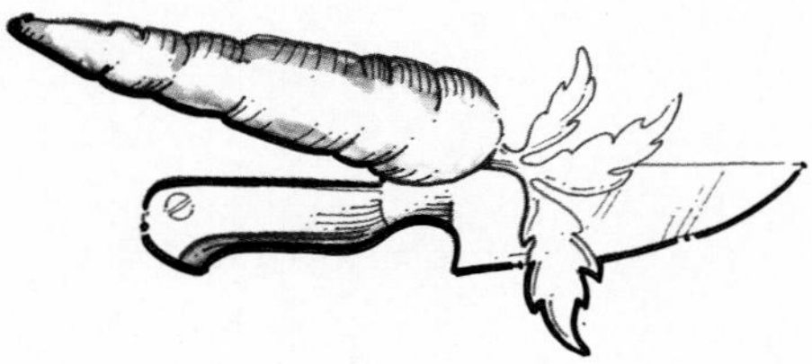

Heating Canned Food

Avoid heating an unopened can of food over an open flame without first puncturing the lid.

Sauces and Marinades

A good sauce makes good barbecued meat taste better. Often the choice of a sauce depends on the taste buds of the cook. Some prefer hot, spicy sauces, while others like a milder version. Generally, we think of a sauce as a mixture which is mopped on the meat as it cooks on the grill.

It's usually a good idea to make extra sauce, for there are those who like to spread extra sauce over their meat, or even to put slivers of the cooked meat in the sauce and spread the mixture on a bun for serving.

Some cooks use catsup, tomato paste, or tomato sauce, and others will not tolerate it on their ingredients list at all. The cook can be as heavy-handed or as stingy as he desires in the addition of seasonings.

Marinades ordinarily, although not always, serve a double purpose. One of the main ingredients of a marinade is vinegar, wine, or lemon juice, which serves as a tenderizer for meat. Other ingredients are added for flavor. Tougher cuts of meat respond especially well to marinades; meats are kept in marinade in refrigerator at least 3 or 4 hours, and often longer.

An aluminum dish should never be used for marinating, because of the chemical reaction of the acid on metal. A plastic bag or a large glass, enameled, or ceramic bowl is ideal. If a plastic bag is used, select the heaviest kind available (or use double thickness). Place marinade mixture and meat in bag and shake occasionally. If a bowl is used, turn meat often so that each side will be exposed to the marinating mixture.

Old Southern Barbecue Sauce

- 1 cup onion, chopped
- 2 cloves garlic, minced
- 1 cup salad oil
- 1 tablespoon dry mustard
- 1 cup Worcestershire sauce
- 1 cup catsup
- ½ cup vinegar
- 2 lemons, finely chopped with peeling
- 1 teaspoon salt
- 1 pod red pepper
- 1 tablespoon Tabasco sauce
- 1 teaspoon black pepper
- 1 teaspoon mixed pickling spices (placed in small cloth bag)

Cook onion and garlic in salad oil until tender; add remaining ingredients and simmer 30 minutes. Remove bag of pickling spices and lemon peel. Yield: about 1 quart.

Red Barbecue Sauce for Spareribs

- ½ cup salad oil
- 3 cups coarsely chopped onions
- 1 tablespoon minced garlic
- 1 (1-pound) can tomatoes
- 1 cup canned tomato purée
- ¼ cup coarsely chopped fresh hot chiles, including seeds
- 2 tablespoons powdered mustard
- 2 tablespoons sugar
- 1 tablespoon white vinegar
- 1½ teaspoons salt

Heat the salad oil in a heavy skillet or Dutch oven over moderate heat. Add the onions and garlic and cook for about 5 minutes, stirring frequently. Onions should be translucent but not brown. Chop the tomatoes very coarsely and add tomatoes and liquid to cooked onions. Add tomato purée, hot chiles, mustard, sugar, vinegar, and salt; bring to a boil over high heat. Cook briskly, uncovered, until the sauce is thick enough to hold its shape almost solidly in the spoon. Remove from heat and adjust seasoning. Use to baste spareribs the last 30 to 40 minutes of cooking time. Yield: enough sauce for 4 pounds spareribs.

Southern Barbecue Sauce

- 1 cup water
- 2 cups vinegar
- 2 teaspoons pepper
- 1 cup margarine, melted
- 2 tablespoons salt
- Garlic salt, if desired

Combine all ingredients in heavy saucepan; heat and place container on grill to use as a mopping sauce for chickens. Yield: enough sauce for 4 or 5 chickens.

Barbecue Sauce for Pork

- Juice and grated peel of 2 lemons
- ½ cup salad oil
- ½ cup liquid smoke
- 1 (13½-ounce) can tomato juice
- 2 tablespoons light brown sugar
- 2 bay leaves

Combine all ingredients in a heavy saucepan. Heat just to boiling, and keep warm to use for brushing on pork on the grill. Yield: about 2½ cups.

Quick Barbecue Sauce

- ½ cup salad oil
- ¾ cup minced onion
- ¾ cup catsup
- ¾ cup water
- ⅓ cup freshly squeezed lemon juice
- 3 tablespoons sugar
- 3 tablespoons Worcestershire sauce
- 2 tablespoons prepared mustard
- 2 teaspoons salt
- ½ teaspoon pepper

Heat salad oil in heavy skillet; add onions and cook until onions are golden. Add other ingredients and simmer for 15 minutes. This sauce may be used on chicken, beef, lamb, or pork. Yield: about 2 cups.

Barbecue Sauce for Beef or Pork

- 1 cup commercial French dressing
- ½ cup commercial chili sauce
- 2 tablespoons light brown sugar
- 1 medium onion, sliced
- 1 tablespoon Worcestershire sauce

Combine all ingredients in a heavy saucepan; cook for 10 minutes. Cool. Use as a marinade for pork chops, beef kabobs, or flank steak. Remove meat from marinade and use as a sauce to brush on meat as it cooks on grill. Yield: about 1½ cups.

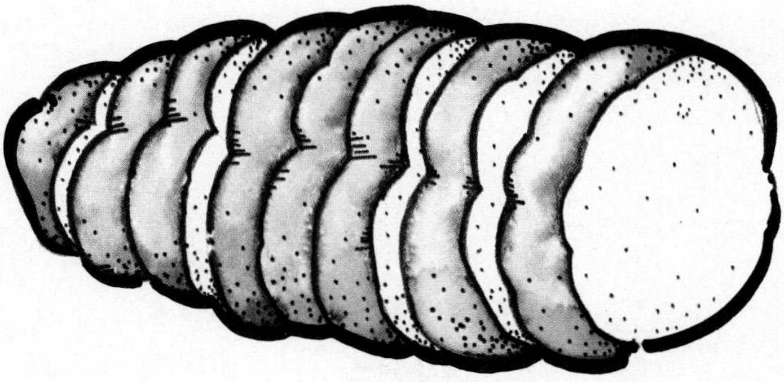

Smoky Barbecue Sauce

- ¼ cup vinegar
- ½ cup water
- 1 tablespoon prepared mustard
- 2 tablespoons sugar
- ½ teaspoon pepper
- 1½ teaspoons salt
- ¼ teaspoon cayenne pepper
- ¼ medium lemon
- 1 medium onion, coarsely chopped
- ¼ cup margarine
- ½ cup catsup
- 2 tablespoons Worcestershire sauce
- 1½ teaspoons liquid smoke

Combine vinegar, water, mustard, sugar, pepper, salt, cayenne, lemon, onion, and margarine in heavy saucepan. Bring to a boil, and boil for 20 minutes. Add catsup, Worcestershire sauce, and liquid smoke; heat just to boiling. Use to baste spareribs on grill. This sauce is better if made in advance, and can be kept in a covered jar in the refrigerator for at least 2 weeks. Yield: about 1¾ cups.

Mild Barbecue Sauce

- ¼ cup margarine, melted
- ½ cup finely chopped onions
- 1⅓ cups water
- ⅔ cup catsup
- ⅔ cup tomato juice
- 1½ teaspoons salt
- 1½ teaspoons paprika
- 1 teaspoon pepper
- 1 teaspoon Worcestershire sauce
- ½ teaspoon garlic salt

Melt margarine in heavy skillet; sauté onions in hot margarine until they turn golden. Add other ingredients and bring to a boil. Use as a mopping sauce for barbecuing chicken. Yield: 3 cups, or enough sauce for 6 chickens.

Basting Sauce for Spareribs

- 1 cup molasses
- 1 cup chili sauce
- ¼ cup prepared mustard
- 1 teaspoon soy sauce
- ½ cup grated onion
- 1 cup beer

Combine molasses, chili sauce, mustard, soy sauce, and grated onion in a small saucepan; bring to a boil and boil for 5 minutes. Remove from heat and stir in beer. Use to brush on spareribs as they cook on grill. Yield: 3½ cups.

Barbecue Sauce for Chicken

- 1 cup catsup
- ½ to 1 teaspoon Tabasco sauce
- 2 tablespoons light brown sugar
- 1 teaspoon powdered mustard
- 2 tablespoons wine vinegar
- ½ teaspoon crushed thyme
- ¼ cup salad oil

Combine all ingredients and heat just to boiling before using to brush on chicken as it barbecues on grill. Yield: enough sauce for 1 (2½-pound) chicken, cut into serving pieces or halves.

Barbecue Sauce with a Difference

- ½ cup salad oil
- 1 cup freshly squeezed lemon juice
- 1 tablespoon salt
- 2 tablespoons molasses
- 1 teaspoon Tabasco sauce

Put salad oil, lemon juice, salt, molasses, and Tabasco in a heavy saucepan. Heat to boiling and use to baste chickens on grill. Yield: about 1½ cups.

Unbeatable Barbecue Sauce

1 (12-ounce) can beer
Juice of 1 lemon
1 clove garlic, pressed
1 medium onion, chopped
¼ cup sugar*
⅓ cup Worcestershire sauce
⅔ cup catsup
⅓ cup orange juice

Combine all ingredients and cook over medium heat until mixture comes to a boil. Lower heat and simmer for 15 minutes. Yield: 3 cups.

* Eliminate sugar in sauce if using on beef.

Wally Boren's Barbecue Sauce — The Gentle Kind

Take a bud of garlic and chop it into little-bitty pieces.
Cut up a whole onion the same way.
Put 2 tablespoons of oil in a saucepan. (Salad oil or olive oil, not linseed or castor oil.)
Dump in the garlic and onion and cook gently for 5 minutes. (If you cook it any longer you'll hear from the neighbors.)
Add 3 teaspoonfuls of Chili Powder. (You know, that *red* powder.
1 teaspoonful of dry mustard. (I don't have to tell you to make all measures level, do I?)
Add a bay leaf. (The Romans called it "Laurel" and *crowned* you with it.)
A pinch of marjoram. (Better make this about ¼ teaspoonful if you're going to be technical.)
Add a No. 2½ can of tomatoes with purée. (Hold it! Run 'em through the sieve first to take the seeds out!)
Next 1 tablespoonful of sugar. (Hurry up, we can't stay in the kitchen all day!)
¼ cup of vinegar. (You're nearly through now.)
½ teaspoonful of celery salt. (Don't ask me why.)
Don't go away. You've got to *stir it* pretty regularly for 40 minutes or maybe a little more while it simmers and thickens.

When it gets as thick as good country gravy, fish out the bay leaves and throw away. Not the *sauce,* the bay leaves.

Put the sauce in bottles or jars 'til you want to use it. It will keep as well as catsup. Yield: 1¼ cups sauce.

If You Want It Hot

Here's all you do to make the *HOT* kind.

Add ½ teaspoonful of Tabasco sauce and stir it in.

Now maybe you want to know how to use this mixture.

Well, take some roasts or broiled beef or chicken or pork and lay it on a slice of buttered bread. Then spread a tablespoonful of the sauce on it and cover it with another slice of bread. You can have it hot or cold according to taste. Of course, good old pit *barbecued* meat is what you ought to have with it but maybe you haven't any pit.

I sure hope you like it because I've had many a real Mexican start callin' me "amigo" after one taste of it.

Super Barbecue Sauce

½ cup red wine
½ cup salad oil
2 tablespoons grated onion
1 clove garlic, crushed
1 tablespoon salt
½ teaspoon black pepper
2 teaspoons Worcestershire sauce
¼ teaspoon thyme
2 tablespoons freshly squeezed lemon juice

Combine all ingredients, but do not heat. Use to brush on chicken or beef as it cooks on grill. Yield: 1¼ cups.

Mexican Barbecue Sauce

1 (14-ounce) bottle catsup
¼ cup water
2 teaspoons powdered mustard
½ teaspoon chili powder
1 teaspoon celery salt
½ teaspoon ground cumin
¼ teaspoon ground cloves
2 tablespoons dark brown sugar
¼ cup wine vinegar
¼ teaspoon Tabasco sauce
2 tablespoons Worcestershire sauce
1 tablespoon grated onion

Combine all ingredients and beat well. This mixture may be used to marinate meat overnight. The next day, remove meat from marinade and place on grill. Brush meat with marinade or sauce as it cooks. This sauce is good for spareribs, pork chops, chicken, flank steak, or ground beef. Yield: about 3 cups.

Super-Duper Barbecue Sauce

1 cup catsup
1 cup water
1 small onion, chopped
1 tablespoon Worcestershire sauce
¼ cup vinegar
1 tablespoon brown sugar
2 teaspoons dry mustard
1 teaspoon paprika
1 teaspoon chili powder
1 clove garlic, minced
½ teaspoon meat tenderizer

Combine ingredients; cover and simmer slowly for 30 minutes. Sauce may be used to marinate meat before grilling or to baste meat during cooking. Yield: about 2 cups.

Bang-Up Barbecue Sauce

1 (10½-ounce) can tomato soup
¼ cup sweet pickle relish
¼ cup chopped onion
1 tablespoon brown sugar
1 tablespoon vinegar
1 tablespoon Worcestershire sauce

Combine all ingredients in saucepan; cover and simmer until onion is tender and flavors are blended. Yield: 1½ cups.

Superb Barbecue Sauce for Pork

⅓ cup vinegar
⅔ cup water
1½ tablespoons prepared mustard
⅓ cup brown sugar
¼ teaspoon black pepper
⅔ cup catsup
1 teaspoon salt
Pinch cayenne pepper
2 slices fresh lemon
1 large onion, sliced
½ cup butter or margarine
1½ tablespoons Worcestershire sauce

Combine all ingredients in heavy skillet. Simmer, uncovered, for 20 minutes. Use to baste pork roast or spareribs. Yield: about 3 cups.

Wine Barbecue Sauce

¼ cup salad oil
½ cup white wine
1 clove garlic, grated
1 small onion, grated
½ teaspoon salt
½ teaspoon celery salt
½ teaspoon black pepper
¼ teaspoon thyme
¼ teaspoon marjoram
¼ teaspoon rosemary

Combine all ingredients and chill for several hours. Marinate chicken or veal in refrigerator for 3 hours. Brush sauce on meat when grilling. Yield: ¾ cup.

Note: Substitute red wine for white wine when grilling steak or lamb.

Onion Barbecue Sauce

1 (10½-ounce) can cream of mushroom soup
1 (10¾-ounce) can onion soup
½ cup catsup
¼ cup salad oil
¼ cup vinegar
2 cloves garlic, minced
2 tablespoons brown sugar
1 tablespoon Worcestershire sauce
⅛ teaspoon Tabasco sauce

Combine all ingredients. Cover and cook over low heat about 15 minutes, stirring occasionally. Yield: 2½ cups.

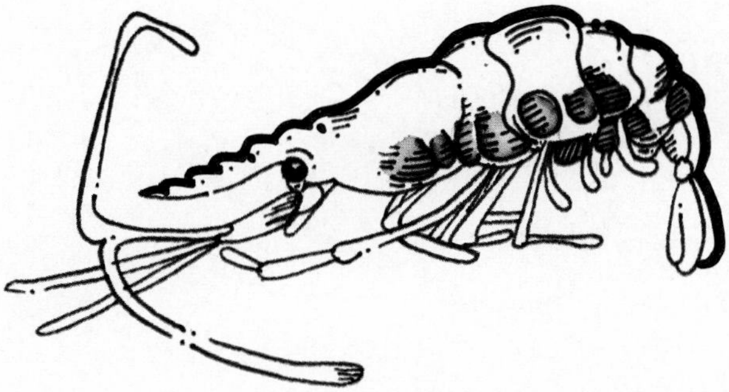

Chili-Pineapple Sauce

1 (14-ounce) bottle catsup
1 cup pineapple juice
¾ cup chopped green onions
½ teaspoon chili powder

Combine all ingredients; stir until well-blended. Baste sauce on meat, fish, or poultry during grilling. Serve additional sauce with meat. Yield: 1½ cups.

Piquante Sauce

1½ cups catsup
3 tablespoons vinegar
2 tablespoons dark corn syrup
2 teaspoons salt
1 teaspoon paprika
¾ teaspoon chili powder
¼ teaspoon pepper

Combine all ingredients; stir until well-blended. Use to baste spareribs, beef, or lamb during grilling. Yield: 1¾ cups.

Honolulu Sauce

- ¼ cup butter or margarine, melted
- ½ cup catsup
- ½ cup orange juice
- ½ cup honey
- ¼ cup freshly squeezed lemon juice
- 2 tablespoons soy sauce
- ½ teaspoon ground ginger

Combine all ingredients in saucepan; cook over medium heat until well-blended. Baste sauce on poultry or pork during grilling. Yield: 2 cups.

Sweet 'n Sour Sauce

- 1 (10½-ounce) can beef broth
- 1 tablespoon cornstarch
- ¾ cup drained crushed pineapple
- ¼ cup chopped onion
- ¼ cup vinegar
- 2 tablespoons sugar
- 1 tablespoon soy sauce
- 1 clove garlic, minced
- ½ teaspoon salt

Combine beef broth and cornstarch in saucepan; cook until sauce thickens, stirring constantly. Add remaining ingredients; simmer 10 minutes, stirring occasionally. Baste steaks and hamburgers with sauce. Yield: 2½ cups.

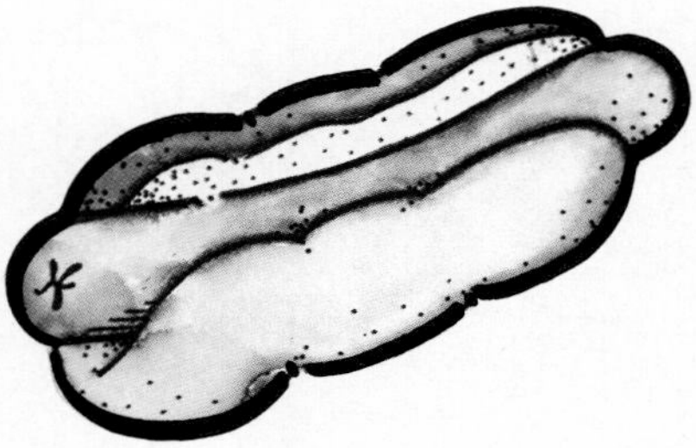

Teriyaki Steak Marinade

- ½ cup soy sauce
- ½ cup brandy
- 1 (1-inch) piece gingerroot, minced
- ¼ cup catsup
- 1 tablespoon mustard
- 1 teaspoon Worcestershire sauce
- ¼ cup brown sugar

Combine all ingredients. Marinate steaks several hours in refrigerator. Yield: 1½ cups.

Beef Wine Marinade

- ¼ cup salad oil
- ¼ cup dry vermouth
- ¼ cup soy sauce
- 1 teaspoon prepared mustard
- ½ teaspoon dry mustard
- 1 clove garlic, minced
- ¼ teaspoon pepper
- ½ teaspoon salt
- 2 teaspoons Worcestershire sauce

Place all ingredients in blender and blend for 2 minutes. Marinate meat in refrigerator for several hours, turning meat frequently. Yield: about 1 cup.

Kabobs Marinade

- 1 tablespoon freshly squeezed lemon juice
- 3 tablespoons salad oil
- 1 clove garlic, crushed
- ¼ teaspoon salt
- 1 teaspoon water
- Dash pepper
- Dash monosodium glutamate

Combine all ingredients. Marinate kabobs in this mixture for several hours in refrigerator. Cook kabobs as desired. Yield: about ¼ cup.

Marinade for Flank Steak

- ½ cup soy sauce
- ¼ to ½ cup freshly squeezed lemon juice (depending on tartness desired)
- ½ teaspoon garlic powder
- ½ teaspoon black pepper
- 1- to 1½-pound flank steak

Combine soy sauce, lemon juice, garlic powder, and pepper in an enameled or glass dish for marinade. Place flank steak in dish, cover, and marinate in refrigerator overnight. The next day: drain well, place steak on grill over low heat, and cook for about 20 minutes, turning once and basting often with marinade. Yield: 4 servings.

Wine Marinade for Lamb

- ½ cup salad oil
- ⅓ cup freshly squeezed lemon juice
- 1 tablespoon tarragon vinegar
- 1 clove garlic, minced
- ½ teaspoon mint
- ¼ teaspoon thyme
- ½ cup dry white wine
- ¼ cup honey

Combine all ingredients; stir until well-blended. Marinate lamb overnight in refrigerator. Yield: about 1½ cups.

Marinade for Fish

- ½ cup freshly squeezed lemon juice
- 3 tablespoons salad oil
- 2 tablespoons brown sugar
- 4 teaspoons soy sauce
- ¼ teaspoon ground ginger
- Pinch black pepper
- 1 pound fish fillets

Combine lemon juice, salad oil, brown sugar, soy sauce, ginger, and pepper in a jar. Shake well and pour over fish which has been placed in a flat dish. Leave in marinade for at least 1 hour. Remove from marinade, drain and cook on grill until done, basting often with marinade. Yield: 3 to 4 servings.

Marinade for Beef Kabobs

½ cup wine vinegar
1 cup salad oil
½ cup grated onion
1 clove garlic, crushed
1 tablespoon Worcestershire sauce
3 pounds lean beef, cut into 1½-inch cubes

Combine vinegar, oil, onion, garlic, and Worcestershire sauce in a large glass bowl. Mix well; add beef cubes and stir. Let stand overnight, turning the meat occasionally. Drain, put meat on skewers and cook over medium heat until meat is desired doneness, basting occasionally with marinade. Yield: about 8 servings.

Mexicali Marinade

¼ cup olive oil
2 cloves garlic, crushed
¼ cup vinegar
¼ cup apple juice
1 teaspoon chili powder
1 teaspoon sugar
1 teaspoon salt
¼ teaspoon pepper

Heat olive oil thoroughly; sauté garlic in olive oil. Add remaining ingredients and cook until heated through. Use to marinate beef, pork, lamb, or veal before grilling; also use to baste during cooking. Yield: ¾ cup.

Oil and Vinegar Marinade

½ cup salad oil
⅓ cup wine vinegar
1 clove garlic, minced
½ teaspoon salt
¼ teaspoon pepper

Combine all ingredients in a jar; cover. Shake well and chill. Shake well before pouring over meat for marinating. Yield: ¾ cup.

Soy-Sesame Marinade

¼ cup chopped onion
¼ cup soy sauce
1 tablespoon light brown sugar
1 tablespoon sesame seed
1 tablespoon salad oil
1 teaspoon salt
1 teaspoon freshly squeezed lemon juice
¼ teaspoon pepper
¼ teaspoon ground ginger

Combine all ingredients; stir until well-blended. Use to marinate beef or lamb before grilling. Yield: ½ cup.

Instant Kabobs

To make instant kabobs, skewer canned cocktail franks with cheese slices, olives, and tiny tomatoes.

Beverages and Mixed Drinks

For successful outdoor entertaining, the smart Southern hostess will prepare cool, refreshing drinks to complement the menu she plans to serve.

Included in the following pages are recipes for mixed drinks as well as non-alcoholic beverages. You can experiment with Orange Spritzers or Apple Blossom Punch, or you can stick to the old tried and true Lemonade or Mint Julep.

The beverage can "sink or swim" an outdoor meal, so make sure you read and follow our recipes carefully. When the guests first arrive, it is important that they be made to feel relaxed and comfortable with a drink of their preference. So it is a good idea to have a variety of beverages to choose from.

Remember that a good drink precedes a good meal, so make sure yours are good and cold (stock up on ice) on those warm Southern nights when you entertain outside.

Pineapple-Lime Punch

- 3 quarts unsweetened pineapple juice
- Juice of 8 lemons
- Juice of 8 oranges
- Juice of 3 limes
- 2 cups sugar
- 4 quarts ginger ale
- 2 quarts plain soda water
- Green food coloring (optional)

Combine fruit juices and sugar. Chill thoroughly. Just before serving, add ginger ale and soda water. Tint a delicate green, if you wish. Yield: 35 cups.

Quick Fruit Punch

- 1 (46-ounce) can sweetened orange juice
- 1 (46-ounce) can sweetened pineapple juice
- 4 cups ginger ale

Chill thoroughly. Mix well. Add ginger ale last. Yield: 30 servings.

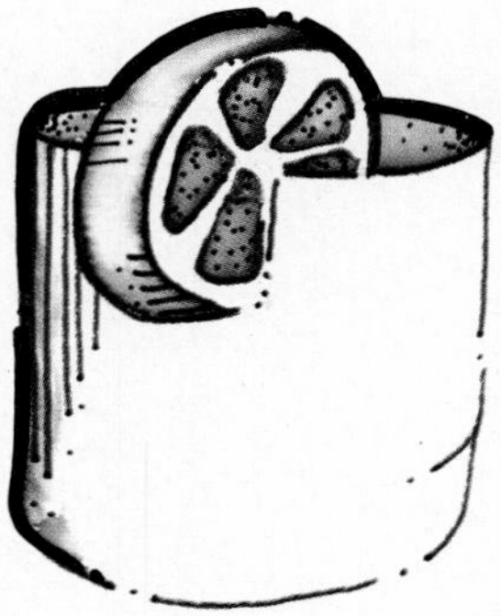

Apple Blossom Punch

- 3 quarts apple juice
- 3 quarts ginger ale
- 3 (12-ounce) cans frozen orange juice concentrate
- Fresh orange slices

Combine fruit juices and ginger ale. Pour over block of ice. Float orange slices on top of punch. Yield: 50 servings.

Fruit Juice Punch

- 3 cups sugar
- 3 quarts water
- 1 cup strong tea
- Juice of 12 lemons
- Juice of 12 oranges
- 4 cups grape juice
- 1 (8-ounce) can crushed pineapple
- 8 cups ginger ale

Boil sugar and water 8 minutes. Chill; add tea, juices, and pineapple. Set in refrigerator to mellow. Just before serving, add the ginger ale. Yield: 50 servings.

Golden Punch No. 1

- **2 cups freshly squeezed lemon juice**
- **6 cups orange juice**
- **8 cups apple juice**
- **4 cups sugar syrup, or sweeten to taste**
- **1 quart orange sherbet (optional)**

Combine all ingredients and chill. Add 1 quart orange sherbet just before serving, if desired. Yield: about 30 servings.

Golden Punch No. 2

- **2 large cans pineapple juice**
- **1 large can sweetened orange juice**
- **1 large can unsweetened orange juice**
- **1 can fresh frozen lemon juice**
- **1 quart water**
- **3 bananas, sliced**
- **2 large bottles ginger ale**
- **1 quart lime or pineapple sherbet**

Mix juices and water and chill. When ready to serve, add bananas, ginger ale, and sherbet. Yield: 40 servings.

Golden Punch No. 3

- **2 (6-ounce) cans frozen orange juice concentrate**
- **½ cup lemon juice**
- **1 cup canned pineapple juice**
- **¼ cup maraschino cherry juice**
- **2 quarts ginger ale**

Combine orange juice concentrate, lemon juice, pineapple juice, and cherry juice; mix well. Pour over ice in punch bowl. Add cold ginger ale. Garnish with berries and pineapple spears if desired. Yield: 25 punch-cup servings.

Cherry Punch

- **2 (3-ounce) packages cherry-flavored gelatin**
- **4 cups boiling water**
- **1 cup sugar**
- **1 quart chilled pineapple juice**
- **1 quart orange juice**
- **1 quart ginger ale**

Dissolve gelatin in boiling water; add sugar and stir until dissolved. Cool to room temperature. (This is very important. Do not chill in refrigerator.) Add fruit juices. Just before serving, add ginger ale. Yield: 25 to 30 servings.

Party Punch

- **1 quart pineapple juice, chilled**
- **1 quart orange juice, chilled**
- **1 quart apple juice, chilled**
- **2 quarts ginger ale, chilled**
- **2 quarts pineapple sherbet**

Pour chilled juices and ginger ale into punch bowl. Top with scoops of sherbet. Yield: 15 servings.

Holiday Punch

Juice of 2 limes
Juice of 1 lemon
3 (6-ounce) cans frozen orange juice
1 (6-ounce) can frozen lemon juice
1 (6-ounce) can frozen lime juice
1 (No. 2) can pineapple juice
½ teaspoon salt
1½ quarts water
1 quart chilled ginger ale
1 pint vodka
Red food coloring, if desired

Several hours ahead mix together the fruit juices, salt, and water, and place in covered container in refrigerator to chill.

At serving time, combine above mixture with ginger ale and vodka. Stir in food coloring, if desired. Serve over a block of ice in punch bowl. Yield: 25 generous servings.

Holiday Fruit Punch

2 quarts boiling water
¼ cup loose tea
2 cups sugar
2 cups lemon juice
4 cups orange juice
1½ quarts cranberry juice
1 quart water
1 quart ginger ale
1 lemon, sliced
2 limes, sliced
Maraschino cherries

Bring 2 quarts of water to a full rolling boil. Immediately pour over the tea. Brew 5 minutes. Strain. Set aside to cool at room temperature. Combine with sugar, fruit juices, and 1 quart water. Chill. Just before serving, pour over large piece of ice or ice cubes; then add ginger ale. Garnish with lemon and lime slices and cherries. Yield: 25 servings.

Grape Punch

2 cups grape juice
1½ cups orange juice
¾ cup sugar
1 cup water
Ice cubes
3 (7-ounce) bottles ginger ale
1 lemon, sliced

Pour fruit juices into 2-quart pitcher. Add sugar and stir until dissolved. Add water and ice cubes. Let stand for a few minutes in refrigerator. Pour equal amounts into 16 tall glasses in which there are a couple of ice cubes. Then fill to top with ginger ale and garnish with lemon slices.

Strawberry Punch

1 (10-ounce) package frozen strawberries
1 (6-ounce) can frozen orange juice concentrate
1 (6-ounce) can frozen lemonade concentrate
3 cups cold water
1 (12-ounce) bottle ginger ale
Ice cubes
1 cup fresh strawberries
3 orange slices

Thaw strawberries. Combine orange juice, lemonade, and water; chill. Add thawed strawberries and ginger ale when ready to serve. Pour over ice cubes in punch bowl. Garnish with whole fresh strawberries and orange slices. Yield: 2 quarts.

Golden Gate Punch

- 2½ cups sugar
- 1 cup water
- 2 (No. 2) cans (4½ cups) pineapple juice
- 2 cups strained lime juice
- 1 quart strained orange juice
- 1¼ cups strained lemon juice
- 2 quarts chilled ginger ale
- Colored ice cubes

Make syrup by combining sugar and water. Heat to boiling. Cool. Combine fruit juices. Add cooled sugar syrup. Chill. Just before serving, add ginger ale and colored ice cubes. To make colored cubes, blend vegetable food coloring with water before freezing. Yield: 5 quarts.

Florida Citrus Punch

- 2 (6-ounce) cans frozen orange juice concentrate
- 1 (6-ounce) can frozen grapefruit juice concentrate
- 1 (6-ounce) can frozen limeade concentrate
- 1 quart ginger ale
- Orange and lime sherbet

Reconstitute the orange and grapefruit concentrates according to directions on the cans. Combine with undiluted limeade and mix well. Add the ginger ale just before serving. Scoops of orange and lime sherbet added just before serving give the finishing touches. Yield: 25 servings.

Citrus Punch No. 1

- 1½ cups sugar
- 3 cups water
- 1 tablespoon instant tea
- 1½ cups lime juice
- 2 (46-ounce) cans blended grapefruit and orange juice
- Ice cubes
- 4 cups ginger ale

Combine sugar and water in saucepan; place over low heat and stir until sugar is dissolved. Add to instant tea. Add juices; chill. Pour into punch bowl; add ice cubes; stir until ice is partially melted. Just before serving, add ginger ale. Garnish with lime slices and maraschino cherries. Yield: 44 (½-cup) servings.

Citrus Punch No. 2

- ¼ teaspoon ground nutmeg
- ½ teaspoon cinnamon
- ½ teaspoon allspice
- 2 cups cider
- ¼ cup sugar
- 6 cups orange juice
- Orange slices
- Cloves

Heat spices and cider to boiling point. Remove from heat. Stir in sugar if desired. Cool. Add orange juice. Serve chilled with ice cubes and use clove-studded orange slices as decoration. Yield: 2 quarts (16 one-half cup servings).

Cranberry Punch No. 1

4 cups cranberry juice cocktail
1½ cups sugar
4 cups pineapple-grapefruit juice
2 quarts ginger ale

Slowly add cranberry juice to sugar; stir until sugar dissolves. Add pineapple-grapefruit juice; chill. Pour into punch bowl; add the chilled ginger ale. Yield: about 32 punch-cup servings.

Cranberry Punch No. 2

6 pints cranberry juice cocktail
1½ quarts strained orange juice
1½ cups water
2½ cups strained lemon juice
3 cups pineapple juice
3 cups sugar

Combine ingredients and blend well. Chill in refrigerator. Pour into a punch bowl with an ice ring and lemon slices. Yield: about 50 servings.

Ruby Red Frost

1 pint bottle cranberry juice cocktail
1½ cups fresh lemon juice
1 cup sugar
2 (28-ounce) bottles chilled ginger ale
1 pint raspberry sherbet
Lemon slices

Combine cranberry juice cocktail, fresh lemon juice, and sugar, blending well. Chill. To serve, pour over ice in punch bowl. Add chilled ginger ale and sherbet. Garnish with lemon slices. Serve at once. Yield: 24 cups.

Cranberry Cooler

½ cup fresh lemon juice
1 cup fresh orange juice
1 pint bottle cranberry juice cocktail
1¼ cups sugar
4 cups ice water or chilled sparkling water
Lemon slices

Combine lemon juice, orange juice, cranberry juice, and sugar; stir until sugar is dissolved. Add ice water or chilled sparkling water. Pour in ice-filled pitcher or punch bowl; garnish with lemon slices. Yield: 16 (4-ounce) servings.

Pineapple-Cranberry Punch

2 pints cranberry juice
2 cups orange juice
¼ cup lemon juice
1 quart pineapple sherbet
1 quart sparkling water or ginger ale

Combine cranberry juice, orange juice, and lemon juice; beat in pineapple sherbet; then chill. Just before serving, slowly pour in sparkling water. Pour over cracked ice and serve immediately. Yield: 14 to 16 servings.

Selecting Fresh Pineapples

When selecting pineapples, pluck a leaf from the pineapple's crown. If the leaf pulls out easily, the fruit is ripe and and ready to eat.

Patio Punch

1 cup strong tea
2 (6-ounce) cans frozen orange juice concentrate, thawed, undiluted
1 (6-ounce) can frozen grapefruit juice concentrate, thawed, undiluted
1 (12-ounce) can apricot nectar
½ cup sugar
Ice cubes
1 quart carbonated water or ginger ale
Strawberries
Mint sprigs

Prepare tea and chill, or use instant tea. Combine tea, undiluted orange concentrate, undiluted grapefruit concentrate, apricot nectar, and sugar in punch bowl or pitcher. Stir until sugar is dissolved. Add ice. Just before serving, add carbonated water or ginger ale. Garnish with strawberries and mint sprigs.

Punchmelon

1 large watermelon
2 cups orange juice
2 cups lemon juice
1 (6-ounce) bottle grenadine syrup
2 quarts bottled lemon-lime beverage, chilled
1 orange, sliced
1 lemon, sliced

With melon standing on end, cut a thin slice off side so it will sit level. Remove top third of melon. Using a coffee cup as a guide, trace scallops around top outside edge. With a sharp knife, carve scalloped edge, following tracing; scoop out fruit, leaving just a trace of red showing in bowl of melon; use scraped-out melon as desired. Chill melon bowl and serve cold.

Combine orange juice, lemon juice, and grenadine; chill. When ready to serve, place a small block of ice, or ice cubes, in melon bowl. Pour juices over ice; pour lemon-lime beverage down side of melon bowl into juice mixture. Float orange and lime slices on top of punch. Yield: 3½ quarts.

Pineapple Punch

Measure into each glass:
2 tablespoons pineapple juice
1 tablespoon lemon juice
2 to 3 tablespoons sugar
¾ cup cooled, prepared tea
Ice cubes

Stir well. Garnish with thin slices of lemon and sprig of mint.

Fruit Punch No. 1

1 cup water
2 cups sugar
1 cup strong, hot tea
2 cups fruit syrup
1 cup freshly squeezed lemon juice
2 cups pineapple juice
Ice water
1 cup maraschino cherries
4 cups ginger ale

Boil water and sugar for 5 minutes; add tea, fruit syrup, and juices. Let stand for 30 minutes; add ice water to make 1½ gallons of liquid. Add cherries and ginger ale. Serve in punch bowl with large piece of ice. Yield: 50 servings.

Fruit Punch No. 2

2 (6-ounce) cans frozen orange juice
1 (6-ounce) can frozen lemonade
1 cup pineapple juice
¼ cup cherry juice (optional)
2 quarts pale dry ginger ale

Mix fruit juices; cover and let stand 12 hours or more in refrigerator. Add cold ginger ale to juices just before serving. Serve over crushed ice or freeze half the ginger ale in refrigerator trays. Yield: 24 servings.

Fruit Punch No. 3

1 (6-ounce) can frozen orange juice concentrate
2 (6-ounce) cans frozen limeade concentrate
1 (6-ounce) can frozen lemonade concentrate
1 (1-pound 14-ounce) can pineapple juice
1 pint cranberry juice cocktail
4 cups cold water
2 quarts ginger ale, chilled
1 pint club soda, chilled
Fruit Ice Ring
Fruits and mint for garnish

Empty frozen concentrates, pineapple and cranberry juices, and water into a large container. Let stand until frozen juice is thawed; stir well. Pour mixture into punch bowl; add ice cubes. Just before serving, gently pour in ginger ale and club soda. Garnish with Fruit Ice Ring and fruits and mint leaves. Yield: 25 to 30 servings.

Fruit Ice Ring

Use any combination of lime, lemon, or orange slices. Arrange in a pattern in the bottom of an 8-inch ring mold. Add water to cover fruit. Freeze. To unmold, loosen ring by dipping bottom of mold in warm water. Float on top of punch.

Ginger Ale-Sherbet Punch

6 quarts ginger ale
7 pints sherbet (mint or orange)
2 or 3 pints vanilla ice cream (optional)

Combine 1 quart ginger ale and 1 pint sherbet, beating well before adding any more. Continue adding in these proportions as needed.

For extra "body" to the punch, add 2 or 3 pints of vanilla ice cream ever so often. Yield: 50 (½-cup) servings.

Hospitality Tea Punch

- 15 tea bags or 5 tablespoons loose tea
- 2 quarts boiling water
- 2 cups lemon juice
- 1 quart orange juice
- 1½ quarts grape juice
- 2 cups sugar
- 2 quarts cold water
- 1 quart ginger ale
- Ice cubes

Pour boiling water over tea. Steep 3 to 5 minutes and strain or remove tea bags. Cool tea. Stir in remaining ingredients except ginger ale. Add ginger ale and ice cubes just before serving. Yield: 2 gallons.

Minted Pineapple Tea

- 1 quart boiling water
- 15 tea bags or ⅓ cup loose tea
- 4 tablespoons chopped fresh mint leaves
- 1 quart cold water
- 1 cup lemon juice
- ⅔ cup sugar
- ¾ cup (6-ounce can) pineapple juice
- Ice cubes
- Lemon wedges

Pour 1 quart boiling water over tea and mint leaves. Cover and let stand for 5 minutes.

Strain the tea into a pitcher holding 1 quart cold water. Add lemon juice, sugar, and pineapple juice. Stir to dissolve sugar, and chill.

To serve, pour the minted tea over ice cubes. Garnish with lemon wedges. Yield: about 2½ quarts.

Golden Tea Punch

- 3 cups boiling water
- 10 tea bags or 10 teaspoons tea leaves
- 24 whole cloves
- 1 (3-inch) stick cinnamon, crumbled
- 2¼ cups fresh lemon juice
- 1¼ cups fresh orange juice
- 3 cups sugar
- 4 quarts cold water
- Orange and lemon slices

Pour boiling water over tea bags, whole cloves, and crumbled stick cinnamon. Cover; steep 5 minutes. Strain and cool. Add lemon juice, orange juice, and sugar, stirring until sugar is dissolved. Add cold water. Pour into ice-filled punch bowl. Garnish with orange and lemon slices. Yield: 50 punch-cup servings.

Spiced Lemonade

- ¾ cup sugar
- ¾ cup water
- 12 whole cloves
- 1 (3-inch) stick cinnamon
- 6 lemons
- 4 cups water
- Decorated ice cubes

Boil sugar and ¾ cup water about 5 minutes. Combine 1 cup of the syrup with spices and cook 5 minutes. Strain. Add juice of lemons and quart of water. Chill. Pour over ice cubes when ready to serve. Lemon-decorated ice cubes or cubes with whole cloves frozen in them will add appeal to this summertime favorite. Yield: 6 servings.

Lemonade

2½ to 3 cups sugar
4¾ cups lemon juice
20 cups water, divided
Ice
Lemon slices
Sprigs of mint

Combine sugar and juice with 4 cups water. Boil for 5 minutes or until sugar is completely dissolved. Remove from heat. Add remaining water and cool. Just before serving, add ice. Garnish with lemon slices and mint. Yield: 25 servings.

Old-Fashioned Lemonade

4 lemons
2 cups sugar
½ cup water
Maraschino cherries
Lemon slices

Cut lemons in thin slices, place in a bowl, and cover with sugar. Mash thoroughly until all juice is extracted. Add water. Let stand 1 hour. Strain. Allow 1 or 2 tablespoons of the strained lemon juice for each serving. Pour into glass filled with shaved ice and add water. Garnish with maraschino cherry and slice of lemon. Yield: 3 to 4 servings.

Citronade

(French Lemonade)

1 lemon
¾ cup sugar
1 cup water
3½ cups water
Maraschino cherries
Lemon slices

Wash lemon; cut into small pieces and remove seeds. Place in electric blender, with sugar and 1 cup water. Blend until smooth. Add blended mixture to 3½ cups water, mixing well. Pour into ice-filled 8- to 10-ounce glasses; garnish with the cherries and lemon slices. Yield: 5 to 6 servings.

Seafoam Punch

½ cup sugar
1 quart cold water
1 (½-ounce) envelope unsweetened lemon-lime soft drink powder
1 pint vanilla ice cream
2 (7-ounce) bottles lemon-lime carbonated beverage, chilled

Place sugar and water in large punch bowl. Add soft drink powder and stir until powder dissolves. Add vanilla ice cream, one spoonful at a time. Pour in the carbonated beverage, resting the bottle on rim of bowl. Serve immediately. Yield: about 16 servings.

Measuring Hints

Before measuring honey, syrup, or molasses, grease the spoon or measuring cup lightly; measuring and pouring will be easier and more accurate.

Grape Juice-Lime Cooler

¼ cup chilled grape juice
1 tablespoon sugar or corn syrup
2 tablespoons chilled milk
Carbonated water

In each glass, blend grape juice and sugar or corn syrup. Slowly stir in chilled milk. Add carbonated water to fill glasses within 1½ inches of top. Top with a scoop of frozen lime sherbet, and serve at once. Yield: 1 (8-ounce) glass.

Blackberry Shrub

4 cups blackberry juice
Sugar syrup
1 cup grape juice
Juice of 2 lemons

Strain juice from canned blackberries, pressing through as much pulp as possible, and measure. If you use fresh berries, prepare juice by cooking berries with just enough water to keep them from burning, and strain. Sweeten to taste with sugar syrup; add grape juice, lemon juice, and chill. Fill glasses one-third full and add water or crushed ice. Yield: 1½ quarts.

Note: Fresh raspberries or loganberries, as well as canned berries, may be used.

Mock Pink Champagne

½ cup sugar
1½ cups water
2 cups cranberry juice
1 cup pineapple juice
½ cup orange juice
2 (7-ounce) bottles lemon-lime carbonated beverage

Boil sugar and water until sugar dissolves; cool. Stir in cranberry, pineapple, and orange juices. Chill. Just before serving, add carbonated beverage. Yield: 14 servings.

Spider Cider

2 quarts apple cider
12 whole cloves
4 sticks cinnamon
Rind of 4 lemons
2 lemons, peeled and thinly sliced
¼ teaspoon ground nutmeg

Combine cider, cloves, cinnamon sticks, thinly peeled rind of 4 lemons, 2 lemons peeled and thinly sliced, and the nutmeg. Cover and heat to boiling. Reduce heat and simmer for about 15 minutes. Allow to cool; then strain. Discard spices. Chill overnight in refrgierator to allow flavors to blend. Heat when ready to serve. Yield: 8 to 10 servings.

Special Mint Punch

1 cup powdered sugar
4 lemons
24 sprigs of mint, chopped fine
1 cup sugar
12 stalks mint
8 cups ginger ale
4 cups water
4 cups shaved ice

Mix powdered sugar, lemon juice, and mint sprigs and set aside for 2 hours. Combine granulated sugar, mint stalks, water, and cut up rind of the 4 lemons. Boil together about 5 minutes; allow to cool. Stir the two mixtures together and strain. To 1 quart of this stock add, just before serving, 2 quarts of ginger ale, 1 quart shaved ice. Stock may be made several days ahead of use and stored in refrigerator. Yield: 1 gallon punch.

Iced Tea-Ade

8 cups boiling water
12 teaspoons tea leaves
24 mint leaves, crushed
1 teaspoon grated lemon rind
1 cup sugar
2 cups water
½ teaspoon salt
⅜ cup freshly squeezed lemon juice

Pour boiling water over tea leaves and add crushed mint leaves. Steep 3 to 5 minutes and strain the tea and chill. Prepare lemon ice by combining lemon rind, sugar, water, salt, and lemon juice. Place over heat and stir until the sugar is dissolved. Then boil for 5 minutes. Place in refrigerator tray and freeze. When ready to serve, fill each iced tea glass one-fourth full with the lemon ice or lemon sherbet. Add the tea. Serve with sugar and garnish with mint. Yield: 8 servings.

Ginger Orange Ice

1½ cups cold water
1½ cups sugar
¼ teaspoon ground ginger
⅛ teaspoon ground cinnamon
1 cup orange juice
¼ cup freshly squeezed lemon juice
¼ cup finely cut crystallized ginger
½ cup top milk
1 egg white

Combine water, sugar, ground ginger, and cinnamon in a small saucepan. Stir over low heat until sugar is dissolved. Bring to a boil for 5 minutes. Let cool. Add fruit juices and crystallized ginger. Pour into freezing tray of refrigerator and freeze to mushlike consistency. Remove to a bowl. Add top milk and egg white beaten stiff. Beat well. Return to refrigerator tray and freeze, stirring every 30 minutes until mixture is set. Serve in chilled sherbet glasses. Yield: 6 to 8 servings.

Orange Frosted

1 (6-ounce) can frozen concentrated orange juice
¼ cup sugar syrup
Shaved ice
About ⅓ cup water

Put 3 tablespoons undiluted concentrate and 1 tablespoon sugar syrup into each 12-ounce glass; mix well. Fill two-thirds full with ice. Fill with water; stir vigorously. Garnish with mint. Yield: 4 servings.

Sugar Syrup

1 cup sugar
1 cup water

Combine sugar and water in saucepan over low heat; stir until sugar is dissolved. Yield: about 1¼ cups.

When Using Oranges

Many recipes call for both orange juice and rind. Always remember to wash and grate the orange before juicing.

Orange Spritzers

2 (6-ounce) cans frozen pineapple juice concentrate
2 (6-ounce) cans frozen orange juice concentrate
3 cups water
½ teaspoon angostura bitters
2 (10-ounce) bottles sparkling water
Gin or vodka (optional)

Empty concentrates into large pitcher. Add water and bitters; stir well. When ready to serve, add sparkling water and pour over ice in old-fashioned glasses. (If alcoholic beverages are desired, add gin or vodka — a small jigger to each glass.) Yield: about 11 (6-ounce) servings.

Bloody Mary No. 1

1 jigger vodka
2 jiggers tomato juice
⅓ jigger lemon juice
Dash Worcestershire sauce
Salt and pepper to taste
Dash Tabasco sauce (optional)

Combine ingredients in shaker with ½ cup cracked ice. Shake until chilled, and strain into a 6-ounce cocktail glass.

Bloody Mary No. 2

2 jiggers tomato juice
2 jiggers vodka
Juice of ½ lemon
Dash Worcestershire sauce
Dash celery salt
Pepper to taste

Combine all ingredients and shake in a cocktail shaker with ½ cup cracked ice. Strain into a 6-ounce cocktail glass.

Note: You may wish to add clam juice to taste or garnish with a thin lemon slice.

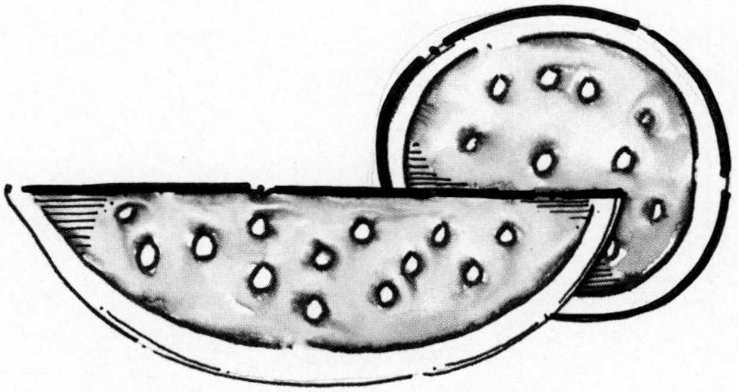

Diamond Head Cocktail

1 ounce vodka or gin
1 ounce rum
1 ounce pineapple juice
½ ounce lime juice
Dash fine sugar

Combine ingredients and shake in a cocktail shaker containing ½ cup ice. Serve in tall cocktail glass with a straw.

Screwdriver

1 jigger vodka
Orange juice

Put ice cubes into an 8-ounce glass. Add vodka; fill with orange juice and stir.

Harvey Wallbanger

¾ cup orange juice
1 ounce vodka
½ ounce Galliano

Stir orange juice and vodka in old-fashioned glass with ice. Splash in Galliano.

Gin Rickey

Juice and rind of ½ lime
1 jigger gin
Sparkling water

Squeeze lime over ice cubes in 8-ounce glass. Add gin, lime rind; fill glass with sparkling water. Stir.

Gin 'n Tonic

Juice and rind of ¼ lime
1 jigger gin
Quinine water (tonic)

Squeeze lime over ice cubes in 8-ounce glass. Add rind, gin; fill with tonic. Stir.

Tom Collins

1 teaspoon sugar
½ jigger lemon juice
1 jigger gin
Sparkling water

Dissolve sugar in lemon juice in a 10-ounce glass, and add ice cubes. Pour in gin. Fill with cold sparkling water, and stir.

Margarita

1 jigger white tequila
½ ounce Triple Sec
1 ounce lime or lemon juice
Salt

Moisten cocktail glass rim with fruit rind; spin rim in salt. Shake ingredients with ½ cup cracked ice. Strain into glass. Drink is sipped over the salted edge.

Sangría No. 1

(Wine Punch)

1 unpeeled orange, seeded and sliced
1 unpeeled lemon, seeded and sliced
Handful strawberries
Handful raspberries (optional)
1 peach, peeled and sliced
2 teaspoons sugar
1 ounce orange or other fruit-flavored liqueur
1 ounce brandy
1 (27-ounce) bottle full-bodied dry red wine

Put all fruit into a large glass pitcher. Stir sugar into the liqueur and add to pitcher along with brandy. Let stand at room temperature for several hours. At serving time, add wine and generous amount of ice. Stir the Sangría with a wooden spoon until it is ice-cold and serve in chilled goblets. Yield: about ¾ quart.

Sangría No. 2

Juice of 1 orange
Juice of 1 lemon
2 tablespoons powdered sugar
4 ounces Cointreau
4 ounces brandy
1 quart red wine
8 to 10 ounces club soda
1 unpeeled orange, thinly sliced
1 unpeeled lemon, thinly sliced

Put orange juice, lemon juice, and powdered sugar into a large glass pitcher. Add Cointreau and brandy, then about 8 ice cubes. Stir well; add red wine and club soda. Stir until ice-cold; pour into chilled goblets, and garnish with thin slices of lemon and orange. Yield: 8 servings.

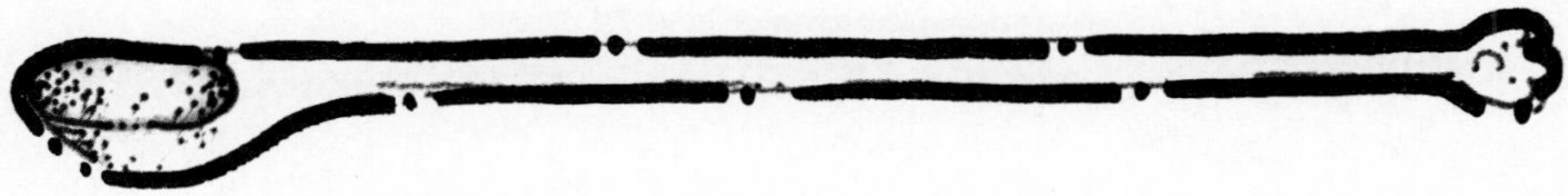

Orange-Champagne Cocktail

1 bottle (4/5 quart) champagne, chilled
4 cups fresh orange juice, chilled

Just before serving, combine chilled ingredients. Serve in champagne glasses. Yield: 12 (5-ounce) servings.

Scarlett O'Hara

1 jigger Southern Comfort
1 jigger cranberry juice cocktail
Juice of ½ fresh lime

Combine ingredients in shaker. Shake with ½ cup cracked ice. Strain into cocktail glass.

Bee-Bites

Juice of ½ lemon
¾ jigger grapefruit juice
¾ jigger orange juice
½ jigger bourbon
Grenadine or sugar

Put all ingredients into shaker with ½ cup crushed ice, adding grenadine or sugar to taste. Shake well and strain into small cocktail glasses. Yield: 2 servings.

Mint Julep

5 sprigs fresh mint
1 teaspoon sugar
Dash water
2 ounces bourbon

Crush 4 sprigs of mint and sugar in water in a tall, chilled glass. Pack glass with cracked ice. Pour in bourbon, and stir until glass is frosted. Insert straw and remaining sprig of mint.

Party Punch

Bottle (4/5 quart) bourbon
2 quarts champagne
4 ounces Jamaica rum
4 ounces freshly squeezed lemon juice
8 ounces pineapple juice
8 ounces grapefruit juice
Orange slices

Pre-chill ingredients; mix in punch bowl, adding champagne last. Add ice; garnish with orange slices. Yield: 25 (punch-cup) servings.

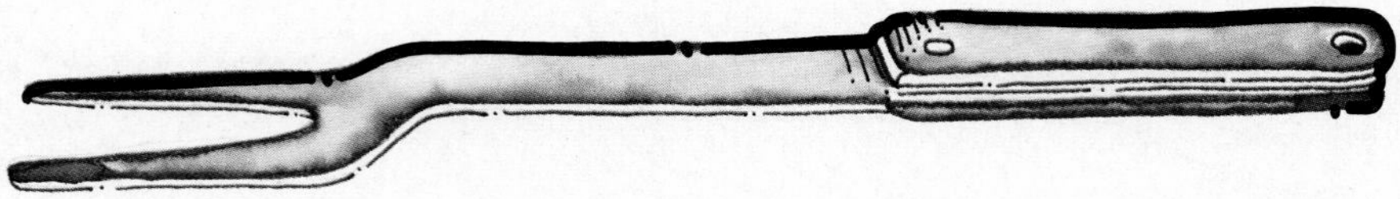

Daiquiri

1 scant teaspoon sugar or 2 scant teaspoons grenadine
Juice of ½ lime
1½ ounces light rum

Dissolve sugar or grenadine in lime juice. Add rum and ½ cup cracked ice. Shake in cocktail shaker or put into electric blender. Strain and serve in 3½-ounce cocktail glass. If electric blender is used, reduce amount of cracked ice.

Peach Daiquiri

2 fresh peach halves (or 2 canned peach halves; omit sugar)
1 teaspoon sugar
1 ounce lime juice
3 ounces light rum
1 cup cracked ice

Liquefy peach halves in blender. Blend in sugar, lime juice, rum, and cracked ice. Serve in chilled cocktail glasses. Yield: 2 servings.

Rum Swizzle

2½ ounces light rum
Juice of ½ lime
1 teaspoon sugar
4 dashes bitters

Mix ingredients in glass pitcher with plenty of finely cracked ice. Stir vigorously until mixture foams. Serve in double old-fashioned glass.

Rum Stinger

1 ounce white crème de menthe
2 ounces light rum

Pour crème de menthe and rum in a shaker. Shake well with cracked ice and strain into cocktail glass and serve.

Planters' Delight

2 ounces rum
1 ounce pineapple juice
1 ounce apricot juice
1 ounce orange juice
1 ounce lemon juice
Pineapple spear

Combine ingredients in a tall glass containing ice; serve with a pineapple spear and a straw. And in Hawaii, you might be served your drink with a small orchid floating on top!

Lelani Sour

2 ounces whiskey
1 ounce lime juice
1 teaspoon sugar
Orange slice

Mix ingredients in shaker with ½ cup cracked ice. Strain into highball glass containing shaved ice. Slit orange slice, slip it onto rim of glass, and serve with a straw.

Mai Tai — Wiki Wiki

2 ounces rum
Dash bitters
1 ounce lime juice
1 teaspoon sugar
Pineapple spear
Mint sprig

Mix first four ingredients in tall glass containing ice. Serve with pineapple spear, sprig of mint, and straw.

Red Velvet Punch

8 cups cranberry juice cocktail
1 (6-ounce) can frozen orange juice
1 (6-ounce) can frozen pineapple juice
1 (6-ounce) can frozen lemon juice
2 cups brandy
2 fifths white champagne

Combine juices and brandy; mix well and pour over a block of ice in punch bowl. Add champagne. Yield: about 30 servings.

Outdoor Entertaining

Outdoor entertaining is a natural for Southern living. It's uncontrived, relaxed, and a welcome détente from formal parties and seated dinners. You've the whole outdoors to entertain you whether you cook out in your backyard or pack a picnic and cycle to a local waterfall or tailgate it at a ballgame.

Those outdoor gatherings, large or small, give you that living-high feeling that even a slight thundershower leaves undampened.

One reason outdoor entertaining is so enjoyable is because it *is* easy. Shortcuts are the road to pleasure and the ingenious always find them. We've collected a few shortcuts and suggestions for you and hope they will spur your imagination to make your parties greater than all outdoors.

Issuing Invitations

Most outdoor entertaining is informal, even casual, and it is perfectly acceptable to issue your invitations by telephone. For larger parties, invitations written on folded informal notes are in order. All invitations should state the occasion, the time, the formality (dress implied), and location: poolside, patio, greenhouse, riverside. Written invitations should be received at least a week in advance of the event. If alternate plans are not possible in case of rain, note should be made that the party will be called off.

There is a real opportunity to be creative in sending out invitations to an outdoor party. You might supply guests with a doggy bag. Simply write the invitation on a brown paper bag, fold it in half, attach the bottom, and address the outside. Indicate in the invitation that your guests should bring the bag along for bones or a few extra ribs and brownies.

Or, make an invitation of a bib or napkin. Use a magic marker to write the party information on a large white bib: "Charlie's bib worn at Mary Brown's Barbecue on July 14 from 5:00 until the food was gone."

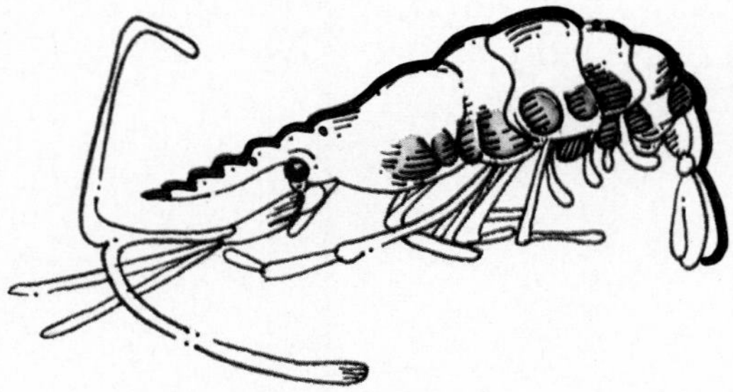

Decorating for an Outdoor Party

Nature is your backdrop and if you've mountains, beaches, flower gardens, or lakes surrounding you, your decorating needs are minimal. But you might place flowering pots or green things around the patio corners or on retaining walls, or hang baskets of flowers in the trees that spread their shade over your table, or decorate the table with an edible centerpiece.

Make the tables fun. Begin collecting unusual pottery and outdoor ware, tablecloths and napkins that set a theme to make the party a little different even if the menu is your favorite Oriental chicken.

A railroad party. Use bandana napkins, enameled tinware cups, pewter plates; make table runners of denim and light the tables and surrounding area with red railroad lanterns. Serve the bread in an upside-down railroad hat.

A garden picnic. When the dinner hour for houseguests varies, pack some hobo suppers. Let them wander into the garden and eat as they please. Wrap the sandwiches in bandanas or serve them on plastic bandana printed trays. Add a cold casserole or salad, wine, and fruit.

A poolside party. Make the pool the centerpiece. Float votive candles on piepan plates camouflaged with magnolias or gardenias. Put small tables around if the party is large enough to allow for intimate groups for a seated meal. If the evening is formal, put down some outdoor carpeting. Leave a portion of the walk uncovered for a dance floor. Set the bar up on the opposite side of the pool from the buffet table to keep the crowd spread out. The buffet table should be surrounded by plenty of space and a little removed from the crowd to facilitate last-minute food preparation and clearing.

We've a steak, come on over. The pleasures of a spontaneous party are multiple. You can relax. Everything doesn't have to be impeccably prepared. And the resulting casualness brings a joy of freedom from protocol's restrictions. The afternoon can linger into dusk and dark — then light the candles and spray away the mosquitoes.

If you've the equipment and a well-stocked larder, you can put together a spur-of-the-moment meal to a guest's delight. It is helpful to have: one tray to keep food hot and another to keep it cool; food covers to keep food fresh and clean, saving the hostess from last minute running in and out of the kitchen; an espresso coffee pot for a warming drink while guests linger and the evening cools.

Fabrics To Face the Elements

Upholstered cushions and chaise covers. Cushions made of heavy-duty, fabric-backed vinyl and stuffed with urethane foam will give the best outdoor wear and can be left out in the rain. Sudsy sponging will generally keep them clean. Don't use an abrasive cleanser or scouring pads.

Heavy-duty cotton cushions, most often found on rattan and redwood seats, do not resist mildew and sun-rot as vinyl does. All cushions should have a welted-seam construction which helps to keep seams from splitting. Buy fabric that has been treated with soil-repellent finish. Surface cleansing with soap and water is usually sufficient, especially if the fabric is soil-repellent. Prop cushions up and set them out to dry.

Webbed furniture. The greater the number of strips, the sturdier the webbing. Look for a close network of well-attached strips. Clean with a vegetable brush and soapy water; rinse with a garden hose.

Awnings and umbrellas. The fabrics available are numerous. Painted canvas is the least expensive and is most often painted with an acrylic-based paint which is water-repellent and fade-resistant.

Vinyl-coated canvas lasts longer and is easy to clean.

Plain cotton usually has the pattern woven into the fabric.

Woven acrylic is mildew-resistant, expensive, but equally durable.

Vinyl-coated glass is mildew-resistant, durable, and flame-resistant.

Clean all types with a sponge or soft brush. To mend, glue a small patch on the top side. A special paint may be ordered to mend pin holes on vinyl.

Outdoor carpeting. Check carpeting recommended for outdoor use. Other carpets may retain water and will gradually deteriorate. The best carpets are of polypropylene or acrylic fibers with polypropylene or treated rubber backings. Clean spills quickly; use garden hose for best results.

Serving with Ease

The nearer to the kitchen you can locate your outdoor party the easier the serving and clean-up will be. Naturally, you may be cooking your meat out-of-doors, but many vegetables, salads, and breads will be prepared inside and carried out along with the flatware and linens.

To aid serving from kitchen to out-of-doors use a roving cart, big carrying baskets, or a little red wagon (if you haven't steps).

Spray-paint apple baskets and other large lightweight containers. Line them with plastic bags and put them in convenient places for guests to dispose of their scraps or paper plates. Have a wagon or large basket nearby for stacking the scraped dishes and flatware and your work will almost be finished before you get the used utensils back to the kitchen.

Keep on hand: throwaway tablecloths in novelty prints, napkins and mats, plastic plates, coasters, candles, paper flowers, and other decorative items that perk up a patio in a moment's notice.

To keep napkins from blowing away before dinnertime, use napkin rings. They also add color and decor to the table. Weight the corners of the tablecloth with fishing leads to keep them from blowing up. Or invest in several clips that slip on the edge of the table to keep your tablecloth in place.

If you're serving corn-on-the-cob and spareribs, furnish kerchiefs for the guests. Paper napkins may fail to absorb all the excess barbecue sauce; so you might also furnish terry cloth fingertip towels. Gay prints and florals are a welcome addition to the table.

Place mats with pockets can be used to hold napkins in place and provide a slot for flatware. Cut off the top of a pair of bib jeans, hem it, and use it for an individual bib. The pockets hold flatware and napkins.

Place mats that roll up and tie with slots for flatware make a neat, easy-to-handle bundle for guests.

Plates with indentions for cups free a hand for self-serving and save a return to the drink table.

A cow bell or old school bell high on a pole signals "time to eat" to chattering guests and wandering children.

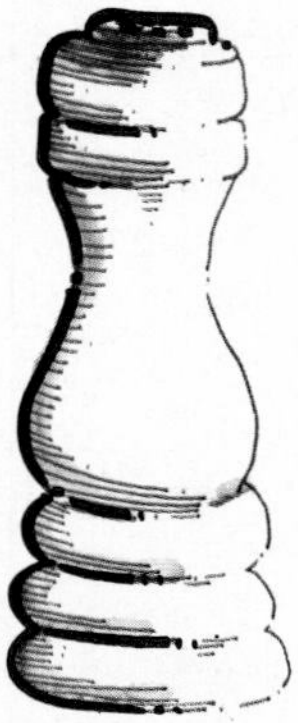

Handy Utensils and Gadgets for Outdoor Entertaining

With today's wide array of outdoor utensils, you can cook as primitively or luxuriously as you please. The most successful outdoor cook assembles all the necessary utensils on a roomy work surface near the fire before he begins his backyard performance. Half the fun of outdoor cooking disappears when you must make numerous trips to and from the kitchen for needed equipment.

Very few tools are needed if they're well-chosen, and built for long and efficient service; quality is usually well worth the cost. Some basic utensils for efficient handling of fire and food: asbestos gloves for arranging briquettes, sharp knives, cutting board, long-handled fork and heavy tongs for turning large pieces of meat, skewers, hinged-grills for ribs or frankfurters, paintbrush or small mop for basting, potholders, large salt and pepper shakers, and a sprinkler bottle for dousing flames. Heavy-duty aluminum foil can be used for everything from a grill windbreaker to making disposable pans. A meat thermometer is a wise investment for checking the doneness of large pieces of meat.

Serving can be simplified with the use of a tray or cart to transport everything from the kitchen to the backyard or patio. When using warming trays or other portable electric appliances outside, special precautions must be taken to use heavy-duty extension cords. Insulated ice chests and containers for hot and cold food are popular. Chemical refrigerants (small cans filled with special chemicals that defrost slowly) can be frozen and will keep food cold for several hours. Particularly if children are present, a first-aid kit and a large "serve yourself" cooler of lemonade or other beverage should be a must on your planning list.

To minimize cleanup problems, have large plastic-lined containers handy. At an informal gathering, most guests are happy to help with the cleanup.

With some preplanning and the necessary outdoor equipment, today's host and hostess should be able to cook and entertain and still have as much fun as their guests.

If the Party Is Away from Home

With the aid of modern picnic equipment, even the most elegant dinner can be served miles from home. Every year more families entertain with picnics at the beach, on a mountain top, or with a tailgate picnic spread at a stadium parking lot. Give some thought to the food preparation and site for your party away from home. If you're inviting guests, be sure that they're as enthusiastic as you are.

Picnic food may be as simple as a sandwich or as elaborate as a multi-course dinner. Special consideration must be given to the foods you're planning to take and to the facilities you have to keep them hot or cold. There are definite dangers in eating certain unrefrigerated foods, particularly dairy products, foods containing mayonnaise, or those high in protein. Hot foods should be kept at 140° or above and cold foods at 45° or below. Temperatures between 45° and 140° are unsafe for some foods, since disease-producing bacteria grow most rapidly at the middle of this temperature range. All perishable foods should be transported in an ice chest with plenty of ice. If dry ice is used, place it on top of the food since the chilling gas (carbon dioxide) is heavier than air. If you don't have an insulated cooler to keep a casserole hot, use a double wrap of foil and overwrap with several thicknesses of newspaper.

When planning your menu, select dishes that transport easily. Tape lids on containers, especially those containing liquids. Wrap each food individually to keep it fresh. Pack condiments in paper cups. This makes for easy storage in an ice chest and easy passing. It may be a good idea to pack a cooler of drinking water just in case there is none available at your picnic site.

It is wise to keep your picnic basket stocked with disposable plates, cups, napkins, eating utensils, salt and pepper shakers, tongs, serving spoons, and potholders. You'll always be ready for an impromptu picnic.

Make a list and include everything you will need for the preparation and serving of food at your party away from home. Don't forget the makings for a fire and any special equipment that goes with it. Be sure the things needed first at the picnic site (any particular food or equipment) are packed last.

As you pack to go home, check-off all the items you brought from home. Leave the party site as clean (or cleaner) than you found it when the outdoor feast is over.

Whether the picnic food is simple or elaborate, there can never be too much of it. For some reason, appetites tend to soar at parties away from home.

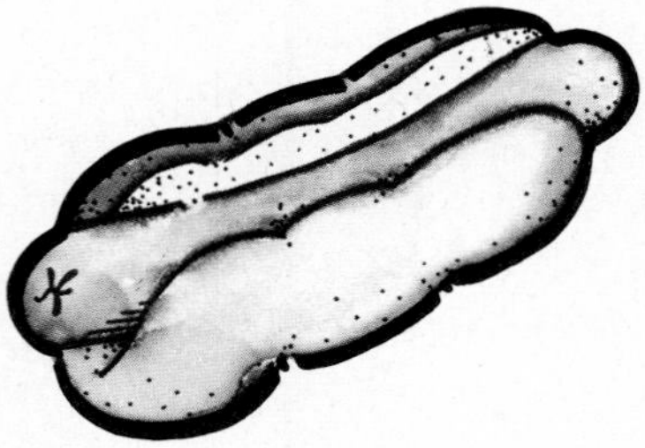

Alternate Plans in Case of Inclement Weather

Bad weather need not spoil your fun, but expect the unexpected and be flexible with your entertainment plans. Have an alternate plan worked out in case the party is forced to move inside. You may wish to limit the guest list to the number you could adequately entertain in the playroom, carport, and den. The wise hostess may put up a tent or tarpaulin in case a shower blows up, drenching guests. If alternate plans are not possible, the party may have to be cancelled. Give some thought to protecting or moving your grill if it is portable, in case of a sudden shower. A large sun umbrella works well in protecting a stationary grill; however, if moving a mobile grill to the porch, breezeway, or garage, make certain the area is well-ventilated.

In spite of inclement weather, the perfect host and hostess will manage to keep spirits higher than the humidity.

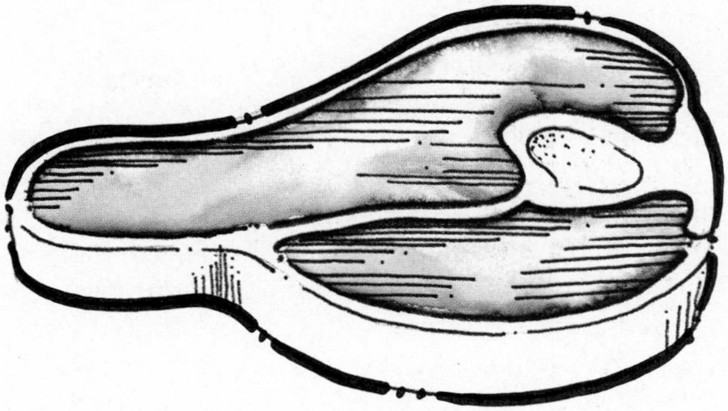

The Guest's Comfort

When cooking out-of-doors be sure there is plenty of food for guests to nibble on. The succulent smells will whet their appetites and they will want something to eat while they drink and watch the chef.

A flappy paper plate and a flimsy fork can ruin the pleasure of a meal. So give a paper plate added appeal and support with rattan holders. And do buy heavy-duty plastic flatware. Some of the pieces are sturdy enough to use again.

Have extra glasses at the bar or drink area for guests and for children who set their drinks down and lose them. The disposable/reusable plastics are convenient and practical for outdoor use. Set up a small, low table for the children's drinks. They can serve themselves and needn't be bothered with making special requests at the adult's bar.

Provide ashtrays and surfaces on which to set drinks and plates. Supply either small tables or individual trays for guests, especially when the food requires cutting.

Have seating and table settings for every guest. Arrange the chair, benches, cushions, and gliders but be sure no one has to sit on damp grass or sand. Folding seats and small tables make for ideal dining proximities. A separate table is usually more fun for children. They can enjoy the freedom of the outdoors without the scrutiny of older eyes. Of course, a favorite aunt, uncle, or family friend can join the children's fun and keep things partially controlled.

If the ground is your table, spread a length of vinyl and cover it with a quilt.

Early in the outdoor season, check your benches and wooden outdoor furniture for splinters and rough areas. A quick rubdown with heavy-duty sandpaper will give a fresh finish and new look to the furniture. Touch up rust spots on wrought iron and other metal furniture. Rough spots are hard on knits and nylons.

Place furniture with a consideration for the predictable elements of nature. Awnings, a lattice or trellis over the porch, spreading trees, and umbrellas can keep the sun from bearing down at mealtime. Hedges, potted plants, and placement of furniture can cut down on wind currents (say, for an afternoon sea breeze). Of course problems of this nature vary with the region, place, and time of day, but practice will soon teach you how to manage your outdoor eating area.

Insect Control

Uninvited guests, such as mosquitoes and other insects, enjoy outdoor parties, too. Spray the party area with an insecticide or fogger about 30 minutes before guests arrive and before food has been displayed. That will give the spray adequate time to work and also time for the odor to dissipate. Keeping food covered until it's time to be cooked or eaten will discourage some flying pests. Citronella candles or torches not only add light and atmosphere, but also help as an insect repellent. Those who entertain extensively outdoors may wish to invest in an ultraviolet lantern designed to attract flying bugs. The bugs are destroyed immediately upon contact with the ultraviolet light. These lanterns can be purchased at most hardware stores.

If you're fortunate enough to have a purple martin birdhouse in your yard, you are probably aware that these birds are adept at helping eliminate some of our insect invaders.

For your guests' comfort, consider some method of pest control to take care of insects who insist on joining the party.

Outdoor Equipment and Accessories

In the South, cooking out-of-doors has never gone out of fashion. Today, the equipment available is equal to the occasion.

Of course, excellent food can be prepared on the very simplest of homemade devices. But for convenience, and for more sophisticated results, a variety of well-engineered grills and smokers and other cooking gear are available. Regardless of what equipment is selected, a successful outdoor chef still needs to understand the principles of meat cookery and the feeding and care of the heat source. In this chapter, we've discussed these principles as well as given you some guidelines for selecting, maintaining, and operating a variety of grills.

We also realize the usefulness of certain small accessories in helping you use your grill effectively and have detailed those for you. Since ice cream freezers, fry pans, warming trays, and woks have found their best friends among outdoor hostesses, we've included a full discussion of selecting and caring for them.

Once you've selected the equipment you need, use and care for it properly. We know it will make your entertaining easier and more enjoyable.

Selecting Your Outdoor Grill

Here are some basic points to consider when selecting your outdoor cooking equipment:

1. What types of food does your family enjoy?
2. Where will you be cooking: in your backyard, on your deck or patio, in parks, or at campsites?
3. How often will you use the equipment?
4. How easy will it be to clean?
5. Where will it be stored?
6. How easy is it to assemble and disassemble?
7. How much are you willing to spend? (Hint: Investing in poorly constructed equipment, even if you are a beginner, is guaranteed to produce disappointing results.)

Before you make any decision as to what you purchase, you should examine the entire inventory of outdoor cooking equipment. Included are gas, electric, charcoal, and woodburning grills and smoking equipment. Each of them has its own advantages and restrictions.

Gas and electric grills with comparable features cost about the same, and for this reason, selection should be based on availability of each utility as well as your family's likes and dislikes. If your home is all electric, then it could be excessively expensive to select a gas grill. On the other hand, if both gas and electricity are used in your home, you would need to explore utility rates, cost of building a gasline to the site, or extending electric connections with a 20-ampere circuit for the grill.

Charcoal grills are less expensive than either gas or electric, and are not limited by the utility available; however, charcoal produces fluctuating heat. Bottled gas grills are also available, but are usually selected for rural areas or when portability is desirable.

Many sizes, styles, and colors are available in all three types. The largest size or double grills should be purchased if you expect to cook for crowds. Cast aluminum grills are rust-proof and are usually dark gray, but are also avail-

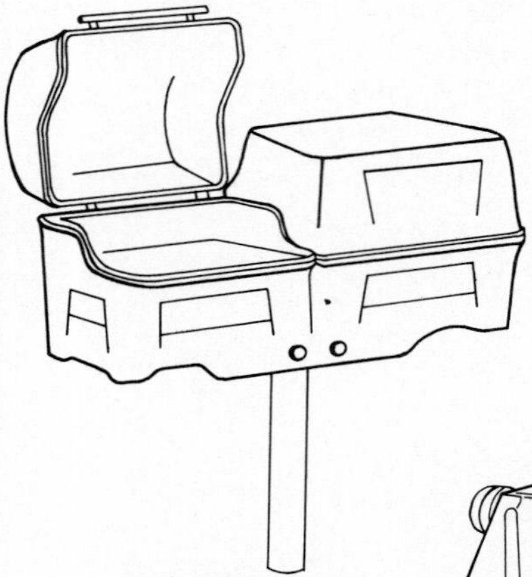

DOUBLE GRILL

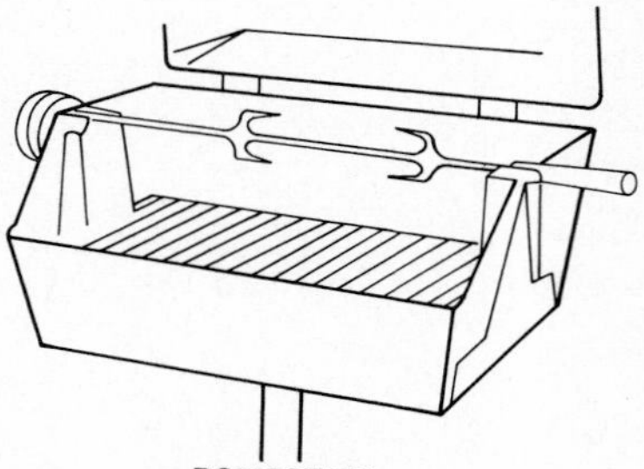

ROTISSERIE

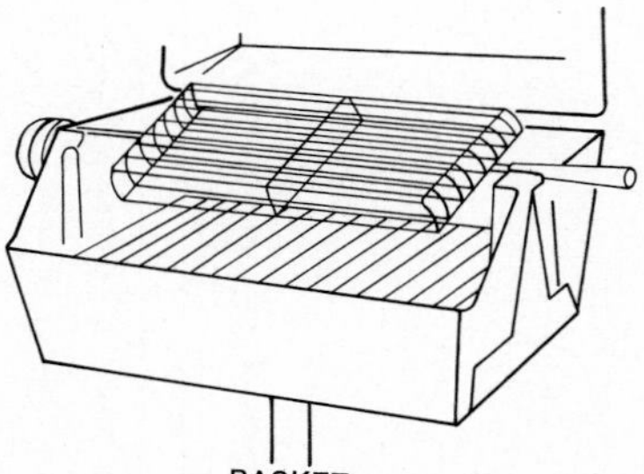

BASKET

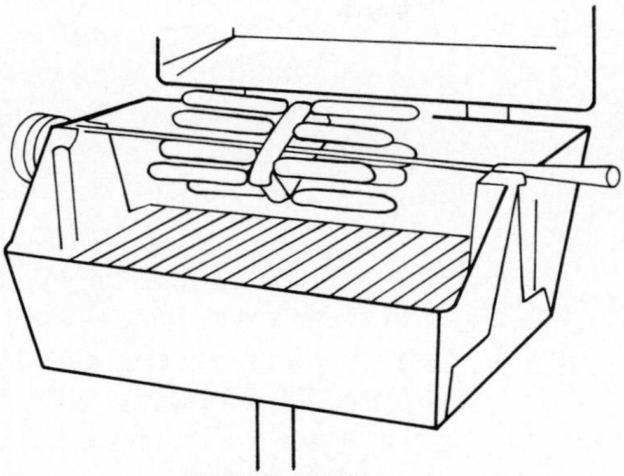

WIENER WHEEL

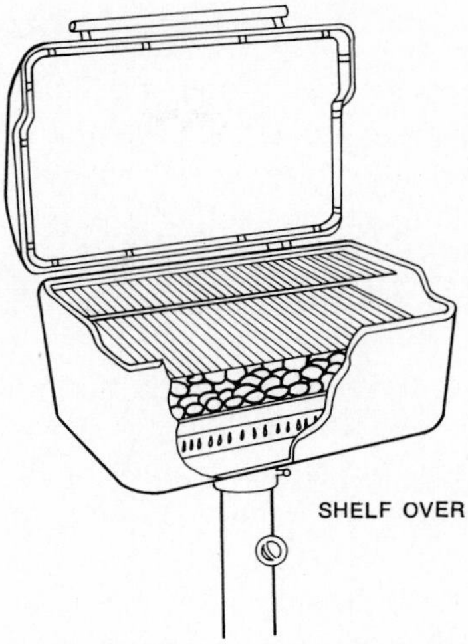

SHELF OVER THE RACK

able in a variety of other colors. Another desirable construction material for grills is heavy-duty steel which is often bonderized with colored enamel to prevent rust. Both metals are weather-resistant, but some care is needed to keep them attractive.

Cast aluminum is rust-free. The exterior appearance is preserved by rubbing with cooking oil while the grill is hot. To remove cooking stains and those caused by dust and rain, use a cloth dipped in a solution of mild detergent and hot water. If the stains are stubborn, use a soft brush with the same solution. Over a period of time, inclement weather and extreme temperatures of cooking may cause white spots of oxidation to develop. These spots can be removed with a steel wool soap pad or a wire brush. The grill may then be sprayed with a special heat-resistant paint. Bonderized steel grills are also cleaned with detergent and water.

Electric- or battery- powered rotisseries, baskets, and wiener wheels can be purchased as additional attachments for all three types.

Whether your grill is gas, electric, or charcoal, a well-built, easily cleaned rack is important. Racks are made of cast aluminum, cast iron, and chrome-plated steel.

Gas racks need only an occasional washing. They can be cleaned by closing the cover after food is removed and turning the unit on "high" to burn off soil. Racks on the electric models can be removed when cool and brushed with a steel brush. Those on charcoal grills should be removed when meat is taken off. If covered with damp paper towels the washing job is not hard. An easier method would be to put the rack in the dishwasher.

Many grills have a shelf over the rack that can be used to warm bread or other accompaniments for the meal.

All three fuel types have models with hinged covers. If you are selecting such a model, look for comfortable, well-placed heatproof handles.

The lava rocks or ceramic rocks in gas and electric grills should be cleaned according to manufacturer's directions as these vary considerably from one model to another.

All grills will last longer and look better if protected by a waterproof cover when not in use, particularly if they are not under a shelter.

Gas Grills

Types to select from: These grills use natural or bottled gas as their fuel. Look for the American Gas Association (AGA) certification on all gas cooking equipment. It is your assurance that the design complies with national safety standards.

Some grills have heat settings marked "low," "medium," and "high"; others have as many as eight heat settings. Many also have a positive screw-type mechanism to lower or raise the grill as an aid in controlling heat intensity. Many of these with motorized rotisseries also have three-position notches on the grill.

Advantages of gas grills: A gas appliance eliminates the muss and fuss of ashes and a smoking fire. Also, when grilling with gas there is an evenness of temperature because the lava rocks absorb the heat and radiate it to the meat.

Using the gas grill: Burners in gas grills come in a variety of shapes ranging from a large round style to an "H" shape. However, the principles of burners in a gas grill are the same as those in a gas range. Combustion depends on the right mixture of gas and air inside the burner. Unless the flame is a clear blue it is not burning correctly and needs some adjustment to the amount of air entering at the base of the burner. Usually this is a simple adjustment and your instruction booklet will tell you what to do. If you are unable to properly adjust the amount of air entering the burner, call your gas utility serviceman.

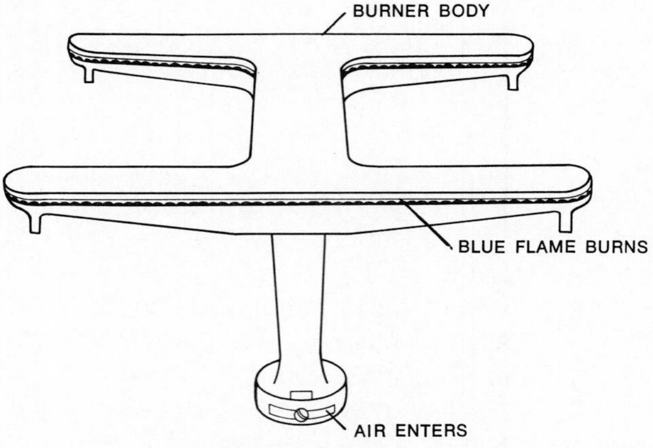

H-SHAPED BURNER

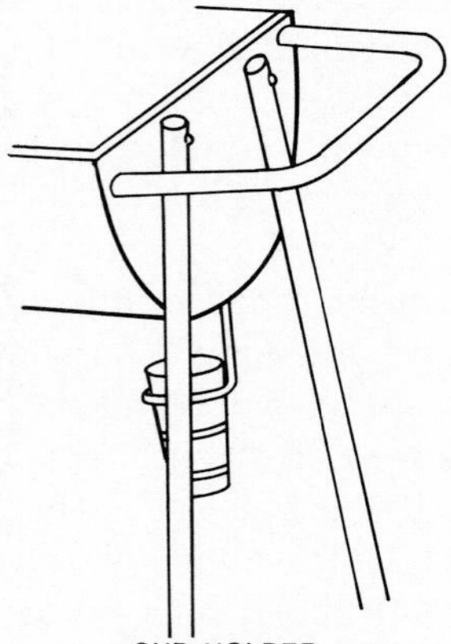

Briquettes made of a lava rock or a ceramic material are spread in the fire box surrounding the burner. These rocks serve to radiate the heat and make cooking more even. Briquettes should be turned occasionally to burn off accumulated grease. After extended use they begin to disintegrate and will need replacing. One brand of replacement lava rocks for the gas grill comes in a bag of 64 pieces and costs less than $10. Replacement will probably not be necessary for at least a year depending on how often you use and how well you care for your grill.

The drip hole in the bottom of the grill is provided to drain off excess fat. If not drained off, fat causes flare-ups which may burn the meat. On gas grills with a cup holder this excess fat can be collected and discarded to prevent staining the surface underneath the grill.

Cleaning the gas grill: The interior of the gas grill may be cleaned by closing the cover and turning the burner on "high" for several minutes. Occasional brushing of the racks and inside the grill cover with a wire brush may be helpful. The racks can be removed for washing periodically. Stainless steel racks may develop a rusty look due to intense heat. The inside of the burners may get scale of oxidized metal from heat and moisture in the air. About twice a year the burner should be lifted out and brushed thoroughly to remove this scale from the burner body and from the holes where the flame burns. Also, check your instruction booklet for location of the air vents and clean them to make sure sufficient air can enter. A few minutes spent in care can add years to the life of your equipment.

Electric Grills

Types to select from: Electric grills come in two voltages — 120-volt and 240-volt. It is important with both types to have a weatherproof, grounded outlet of the appropriate voltage. According to the Association of Home Appliance Manufacturers, 80% of the 15- and 20-ampere outlets are improperly grounded.

The various models available are either permanently installed, portable, or tabletop. The use you plan to make of the grill and your family's needs should determine which you select.

Features to look for: The Underwriters' Laboratories (UL) seal of approval should be present. Vents should be adjustable to aid in controlling moisture and smoke inside the grill. Look for a unit with sturdy construction as discussed on page 162 with accessories available that you need and will use.

Well-marked temperature controls that are weatherproof and designed for outdoor operation are essential. This control usually operates like that of a surface unit on an electric range. Also make sure the unit you select has heatproof handles to protect your hands when lifting the lid.

Cost characteristics: There is a wide range of prices in electric grills beginning at about $30 and climbing up to $130 for those operating on 120-volts. These prices are about the same level as for similar quality in gas grills. All electric grills require a grounded outlet for safety and this may add to the total cost if one is not available at the time of purchase.

The grills that require 240-volt wiring (this is the same as that required for an electric range) will cost from about $130 to $150. But there might be the addi-

240 VOLTS GROUNDED RECEPTACLE

tional expense of having the electrical wiring installed, which is usually more expensive than adapting for the 120-volt grill. All outdoor circuits should be grounded regardless of the voltage used.

Advantages of electric grills: "Charcoal" flavor is produced without the use of charcoal. An electric grill is safe because there is no flame and matches are not needed to ignite it. The electric grill is for the most part self-cleaning, if the manufacturer's directions are followed. However, this does not mean that you will *never* have to clean it.

Using the electric grill: Depending on the house current load and the distance of the grill from the power source, cor-

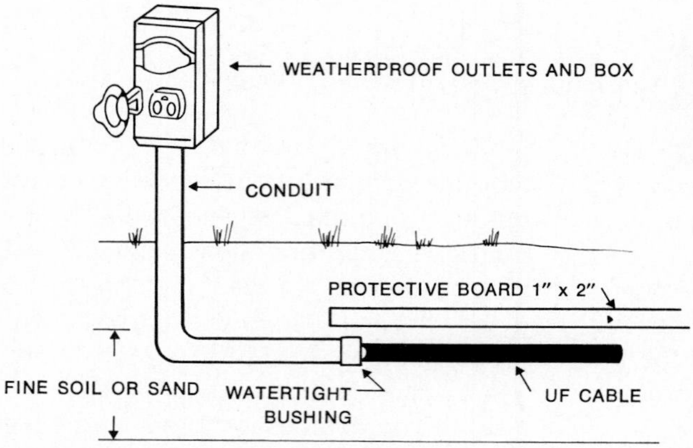

UNDERGROUND WIRING FOR WEATHERPROOF DUPLEX RECEPTACLE

120 VOLTS PORTABLE DUPLEX GROUNDED RECEPTACLE

rections in the temperature settings may have to be made to maintain the desired heat.

Do not use an ordinary extension cord; this wire is too small-gauged to carry the amount of current needed. Use only a heavy-duty, three-wire, No. 14 extension cord, not more than 12 feet long. The longer the cord, the less heat from the grill. If you have a choice of outlets, or have an outlet installed, remember the nearer the meter box the less the voltage will drop. Lower voltage results in inefficient use of the electrical current and heat is decreased.

The grill user should never use the rotisserie outlet for heating appliances such as coffee pots or fry pans. The wattage the grill requires plus that of a heating appliance will overload the circuit and decrease the heating efficiency of the grill.

Water should never be used to relieve flare-ups because of the hazards of shock, and the sudden temperature change on the heating element can reduce its life. When flare-ups occur, turn the unit off.

Hickory flakes may be used to produce a smoky flavor. Place these flakes on top of the ceramic briquettes.

Metal cookie sheets and large pans should not be placed on top of the grill because they may trap the heat and cause the heating element to burn out. A sheet of aluminum foil may be used as long as care is taken not to cover the entire grill. Be sure to leave some areas around the foil to let the air circulate.

Charcoal Grills

Purchase hardwood charcoal briquettes for use in the grill. The amount used is determined by what you are cooking. A roast, chicken, turkey, or any large mass of meat will require 20 to 30 briquettes. A steak or two, or four to six hamburgers, will require about 12 to 15 briquettes.

Charcoal is lighted in a variety of ways. You can put a half a dozen charcoal briquettes in a coffee can, pour in about a cup of charcoal lighter, put the lid on, and let them soak for about 20 minutes. With tongs, pile the soaked charcoal in a small pyramid, placing about six more untreated briquettes over them. Light near the bottom of the pile. As soon as they are burning well, add the rest of the briquettes that will be needed. This method will take about 45 minutes for grayish ash to form, signaling time to start cooking.

You can get a fire in about 30 minutes by using a gallon can with both ends cut out and a few large holes cut 1 inch from the bottom. This can is placed in the fire bowl with holes nearest the bottom. Fill the can with briquettes and soak with charcoal lighting fluid. Let stand for a minute, then light. When briquettes are covered with gray ash, lift the can off with pliers or tongs and spread over cooking area. Methods of spreading coals for various foods on all types of grills are discussed under "Cooking on all Grills."

For the confirmed outdoor cook there is a gadget that fires things up in a hurry. This is the electric starter. To use it, lay out about a dozen charcoal briquettes, put the starter over them and put about 12 more briquettes on top. Do not use any liquid charcoal lighters. Now plug the starter into an appliance outlet. After a few minutes the coals will begin to burn. Leave in place according to directions on starter or until ashes begin to show along both edges of the starter. Do not exceed time limit given in instructions. At this time, unplug it and lift from the coals. After a few more minutes coals can be arranged.

Stubs from leftover candles make good starters too. To use them, or to use the liquid fire starters, charcoal should be heaped into a pyramid. Squirt liquid starter on the coals, then after a minute carefully light the coals. Never put a liquid starter on hot coals or use gasoline or kerosene to start fires.

As soon as coals are about two-thirds covered with ash they are ready to be spread into the pattern required for cooking your food.

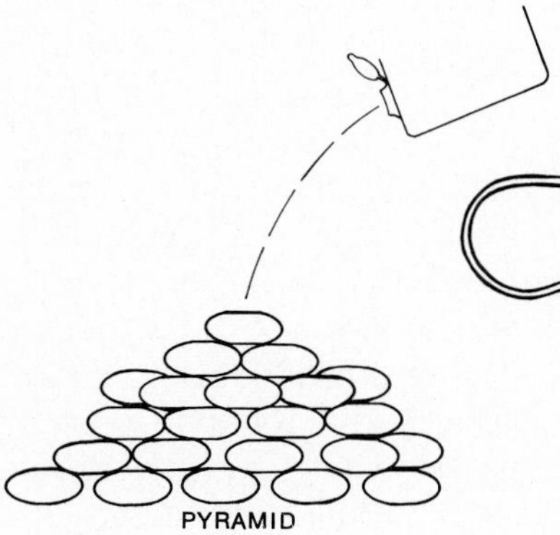

PYRAMID

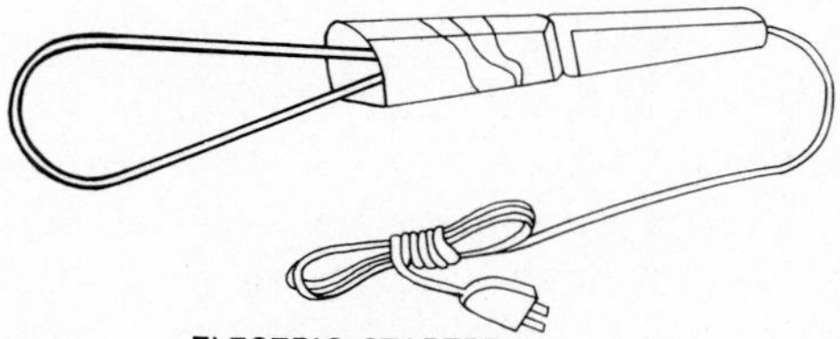

ELECTRIC STARTER

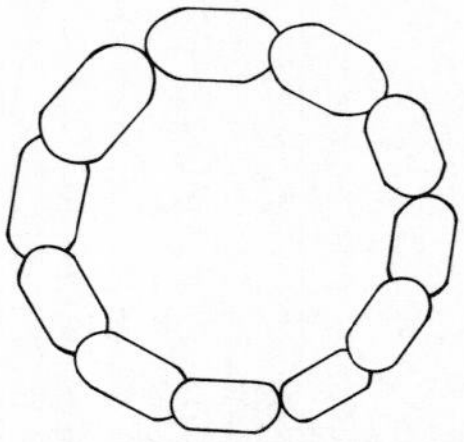

COALS ARRANGED IN A RING

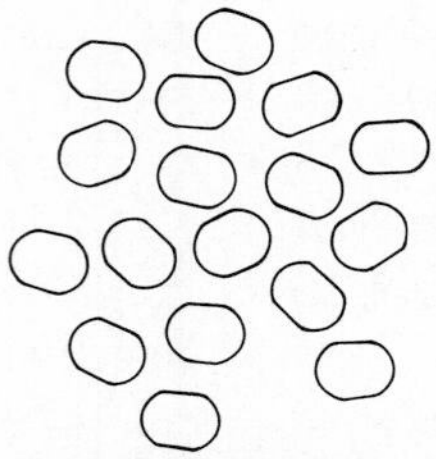

COALS ARRANGED IN A POLKA-DOT PATTERN

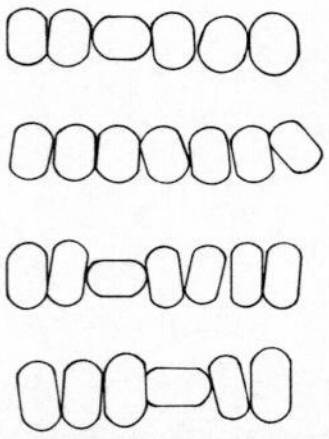

COALS ARRANGED FOR COOKING FOOD ON SKEWERS

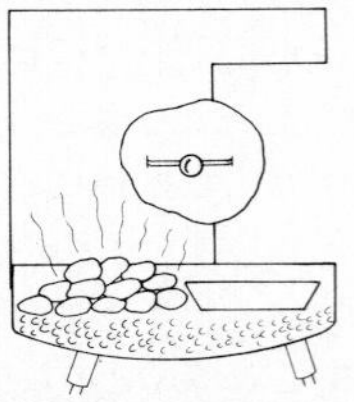

COALS AT THE REAR OF THE FIRE BOX

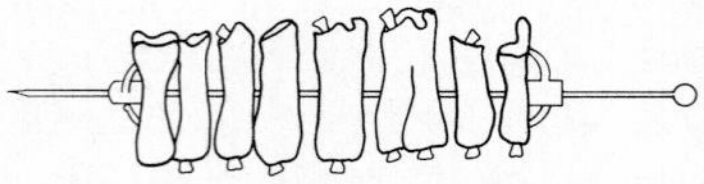

RIBS LACED ON SKEWER

Cooking on all Grills

When the charcoal briquettes are covered with a grayish ash, gas lava rocks are red hot, or the ceramic briquettes in the electric grill are thoroughly heated, they will need to be arranged according to the meat being cooked.

Roast, turkey, and chicken require long cooking with low heat (gas and electric heat controls are placed on the lowest setting). When using a spit over an open grill of either of the three fuels, coals are arranged in a ring or oval extending well beyond the outer edges of the meat.

If using a grill with a hood, coals are placed at the rear of the fire box with the space underneath the meat left open. A rotisserie is usually used with a hood.

For grills with lids, the coals should be spread well over the fire box surface with heat settings as low as possible. Those that do not have a rotisserie or spit will require manual turning of the meat several times during cooking.

For shish-kabobs or foods on skewers, the various types of briquettes are laid in parallel lines below, in between skewers with kabobs, and around the sides of the fire box. Since these foods are cooked fast, heat can be set on "high." If charcoal is used it can be placed within a few inches of the food. Skewers should be turned several times if rotating skewers are not used.

For steaks, chops, hamburgers, or other foods being broiled, arrange coals or briquettes in a polka-dot pattern with 1 or 2 inches between each briquette. Broiled meats are cooked with the cover open unless smoke flavor is to be added at the end of the cooking period.

If a smoke flavor is desired for any of these foods, damp chips from hickory or other nut or fruit trees may be added to the briquettes. Small bits of garlic, rosemary, or other favorite aromatic herbs may also be added. After these flavors are added, the cover is closed. If the grill is an uncovered type, an improvised lid may be used to hold the smoke around the meat.

Smokers

Several manufacturers have developed smokers made of heavy cast metal or rolled steel. They are built on legs, and a fire pan with air vents in the bottom is suspended from the sides. This fire pan can use charcoal briquettes and one or two hardwood sticks, 3 to 4 inches long and about ½ inch in diameter. A water pan is hung directly under the rack. Some models have two racks available with a domed lid that lifts off to complete the unit.

This type of cooking is quite slow as compared to the more open grills because the smoker depends on heat and steam over an extended length of time. Cooking times are from 2 to 3 hours for 4 pounds of fish or 4 pounds of link sausage, and up to as long as 12 or more hours for a large turkey. Cooking on the double grill requires an even greater length of time.

Food is seasoned before placing in the smoker. All meats are self-basting because steam is created by the water in the pan. Meat drippings in the water pan make an excellent base for sauces. Meat cooked by this method is not only smoky tasting but more juicy and tender than most grilled meat.

Directions with the smoker give approximate fuel requirements and cooking times. With any of the units available the heat can be controlled by raising or lowering rack level and by opening and closing the drafts. To obtain the highest heat, open drafts or dampers as wide as possible. A good tip to remember is "the more air, the hotter the fire." Close dampers almost completely for low heat. Never close them completely since fresh air movement is necessary for browning and to keep fuel burning.

Use a meat thermometer to determine when meat is done.

Using the smoker: Remove dome, rack, and water pan. Place charcoal briquettes as specified on the cooking

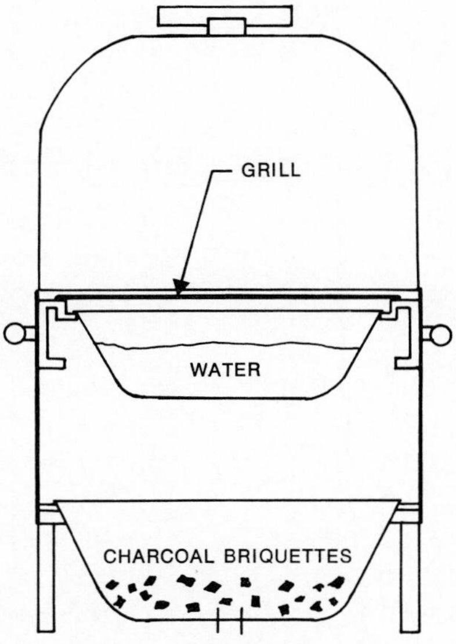

SMOKER

STEP-UP RACK

chart. Start fire with an electric starter or put about 1 cup of non-odor producing liquid fire starter on the briquettes and let them soak for 3 minutes before lighting with a match. Allow the briquettes to burn until they are without flames and you have a bed of glowing grayish coals. This will take about 25 minutes.

Pieces of hickory, pecan, mesquite, apple, or other flavor-producing wood may be added. Replace the water pan and fill to the directed level.

Put seasoned meat on the rack. If meat is in more than one piece, leave space between the pieces to allow steam and smoke to reach all surfaces. Replace the dome and remove only after 4 hours to check the water level.

When smoking meats that take no longer than 6 hours or no less than 4 hours to cook, a wide variety of vegetables can be cooked at the same time. Vegetables are cooked in the water pan where they take on a new and delightful flavor. You may cook just one vegetable or a combination of vegetables. When cooking vegetables, fill the water pan to the brim, then check the water level after 3 hours, and add more water if needed. Add salt to the water, then try one or more of the following raw vegetables: whole carrots, whole medium onions, fresh mushrooms, white potatoes, sweet potatoes, quartered cabbage, whole okra, or let your creativity guide you to try any of your favorites. The flavor will amaze you.

If you have a double rack model or a single rack and buy the extra step-up rack, try cooking meats on the top and an uncovered vegetable casserole on the lower shelf. No fat will be needed in the casserole as the smoky drippings and misty steam will season it for you. Casserole dishes will need 4 hours or more to cook, so be sure your meat takes that long too.

No matter what sort of outdoor cooking equipment you select, let your personality show through the creative and imaginative foods you prepare. Anybody can follow a prescription: only a genius can make one.

Time and Temperature Chart for Cooking on all Grills

Meat	Size	Heat	Approximate Cooking Time
Steak	1-inch	High	12 to 15 minutes
Hamburgers	1-inch	High	8 minutes
Chicken	pieces	Medium to High No flame	45 minutes
Pork Chops	1-inch	Medium to High No flame	35 minutes or more
Spareribs	whole	Low to Medium	45 minutes or more
Ham, Smoked	7- to 8-pound	Medium	2 hours
Fish Fillet	1-inch	Medium	16 to 20 minutes
Beef Rolled Rib Roast	4- to 5-pound	Medium or 15 minutes on High then reduce to Low	2¾ hours or more at 170°

Useful Utensils and Tools

Long handled two-prong fork
Tongs for turning food
Heavier tongs for arranging charcoal, lava rocks, or ceramic rocks
Meat thermometer
Skewers
Basting brush or mop
Hinged wire basket for hard-to-handle foods
Large cutting board
1 or 2 good slicing knives
Cordless slicing knife can be electrically charged inside and taken outside
Asbestos gloves
Hot pads
Long handled salt and pepper shakers
Long handled spatula
Plastic bottle filled with water for squirting flare-ups on charcoal fire
Rolls of paper towels

Selection and Use of Small Electrical Appliances

Whether you're using an electric skillet, a hot tray, an electric wok, coffee pot, or fondue pot, there are some basic factors that need to be kept in mind.

Always purchase a product made by a reputable manufacturer and backed by a warranty. Return warranty card as soon as appliance has been purchased so that repair or replacements, if needed, can be made without charge before warranty period is up.

Carefully study the use and care booklet that comes with each appliance. Keep the booklet handy and refer to it often.

Select equipment with heat-resistant handles, and check to see if it has a self-grounding electrical cord. This feature is new, and may not be available on all pieces of equipment, but it has a definite advantage in preventing shocks.

Be sure that you have sufficient circuits to supply convenience outlets with ample electricity to operate the appliances with maximum efficiency. Check the wattage rating stamped on each appliance and never overload any electrical circuit.

Keep a supply of extra fuses on hand in case a fuse should "blow." Never replace a fuse with one of a larger voltage, just reduce the number of appliances used on the circuit giving the trouble.

Some appliances come equipped with the three-prong cord; never under any conditions should you file off the extra prong so that it can be used on an ungrounded circuit. The extra prong means this appliance should be plugged into a grounded outlet.

If extension cords are needed, use heavy-duty extension cords rated for 15-amperes. An ordinary extension cord will overheat the appliance and probably "blow" a fuse.

Never stand on a damp surface when using electrical equipment and be sure that the equipment itself is used on a dry surface.

Never immerse an appliance in water unless it is clearly marked "immersible."

When using an electrical appliance with a detachable cord or temperature control, plug detachable cord into the appliance first, then into the wall outlet. Unless this procedure is followed, the points of the cord, carrying a full load of electricity, may burn out very quickly or burn out the appliance.

Reverse this procedure after using the appliance: unplug from outlet, then remove detachable cord from appliance.

Ice Cream Freezers

Most of the ice cream freezers on the market are powered with electricity although the manually powered models are still available. Most freezers are available in 4-, 5-, and 6-quart sizes and powered by 115- or 200-watt motors. The exterior bucket is made of either wood or plastic insulated with polypropylene. The inner containers are made of plastic or tin-plated steel.

Points to consider when purchasing an ice cream freezer: Moisture will not condense on a wood or well-insulated container and this might be important if you will be using the freezer in the kitchen. If you would like to watch the freezing process and be better able to check freezing progress, select a "see through" lid. Make sure that the dasher has at least ¼-inch clearance in your freezer bucket. Be certain that you understand the terms of the guarantee or warranty. This is especially important with this appliance. If the motor is allowed to run after the ice cream is frozen, it may cause the motor to overheat and burn out. Would this be covered in your warranty?

Using and caring for your ice cream freezer: Learn how to use and care for your freezer by reading the instruction booklet for your particular appliance. Clean freezer immediately after each use. Your ice cream will freeze more rapidly if you chill the container and all the ingredients before beginning to make ice cream. Allowance must be made for expansion, so be certain that you fill the inner container only one-half to two-thirds full. Attach top firmly on the container before plugging in the motor.

The ice and salt should be packed according to the manufacturer's instructions. Additional ice and salt may need to be added during the freezing period. Let the motor run half an hour or until it begins to labor. Then the freezer should be unplugged, so that it does not stall and cause damage to the motor.

Drain off water, remove dasher, cover securely, and repack with salt and ice. The freezer should stand for an hour longer for ice cream to harden.

Cleaning all parts of the freezer is of utmost importance. Rinse off all salt from metal parts. Do not immerse the motor in water or allow it to get wet. Simply wipe it off with a damp cloth.

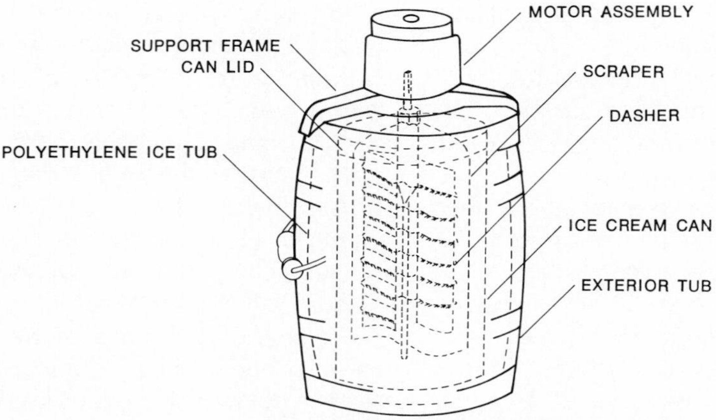

ELECTRIC ICE CREAM FREEZER

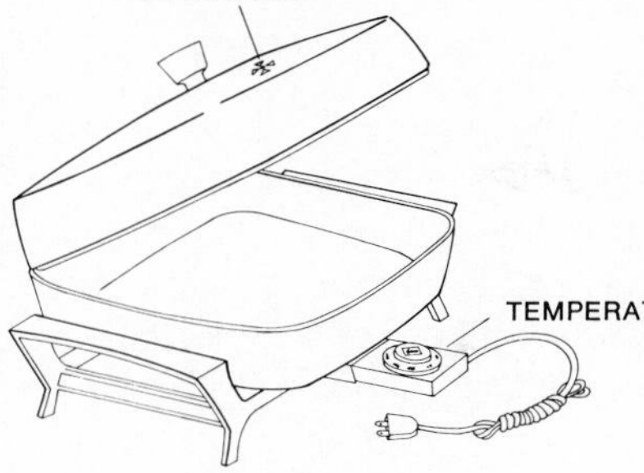

Fry Pans

Portability of an electric fry pan makes it an excellent appliance to use outdoors. The fry pan has thermostatically controlled heat which gives dependable results without constant watching. Most fry pans will use from 1000 to 1500 watts which makes it essential that they be plugged into a grounded appliance outlet. Some of the newer models have grounded wires; these are the safest kinds to use. Remember that the fry pan should not be plugged into the convenience outlet on the electric grill since the grill plus the fry pan will be more than the circuit can handle — or the efficiency of both will be decreased.

Features to look for: Rectangular and square pans have greater cooking areas. Look for a model with a signal light that will tell you when the desired temperature has been reached. If it is important to you to wash your fry pan in the dishwasher, select one that has a removable heat control and is completely immersible. Caution: Wash in the dishwasher only if the manufacturer recommends it.

Fry pans are available in many materials, colors, and sizes; therefore, you may select the one that meets your special needs and preferences. Select a model with heat-resistant handles and feet, especially if you are planning to carry it to the outdoor cooking area. A convenient temperature guide on the handle may be very helpful. Some pans are equipped with a warming tray that slides under the fry pan itself; this is a nice feature for your outdoor food preparation such as for warming rolls, etc.

Use and care of the fry pan: If you have selected a fry pan with a non-stick finish, it is essential to season it with unsalted oil before using it. Set the temperature control to the "off" position before plugging heat control unit into the fry pan; then plug it into the convenience outlet.

Foods should not be overcrowded when browning. You might need to brown in batches, but wait for the indicator light to go on before adding another batch.

The heat control unit should be handled carefully. The calibration might become inaccurate if it is jarred.

An aluminum cooking surface may be cleaned with soap-filled pads. If the aluminum has darkened, 2 tablespoons of cream of tartar and 2 quarts of water may be boiled in the fry pan, then emptied, rinsed, and dried.

Stainless steel cleaner or sudsy water should be used to clean the stainless steel fry pan.

Never store the fry pan in the oven of the range, since the oven temperature will damage the handles and the heat control unit. It is very easy to accidentally turn on the oven not realizing or remembering the pan is in there.

Woks

The wok is perhaps the most versatile cooking utensil ever invented. It may be available in an electric model or one that is used on your kitchen range. Its unique shape makes it a skillet, a sauce pan, and a sauce pot. Because it has controlled heat in a small base, it is the ideal stir-frying, steaming, and stewing appliance.

Woks are made of a heavyweight aluminum coated with a fired-on, no-stick finish.

Care of the wok is essentially the same as that of the electric fry pan. Whenever oil is heated in the wok, make certain it is uncovered. Do not carry a wok when it is filled with hot liquids.

Always use the wok on a flat moisture-free surface, and make certain the terminal pins (to which the heat control unit is attached) are dry. Do not handle wok with wet hands.

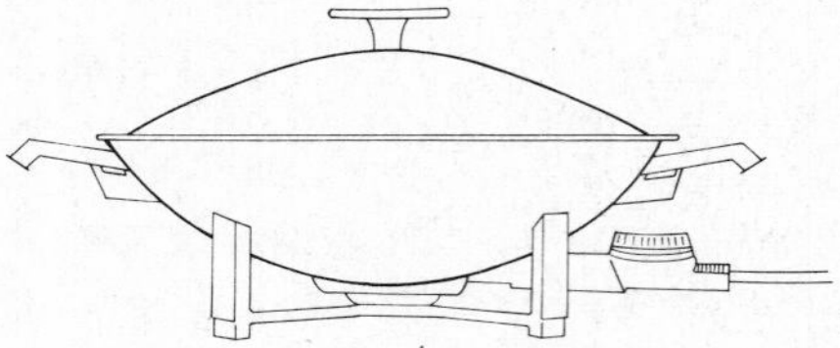

WOK

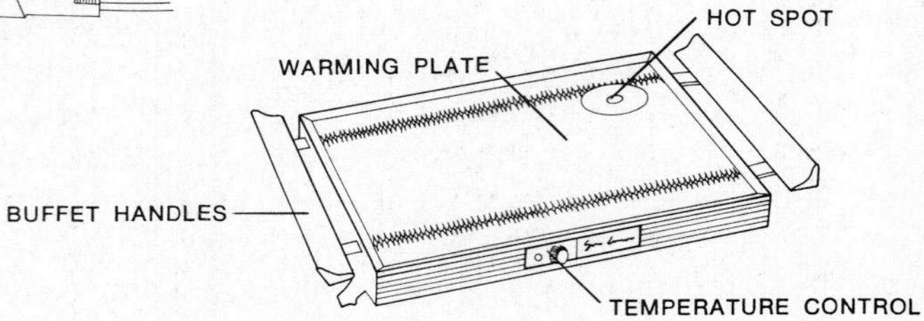

HOT TRAY

Hot Trays

Hot trays come in various sizes: one with a single heating unit for the coffee pot; a family-size to heat several items; and the 52-inch hostess model, appropriate for large crowds.

Features to look for: Consider the size and shape of hot tray in relation to your needs and available space. Select a color and design to harmonize with your decor. Check to see that the hot tray has an adjustable thermostat and an "off-on" switch. Other features you may desire are the hot spot, a pilot-light, warming drawer, and bubble dome.

Use and care of hot trays: Read the use and care manual carefully before using. Be careful not to drop your tray. Even shatter-resistant glass will break under some circumstances. Plug into a grounded small appliance circuit, if at all possible. This is essential with the larger sizes. After using, cool and wipe with a damp sponge or cloth. Never immerse a hot tray in water or allow water to seep under the glass top.

This delicately browned Rolled Rib Roast (recipe on page 4) garnished with parsley makes for elegant dinnertime enjoyment in an informal, casual setting.

Outdoor Lighting

When night comes, the home landscape no longer has to disappear in the darkness. Not when landscape lighting is available, as it is today. A series of well-placed outdoor lighting fixtures will highlight the best features of a garden making it a lovely backdrop for outdoor entertaining.

The photographs and text in this chapter illustrate the ways and means of extending garden enjoyment into the night. There is a general description of landscape lighting as a new art, some specific discussion of how to gain special effects, and information about equipment and installation ranging from the inexpensive do-it-yourself kit up to professionally designed and installed systems.

Landscape lighting is an art that seems made for the South with its diverse and often spectacular home landscape settings that can be a pleasure to look at year-round. And while garden lighting makes special entertainment occasions that much more special, it is also available for family and friends to enjoy all the time.

For those who have never seen outdoor lighting treated as an art, the examples shown here will be a revelation.

A single specimen tree like this one can set the theme for a nighttime garden, while a downlight illuminates the outdoor dining group.

For any kind of outdoor entertaining a proper setting is an important factor. An ample terrace or deck easily reached, attractive landscaping, and comfortable seating all contribute to making family or guests feel as at home outdoors as they would be within the house.

Most of these necessities for successful outdoor living are taken care of in the South where the gracious terrace in a handsome, man-made or natural landscape setting is a tradition. But there is a new, growing art — landscape lighting or illumination — which may soon become a part of this tradition.

Landscape illumination, the art of lighting a home garden setting, seems a natural for the South and its outdoor living. Much entertaining, if not most, is done after dark. To bring the garden to life at night for enjoyment and practical usage makes excellent sense, and there is the additional advantage that a lighted landscape setting can be enjoyed year-round as something to be seen from inside as well.

There are, of course, many ways to use candles, torches, and other occasional lighting for outdoor entertaining, and these remain valid. But landscape lighting reproduces in nighttime form, the garden itself. To realize what the difference entails you need only look at the accompanying photographs. Landscape illumination is still, as described above, a rare art. The gardens shown here were all designed by John Watson of Dallas, who introduced landscape lighting as an art some years ago and continues to be its leading practitioner. The artful lighting approach pioneered by Watson goes far beyond the strictly functional fixtures found in many houses: a floodlight, a front porch light, possibly one light above the garage, and a post lamp out in the lawn. These are for utility only, as anyone who has destroyed the mood of a party by switching on a terrace floodlight soon discovers.

The basis for any successful landscape lighting must be the house and its garden setting. The features of the garden, the way it is used, how the landscape is viewed from house or terrace should be an integral part of a complete lighting program. Ideally, the practical needs for illumination of a terrace, walk, or entry are also handled by general aesthetic lighting so that what pleases also serves real needs.

"The best features of a garden — its specimen trees, paving, background — should be the foundation for night lighting," according to Watson. "And we always try to go with understatement. The common tendency is to have the light level both inside and outside the house too high. You really don't need great powerful spots in a garden, but rather a soft overall effect."

A professional design and installation for a home garden can cost anywhere from a few hundred dollars for a very small garden on up to $1,000 to $2,500 range for more typical medium-sized gardens. The advantages in this approach are that the results are truly artful, light sources are used efficiently, and the homeowner has only to enjoy the results.

Many homeowners, however, might prefer the more modest do-it-yourself approach possible with low-voltage lighting systems now available. Such systems consist of a transformer, wiring, and small light fixtures that are usually moveable. The transformer, when plugged into an exterior all-weather outlet or other safe source of electricity in

Soft lighting filtering like moonlight from trees illuminates a terrace and lawn beyond. John Watson, Dallas, landscape illuminator.

the home, converts standard 120 voltage to 12 volts. Because of its low-voltage features, the homeowner can safely install or rearrange the system himself, once a proper 120-volt connection is made for the transformer. Normally, no more than 100 feet of wire and six fixtures should be run from a single transformer. Due to this fact, and the generally lower light level produced by a low-voltage system, the do-it-yourself project would best be limited to a relatively small, contained portion of the garden. (A completely satisfactory landscape lighting project would include full-power fixtures as well as low-voltage.)

As with garden design itself, night lighting will draw upon the effects of composition, contrast, texture, and the like in order to be attractive. The extremes of overall flat lighting from a single source, on one hand, and a clutter of isolated pools of light, on the other, are to be equally avoided. A good guide from professional designers is to have three levels or intensities: dominant lighting, such as that on a feature tree or object; secondary lighting, to form a backdrop for the dominant feature; and fill lighting, a light wash of light to tie elements together. These will, of course, vary from garden to garden.

In many areas of the South, where wooded residential lots abound, the most effective landscape illumination is that done of and in major trees. Uplighting into the trees' branches brings them to life, while downlighting from a tree enlivens the surrounding area with light and shadow. The result is particularly striking when light blue filters or mercury vapor fixtures are used to simulate moonlight. Because of its complexity and the type of fixture needed, major tree lighting does not fall within the do-it-yourself class, though such an installation could form the framework for additional low-voltage experimentation by the homeowner.

One of the great advantages in tree-mounted landscape lighting is that fixtures are readily hidden from view. The placement and appearance of garden lighting fixtures are important. Their finish and design should be such that they are inconspicuous by day and create no glare or distraction at night. In landscape lighting, the landscape should be the subject of attention, not the light source. Installation by a professional lighting designer can be expected to take concealment into account. The homeowner buying fixtures for a low-voltage system will want to avoid those without hoods that shroud light sources and direct them to garden features.

Experimenting with night lighting will give the homeowner some feeling for what potential there is in bringing the garden to life at night, whether a professional or do-it-yourself approach is being followed. A weatherproof extension cord and a hooded, clamp-on utility lamp can be used for this purpose. The clamp will allow the lamp to be held in place while the effect is viewed from a distance. Besides changing location the light level can also be varied while the result is registered. Such experimentation should be done when the site is as dry as possible; and equipment should be in good condition. Bulbs should not be changed until the extension cord is unplugged.

In the process of experimenting with night lighting, a number of techniques should be tried:

Uplighting — The light source is concealed on or in the ground below the plant or nestled in the lower branches of a tree so the light flares up dramatically, picking out some parts of the

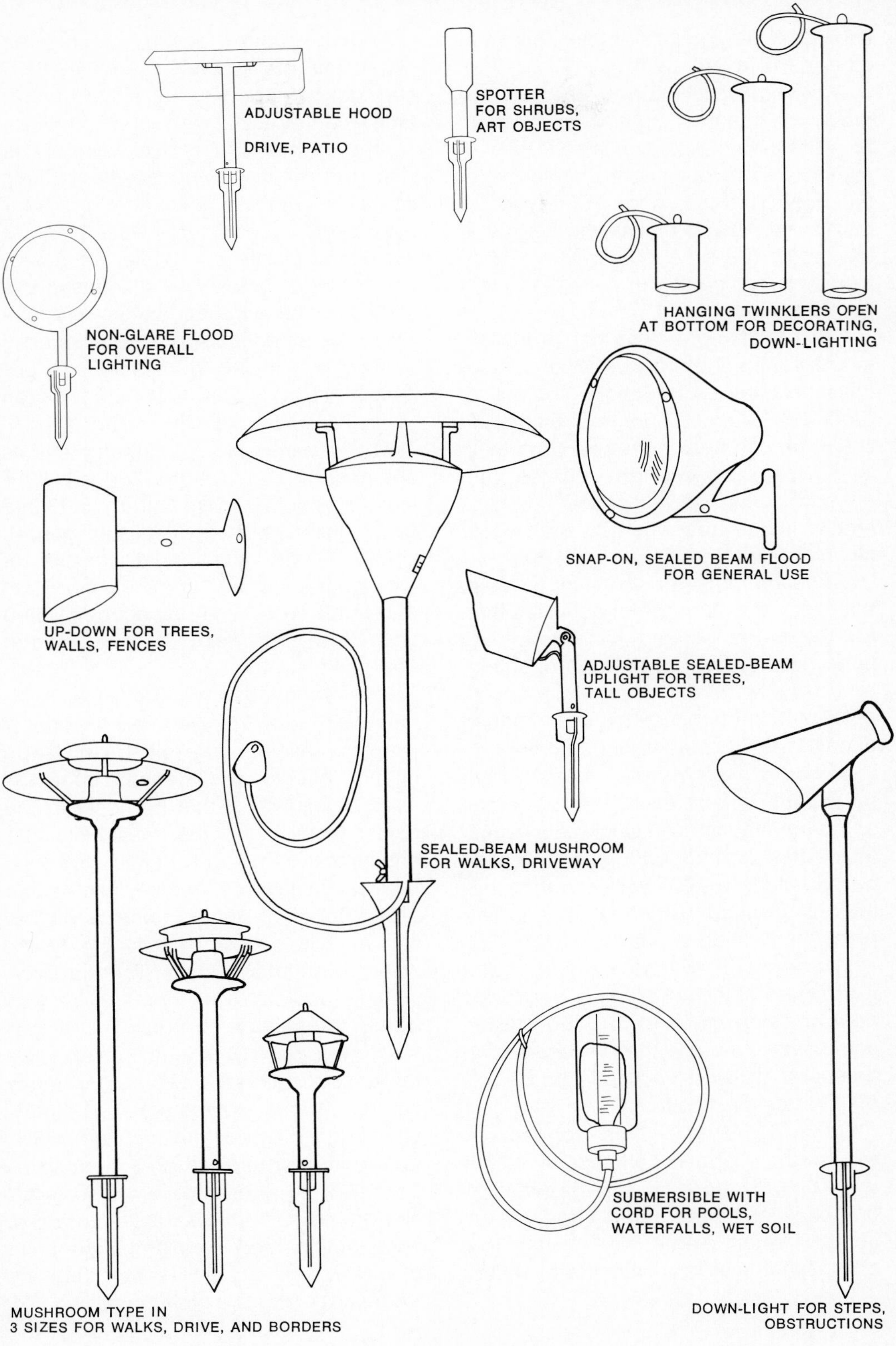
ADJUSTABLE HOOD
DRIVE, PATIO
SPOTTER
FOR SHRUBS,
ART OBJECTS
HANGING TWINKLERS OPEN
AT BOTTOM FOR DECORATING,
DOWN-LIGHTING
NON-GLARE FLOOD
FOR OVERALL
LIGHTING
SNAP-ON, SEALED BEAM FLOOD
FOR GENERAL USE
UP-DOWN FOR TREES,
WALLS, FENCES
ADJUSTABLE SEALED-BEAM
UPLIGHT FOR TREES,
TALL OBJECTS
SEALED-BEAM MUSHROOM
FOR WALKS, DRIVEWAY
SUBMERSIBLE WITH
CORD FOR POOLS,
WATERFALLS, WET SOIL
MUSHROOM TYPE IN
3 SIZES FOR WALKS, DRIVE, AND BORDERS
DOWN-LIGHT FOR STEPS,
OBSTRUCTIONS

subject in luminous glow and showing other parts in dark relief.

Downlighting — Light sources are mounted in a tree, on a wall or fence, or — if nothing else is available — on a standard. The downlight should be of the controlled beam or spot type for maximum impact, unless the source is low, as in the case of mushroom lamp fixtures which create a pool of light near the ground.

Cross Lighting — Also called modeling, this technique focuses two or more light sources on a single subject of particular interest such as a garden sculpture or a specimen tree. Care must be taken to prevent light sources from creating glare, particularly if the subject is in an area where people sit or move about.

Floodlighting — In the usual sense, this technique is more for activities than for the mood desired for entertaining and viewing. Very soft floodlighting, however, can be used for fill lighting to prevent accented subjects from floating uncomfortably in a sea of darkness.

Silhouette Lighting — A technique particularly effective when a plant has an open, angular form, such as a yucca. Instead of light being thrown directly on the plant, a light wall or fence behind is washed with light setting the plant out in relief.

Shadowing — Shadows can result from most kinds of lighting described here and can be used to good end. In some cases, though, the shadow thrown against a wall or fence can be of primary interest in itself.

Back Lighting — This technique, where the light is placed to shine through or bounce off leaves or branches can have great impact, particularly when plants have translucent or glossy leaves that transmit or reflect light.

Mirror Lighting — For use around water, this method lets the water itself stay dark to function as a mirror surface. Plants beyond a pool or pond are lighted so that they reflect in the water from the main viewing position. Since lighting in water is difficult, mirror lighting makes a good alternative.

Accent Lighting — While accentuation is what landscape illumination is all about, fine accent lighting of pinpoint character stands out as its own special method of showing off a particular object, much as you would call attention to art objects inside the home.

These categories of lighting effects are general descriptions and are subject to almost infinite variation. Some of the most pleasing results of garden lighting — the illuminated texture of bark on tree trunks, for example, or that of a brick wall — may be accomplished with one or more of the above approaches.

Experimenting with a hooded bulb fixture can be worthwhile, but obviously the more refined and exciting landscape lighting effects must depend upon fixtures designed for that purpose. In the past several years the availability and choice of such equipment has expanded rapidly. Today the homeowner or the professional designer doing a project has a wide selection of fixture types, sizes, finishes, and costs. There are adjustable spots, downlights, and hooded lights, mushroom lights of differing sizes, non-glare floodlights, small spotter lights for pinpoint effects, and many others. Some equipment has interchangeable lenses that can turn a fixture from spot to flood or vice-versa as the need arises. Lamps are also available in varied forms for specific tasks. For example, long-lived lamps are much preferred for hard-to-reach fixtures where changing is a major task.

Warm lighting for the terrace and cool moonlight illumination for the garden beyond create an outdoor setting for a Ft. Worth residence. John Watson, Dallas, landscape illuminator.

There are a number of other considerations for the homeowner who plans to install a low-voltage system. One advantage in amateur use of these lighting systems is that the wire does not have to be placed underground. And since most fixtures come with metal stakes as a base, they can be easily moved until the right position is found. For a permanent or semi-permanent installation, the wiring can be put in the ground but should either be protected by strips of 1 x 3 lumber atop the wire (to prevent damage from digging) or run-along walks, fences, or other edges where soil is not disturbed.

For safety, most codes now require that any fixed or portable equipment, like lighting systems, be electrically grounded. Once installed, equipment should be checked periodically to see that wires are covered and in place. Even with safe low-voltage systems, a transformer properly grounded and in good working order is important to maintain safety.

Consideration of neighboring property is, of course, another aspect of landscape lighting not to be overlooked. Sources should never be located where they will shine into adjoining property.

Options available for landscape lighting systems include dimmers which enable the entire system or particular parts to be raised or lowered in brightness as desired. Photocells and timers are also available which will automatically turn lights on and then turn them off. The photocells are regulated by brightness, the timers by a dial setting. Lenses in color are also available, but except for the light blue moonlight effect it is recommended that color not be used. White light or moonlight will bring out the best features of a garden and are easy to live with, while colors tend to distort the natural setting and are too carnival-like for home surroundings.

Durability is an important consideration in outdoor lighting equipment since fixtures are exposed to weather, and the cost of equipment is usually proportionate to quality and durability: something to keep in mind when shopping or specifying. Equipment must also withstand the normal abuse of the outdoor location such as that from lawnmowers, dogs, and children. Fixtures normally have a green or black finish which allows them to be camouflaged more easily in the garden.

A homeowner, interested in having a landscape lighting system installed, may start an inquiry by checking the commercial listings in the telephone directory under "Lighting". A landscape architect may also be of help, and in some cities local power companies have personnel trained to assist in such projects.

The advantage of uplighting trees like this is that light sources are above eye level, mounted in the lower branches of the trees.

Index

Salads

Sauces and Marinades

Soups

Stews

Tips

Vegetables